RETHINKING KAZAKH

— AND —

CENTRAL ASIAN NATIONHOOD

A Challenge to Prevailing Western Views

Rethinking Kazakh

— and —

Central Asian Nationhood

A Challenge to Prevailing Western Views

R. Charles Weller

Asia Research Associates
Los Angeles

Central Asian Historical-Cultural Research Center (CAHCRC) and
Asia Research Associates (ARA)
www.ara-cahcrc.com   ara@ara-cahcrc.com

This book was printed in the United States of America.
2nd Print Release, July 2006

To order additional copies of this book, contact:
Xlibris Corporation
1-888-795-4274
www.Xlibris.com
Orders@Xlibris.com
32067

Cover image: Bronze relief depicting the December 1986 demonstrations in Republic Square, Almaty, defending Kazakh rights to political power in Kazakhstan by protesting the appointment of a Russian replacement of the former Kazakh head of state. Photo by R. Charles Weller. All rights reserved.

Contents

DEDICATION

In memory of a personal hero,
Martin Luther King, Jr.
and all he stood for
in defending ethnonational
civil and human rights
as well as dignities
in our world.

Foreword[1]*

Whatever the person who takes a pen into their hands writes, if he writes with knowledge of what he is talking about, errors and strayings from the path in our world would be few. But, in today's "age of information," the situation is not so. Those who take up the pen, rather than delivering humanity from its erring and straying, are further confusing people's minds as misunderstandings and misconceptions are being spread about without pause. If we ask the cause of this predicament, we should focus our attention on two problems. First, those who take up the pen might speak or write from lack of knowledge. The absence or lack of knowledge becomes the foundation for the increase of misguided writings. Secondly, those who take up the pen evade telling the truth with the intention of serving some particular assignment or aim. Sitting down and carefully reading Charles Weller's work entitled "Rethinking Kazakh and Central Asian Nationhood," this is the thinking, the conclusion to which I came. The idea of the Western and Eastern European writers quoted in this work who say that the ethnonational identities of Central Asia are the imagination or invention of Russian colonialists or communists is ignoble and offensive for the person in their right mind, they are surely connected with the two causes just named. What makes a ray of hope shine down on me[2] is the inquiry of a researcher like Charles Weller. He is not an outside observer of Central Asia or especially Kazakhstan, he is one who has mastered the Kazakh language, who is acquainted with Kazakh culture and history, an honorary citizen of the nation who mingles hand-to-hand with Kazakh scholars.

Of course, as he himself acknowledges, he was not born a Kazakh, he is an American citizen. The system of American thought can be observed clearly in his work, and perhaps that is even one its valuable contributions. The study of nationhood is not a trivial undertaking, Charles himself sees the complexity of it. But he has commenced his study of nationhood on the right foot. In order to study nationhood, he has mastered for himself the language of the nation which communicates its worldview. The learning and study of national treasures comes first and foremost through the national language. Of course, simply learning the national language itself does not make it possible to become fully and completely acquainted with the nation. In order to become acquainted with the nation you must be together with the people for a long time, because the people continue to bring forth and unveil their treasures in relation to all kinds of eras and times.

The Kazakh people have themselves experienced such times and eras. The Kazakh people who had been associated with the Kazakh State established in 1466 were cut off from their nationhood through the official resolution of the Russian Empire in 1822. But to the point, 356 years of statehood experience does not go off into sudden oblivion, it becomes the foundation for historical stories, poems, songs, compositions, folktales, etc, and is passed down from one generation to the next in oral, and when possible written, form. Historical memory does not go off into complete obliteration. Charles Weller has raised these issues in appropriate fashion. He endeavors hard to explain them through the concepts of 'ethnos' and 'nation' (lit. 'ult' and 'yel'). He tells the truth, the fact of the existence of the ethnonational identity of the Kazakh people, that its political yearnings and strivings to be a nation have never died out.

The Kazakh people became a colonial nation in two historical circumstances. In one of the those—the period of the Russian Empire, from 1822 (when the Khanate, that is the Kazakh State, was done away with by official resolution) until 1917, in other words for one entire century—it was a colonial nation. Clearly it ceased from being an independent, sovereign nation. Its nationhood was done away with through the liquidation of the State. The Kazakhs began living as a social group. Through the ethnonational liberation movement of 1837-47 Kenesari attempted to bring the Kazakhs to independence, but the hope of the nation at that time was left unfulfilled. Likewise, though the Alash Orda brought the Kazakhs to independence and re-established the Kazakh nation between 1917-20, this was only a fleeting moment in national history. Nonetheless, their short-lived success became the foundation for the Kazakh SSR as an autonomous nation in the Soviet Union in 1936, and this nation in turn became the base for today's nation of Kazakhstan. In this way, today's sovereign nation of Kazakhstan can be viewed as the rebirth and continuation of the Kazakh State with its 356 years of independent statehood experience, though of course with significant adjustment to the modern age.

But a great many foreign scholars commence the history of the Kazakh nation from the period after the Russians came; this is a mistaken understanding. The formation of the Kazakhs as an ethnos starts, as Mirza Haidar Dulati has shown in his work entitled *Tarix-i Rashidi*, from 1466, from the laying of the foundation stone of the Kazakh Khanate. Those are the roots of today's nation of Kazakhstan and the Kazakh people therein. Denying or not knowing anything of this clear and well-known history is the basis for mistaken opinions taking hold of pastureland in people's minds. It seems to me that Charles Weller has taken up the task of correctly explaining this issue.

An American scholar takes interest in this kind of undertaking, and there are those in Kazakhstan who look on with respect, I myself am one of them. Of course, on occasion concrete information falls short even for Charles, that is an understandable and natural thing. On top of this, in the study of the Kazakhs and Central Asians, even that which the local scholars, journalists and writers say or write varies; if some write with knowledge, some confuse the nation, and the purposes in such vary. It is of course understandable if an American scholar sometimes runs into difficulty in his ability to discern this.

Secondly, then, the Kazakh people were part of the composition of Communist Russia from 1917 until 1991. This was a different type of colonialism. During this period, the most important treasure was not the ethnos (lit. 'ult'), to the contrary, it was 'non-ethnos-ness' (lit. 'ultsizdik'). This was called 'internationalism'. In these years, the Kazakh people began to forget their native history and language, because intentional policy was carried out in order for it to be that way. During these years spiritual-cultural colonialism was a powerful force. During these years there arose those who rejected their own ethnicity and its value as contrary, they were opposed to Independence. That opposition is still observable.

The situation now is different. Since 1991 a new younger generation is taking shape. They are being trained up on the foundations of national values, and in this effort Charles Weller, in spite of being an American, also has a part; the proof of this is in his work which is now being recommended to the reader.

But Charles is not alone in researching Central Asia and Kazakhstan. His Japanese wife, Yumiko, is likewise one who has mastered the Kazakh language. To have two foreigners in one family who know the Kazakh language is a wonderful thing. Knowing the language brings people together. When Charles and Yumiko speak in the Kazakh language, we marvel at their persistent labor. Learning a language is not an easy thing, for that the people have to be of interest to you. In knowledge of the peoples of Central Asia, especially the Kazakhs, this work now being published is a piece of material which will not be found elsewhere. Its main ideas have been presented by the author to the public in a number of scholarly conferences in Kazakhstan and now in published form. The author is known to the people of Kazakhstan, and his achievement in mastering the Kazakh language has not gone unnoticed; many of the television stations, radio programs and publications which come forth in the Republic of Kazakhstan have made his work known.

This work of Charles Weller should not be received from one, narrow perspective. Drawing to the best of his ability on world experience, he has written the work in objective fashion. Therefore, even in times to come, I wish success for his labors in his purpose of making known nations to nations!

Garifolla Yesim
Post-doctoral graduate of Philosophy,
Dean of the Faculty of Philosophy and Political
Science at Kazakh National (State) University,
Scholar of highest honors in
the National Academy of Science
for the Republic of Kazakhstan

Introduction

In this work, R. Charles Weller raises issues of exegeting the historical unity of the nation-states which came into being after the collapse of the Soviet Union in Kazakhstan and Central Asia. With this purpose in view, he thoroughly analyzes the publications of certain scholars in Russia and the Western nations which have been written from a Eurocentric perspective. According to Weller, the main error of these authors is in their nullification of the history of the Central Asian nations by considering them imagined or invented republics which were fabricated in the Russian Tsarist and/or Soviet communist era.

Here the Western and Russian authors have put out of mind the fact that the Central Asian peoples are Eastern nations, that their formation has been within Islamic culture. They are imposing Western modernism upon the Central Asian nations, and among them Kazakhstan, without any kind of modification. The Western authors completely write off the past history of the Kazakhs and other Central Asians or give partial evaluations of them from a Eurocentric perspective. They want to move those peoples (or nations, lit. 'haliktar') to the secular and/or Christian "Western model." They consider that the Central Asians (and among them the Kazakhs), like the peoples of the Baltic shore, do not have the ability to establish national states, (or) when they are founded they will divide according to ethnic groups (lit. 'taipalar') and regions and make war with one another.[3] Therefore, in order to establish "genuine equality" in their nations, these states must be "multiethnic," that is, they recommend that special rights of equality must be given, not to the indigenous ethnonational groups, but first to the Euroslavic ethnonational groups. Here one thing in particular which they wish to draw attention to is the issue of the official (state) language. In their opinion, the native languages cannot be official languages, because "the ethnic situation of the Middle Ages, including ethnonyms, cannot be superimposed on the contemporary."[4] That is to say, in their view, Russian language and culture must function as the common language and culture for all the peoples of the state.

In his work, R.C. Weller refutes these views from their very roots. Leaning upon the works of Kazakh scholars, he offers the idea that the State of Kazakhstan is, first and foremost, the legal-rightful heir of all past states which have been established here, including first among them the Kazakh khanate. This is a work of top-level scholarship, I consider its release to the public a good and right thing!

—Burkitbai Ayagan, post-doctoral graduate
and professor of history, academic of highest honors,
president of 'Kazakh Encyclopedia'

Review Statements
by Kazakh Scholars

The historical and social importance of this book is immense. It will take a special place among the many books which have been published in the field of history and sociology in recent times. It elevates the status and level of the Kazakh nation and the right of statehood for the Kazakh people and produces confidence in the reader as to the ability (of Kazakhstan) to be placed alongside the states of Europe and Asia. This work needs to be made public and distributed widely in universities and other educational institutions. Without question it instructs people in love for (their) fatherland and ethnonational identity and reinforces confidence in the bright future of the Kazakh nation in accordance with a national policy that does not marginalize or offend the multiple ethnic groups living in Kazakhstan.

> *—Kadrahman Duisembin, academic of highest honors,*
> *post-doctoral graduate and professor of biology*

Western researchers typically receive their cultural-civilizational understanding about Central Asia through Western and Russian lenses. They have not yet been able to graduate from the erroneous view which holds that the nomad Turkic people did not have their own comparable civilization, government, laws, etc. The idea of the naysayers that "the Kazakh people are not ready to accept democracy in its modern, civilized form" results from this. Just as Shokan Ualihanov did in his time, Charles Weller strives to explain the Turkic civilization to the world with integrity and braveness. According to the author, democracy, like civilization itself, is a well established tradition in world history, but neither are monolithic structures. We believe strongly that the Turkic peoples, who have contributed significantly to world civilization, stand among the politically-socially advanced nations. . . . We share the conclusion of the author: the Creator God never wants to see the valuable aspects of national culture vanish or be unduly conformed to the national culture of another people or nation. Preserving our own civilization, including its heritage of culture, language and statehood, is a necessary part of the democratic vision in Central Asia.

—*Tursin H. Gabitov, post-doctoral graduate*
and professor of philosophy and culture

The essence and uniqueness of this work is due to a great many things. First (with a view to the Kazakh version), a foreign American scholar knows how to drive home his thoughts and reflections in our State language, the Kazakh language. Second, he, together with the Kazakh people, genuinely sympathizes with the peoples of Central Asia and, with a view to the present and the future, puts forth the issue of defending their nationhood, making the effort to thoroughly analyze the problems involved. The author analyzes in comparative fashion the Marxist and Western modernist trends, elucidating how important they are for today's nation of Kazakhstan. There are sure grounds for evaluating his use of recent Western works alongside authors from Kazakhstan and Eastern Europe, and his putting of these together into circulation, as a new contribution to scholarship. This work, which stimulates a number of thoughts and which raises a number of essential issues, creates exceptional interest in the reader.

—*Nagima Zh. Baitenova, post-doctoral graduate*
and professor of philosophy

This work immediately captures one's attention, displaying its importance and scholarly sharpness. Weller says that two of the primary imperatives of democracy in our day—the separation of religion and state and the separation of ethnicity and state—trace their roots to Western democracy (including Western Protestant Christianity) and I agree with this view. He notes that Western democracy, which is founded upon the doctrine of a territorial political nation, is not entirely suitable to Eastern democracy, which is founded upon the doctrine of ethnic nationhood. Indeed, as Weller himself points out, the contributions to democracy which the "Alash" party had in view (in the early 20th century) are not the same as the Western ones. The very processes which are underway today in our society seem to demonstrate this view. . . . When Weller emphasizes that the Kazakh people, who (historically) came to possess the wide-spacious steppe, still to this day have a historical, legal right to this land, you are left with the impression that one of the Kazakh's own genuine sons has written these things. This is not blind partiality, I know it to be his objectivity as a scholar, and even his cultural cordiality. . . . I know him as a person helping to connect and forge the process of establishing dialogue and genuine mutual respect for one another between two nations, two cultures, two continents.

—Aktolkin T. Kulsarieva, PhD
and associate professor of philosophy and culture

Charles Weller's work focuses upon one of the most vital issues that Kazakhstan is currently facing as a nation. Together with the sunny side of a nation which, after achieving independence, is pressing ahead on the road of democracy, it lays bare the shadowy aspects as well. The author comes to tell us that (scholars) are not simply looking on with impartiality at the situation of our nation which has soaked into its stature both the necessary as well as the harmful aspects of Western democracy. Then he focuses his attention on the (two) imperatives of (Western) democracy, the separation of religion and state and the separation of ethnicity and state, giving primary attention to the latter.

The issues raised by the author are crucial. It is the fruit of one who is a sympathetic, spiritual brother who wishes to come to the aid of defending the Kazakh (people's) ethnic-national identity through these kinds of his own works which critique those, including albeit a few citizens encountered on occasion in our own midst, who today look indifferently and apathetically upon the indigenous culture of the (Kazakh) ethnos. The author's own word testifies to this: "it is (historically) self-evident that the Kazakh people hold a special place in the nation of Kazakhstan."

—Ainur D. Kormanalieva, PhD
and associate professor, eastern and Islamic studies

When I first learned from Charles Weller about the views of Western modernists, i.e. the idea that the Kazakh ethnos has no (real) history of independent nationhood and no (genuine) cultural heritage or language, but these are rather attributed to the Russians as a colonial creation, I went about for a long time unable to get a hold of myself. When he showed me a number of books espousing that view and lent me a few of them to look at, I not only heard from him, but experienced the sense of reading with my own eyes works which cast doubt upon not only the past, but the future of the Kazakhs. I said, "This concerns the destiny of an entire nation."

. . . If someone wishes to say something about the Kazakhs, then the wisest thing to do would be to write as they work on learning their language, read their publications in the original language, understand their outlook and mentality and become familiar with their nature. The best scholars do not study particular ethnonational groups via the material written about them in other languages. From this vantage, this work, *Rethinking Kazakh and Central Asian Nationhood*, is an exceedingly profitable study written by someone who has learned the Kazakh language, understood their heart and soul and who is (thus) able to give a sound, relevant answer to those in view. I have full confidence that the gratitude of the Kazakh people, whose quality is that of a peaceful people, and that of the other peoples who share their lot, will be apportioned to him. I am of the opinion that all scholars will do well to consult this work.

—*Nursaule Rsalieva, PhD candidate*
and instructor of linguistics and translation theory

Preface

With the weather still warm in early September (2005), I was enjoying my usual walk to work up Aimanov Street in Almaty. I was feeling somewhat good about having finished the main text of this book and was thinking of the details remaining before getting it off to the publisher. As I passed by one of the newspaper kiosks along the way, I decided to have a look, as I often do, at the various headlines. The phrase 'The Ethnonational Idea' (lit. 'Ulttik ideya')—a common household phrase heard often in scholarly and political discussions as well as the media—caught my eye in large bold print in the center of one particular front page. Then, as my eyes scanned across the rest of the page, up in the lefthand corner was another article title, the catch-phrase sense of which can be rendered: 'There Before, and Still There Later too' (lit. 'Burin da bolgan, keiin de bola beredi').[5] It turned out to be a brief article on the historical depth of Kazakh nationhood, particularly in its political dimensions (i.e. 'statehood'). Upon turning to the page with the article, the opening paragraph was highlighted, reading:

> In recent times some political figures are going about determined to commence the [Kazakh] nation's history from their own birthdays. If you sit and listen to their words, these Kazakhs have had neither state, nor borders, nor [political] authority until this [beginning of the nation's history on their birthdays]. Oh my, from where then did these Kazakhs emerge?[6]

Whoever exactly the writer may have in view here and whatever his own purpose(s) in writing about them, these are not of concern to us. We do not quote his comments to support whatever agenda he or the newspaper itself may have in mind. Our concern is with *the view* attributed to certain Kazakhs—whether accurately or inaccurately, whether political figures or otherwise—

who are said to "commence the nation's history from" some time very late, namely the 20th century, and that, in the minds of such Kazakhs, there were "neither state, nor borders, nor [political] authority" before this time.

To be carefully noted here is the intimate relation between the beginning of 'nationhood' and the idea of 'state' and 'borders' and 'political authority'. Of course, 'nations' are commonly called 'states', i.e. the two terms get used interchangeably as synonyms on a regular basis. Thus, for example, the political 'states' of the world attempt to work together in an organization which is called 'The United *Nations*'. But more than that, we even find the two terms combined into the one compound term 'nation-state' which is then even compounded further with the adjective 'political' which itself becomes still further modified with the prefix 'geo'. Ultimately we wind up with phrases like 'geo-political nation', which could be repeated in connection with state and/or nation-state. Whatever precise term is used, the emphasis of usage for the term 'nation' in these cases is upon '*political* nationhood'. 'Political nations' of course have to deal with issues of territory (i.e. 'land') and language, not to mention culture, economy, history and other things.

Yet 'nation' is also used in reference to 'ethnic group'. Indeed, the term 'nation' (or plural 'nations') has been commonly used to translate the Greek term 'ethnos' (or plural 'ethne') which lies behind our concept and study of 'ethnicity' via 'ethnography', 'ethnology' and the like. And so we speak of 'ethnic nations'. Of course, 'ethnic nations' and their 'ethnicity' are inseparably tied to 'culture'—'ethnic culture' to be specific. Therefore, we also speak of 'cultural nations'. And these 'ethnic nations' or 'cultural nations' involve issues of land, language and other matters of 'ethnic cultural being and identity'. Land and language as well as history, culture, society, economy and politics all become uniquely and intimately related to the 'ethnic' or 'cultural nation'.

And so the question arises: What do 'ethnic nation' and 'political nation' have to do with one another? Are they one and the same thing? Are they two entirely distinct and separate things? What is their proper relationship with one another? When we speak of 'national language', 'national culture', 'national territory', 'national government' and the like are we talking about 'ethnic nations', 'nation-nations' or 'nation-states'? Consider 'the nation of Kazakhstan' for example. The term 'stan' means essentially 'land' or 'nation' (cf. also 'country'). When speaking of 'Kazakhstan' then, are we talking about 'the Kazakh nation' or perhaps 'the land of the Kazakhs'? It would seem so, otherwise why have the *ethnonym* of the 'ethnic nation' lying at the heart of the name of the 'political nation'? It would seem just from the name itself that the modern 'political nation' of '*Kazakh*stan' is somehow uniquely and intimately tied to, not 'the Russian nation' or 'the Ukrainian nation' or 'the German nation', but 'the Kazakh nation', i.e. the 'ethnic nation' known as 'Kazakh'. And if that is the case then it would seem quite normal and appropriate that the 'national language' of the 'political nation' would and even should be the same as the 'national language' of the 'ethnic nation', in this case namely 'Kazakh'. The same could be said for the (primary) 'national culture'. And it would seem that the political authority to make this decision for the 'nation' would rest, first and foremost, with the Kazakhs in their own historic homeland which bears their own ethnic name.

Yet, as just alluded to, the 'political nation' of 'Kazakhstan' *has become* home to more than one 'ethnic nation'. That is, it is home to more than just 'the Kazakh nation', it has also *become* home to large numbers of people from 'the Russian nation', 'the Ukrainian nation', 'the German nation', 'the Uzbek nation', 'the Uighur nation' and so on. This means 'Kazakhstan' is in reality a 'multiethnic nation'. Is it fair then that the 'political nation' should bear the name of only one of the 'ethnic nations' which call it 'home'? Likewise, is it fair that the 'national language' and 'national culture' of only one 'ethnic nation' living in that 'political nation' should have the right to be named and used as the 'national language' and/or 'national culture' of that 'political nation'?

These questions are more than merely academic. They *remain* burning but still unresolved questions of the hour for Central Asia, a rather lo-o-o-o-o-ng hour which has stretched from at least 1991, when Russian imperialism in Central Asia finally came to end and the Central Asian peoples became free to pursue independent nationhood. Or did they? The *foreign* political, cultural and even linguistic not to mention economic forces which once held them in bondage still seem to be operating at slightly reduced but nonetheless significant levels. They have only been re-channeled and now been joined by, as well as themselves joined in with, new 'international' political, cultural and linguistic not to mention economic forces which all seem to have their will, standards, values and ideals which they want the Central Asian peoples to follow, indeed which they even insist they must follow or be in 'violation' of human rights and ethics. The resolution of these questions, therefore, involves further questions of not only philosophical ideology regarding 'nationhood', but international human rights and ethics. And these questions involve still further questions of history, or more accurately, to borrow the subtitle of Anthony D. Smith's important 2001 work, 'historiographical debates over ethnicity and nationalism'. Indeed, together with defining and relating 'ethnic nation' and 'political nation', the entire question of history and its proper understanding and interpretation looms large in the whole debate, as can be seen in the quote from the article noted above.

For those who are not aware that there even has been or remains such a debate, now is the time to 'arise, shine' and be educated about it. With respect to those who "commence the nation's history from" some time in the 20th century and believe that there were "neither state, nor borders, nor [political] authority" before this time, the same article asks "from where . . . did these Kazakhs emerge?" Indeed, as we shall see, it is not only Kazakhs—albeit certainly a minority of them—who hold this view, but there are a far greater majority of Western, including Euroslavic, scholars who hold it. Not only do they 'hold it' though, they actively, even aggressively at times, promote it to the point that the Kazakh and Central Asian peoples and nations are bombarded from nearly every side with theories that insist that both their 'ethnic nationhood' and their 'political nationhood' are 'imagined' or 'invented' constructs of the Russians which have no real connection with their former historic identities. Thus, they are left with no grounds for establishing 'political nationhood' on 'ethnic nationhood' in the modern global age. Indeed, they are accused of an 'unfulfilled promise' for not conforming to the standards, ideals and values of 'nationhood' defined for and assigned to them by these foreign scholars. Meanwhile, the majority of native Kazakh and Central Asian peoples hold a very different view, one which sees their ethnic as well as political identity going back into history well beyond the coming of the Russians and *continuing*, amidst the many changing circumstances of the times, up until the modern day when *rights* for (reasonable, adjusted) restoration of that nationhood should be granted to them in the wake of new found freedom.

It is towards understanding much more thoroughly and accurately both those views, along with others involved in the 'clash of paradigms' over ethnicity and nationhood in the modern global age, which this book hopes to move. From there, one can only hope and pray that genuinely ethical and practical solutions can be found for the ethnic as well as political 'nations' involved, including the Kazakh and Central Asian 'nations'. With a view to genuine 'liberty and justice for all' based on respectful and integral treatment of ethnonational history and identity in Central Asia and, likewise, with an earnest interest in avoiding the repetition of historical injustices while seeking reasonable resolution of and recompense for them, this book aims at *Rethinking Kazakh and Central Asian Nationhood*.

Background

From one angle, my own interest in these matters can be traced back to my first trip to Kazakhstan in the early 1990s when I visited on a culture exchange and toured the country as part of an amateur American folk music group. That was a day and time when I had more opportunity for music enjoyment, something I miss these days amidst academic pursuits. Regardless, it was also a day and time when 'Negro spirituals' were a core part of our repertoire because they are rightful heirs to the American folk music tradition. They share a great deal in common with the Kazakh folk music tradition in that both give expression to the ethnonational aspirations of a people flavored by the suffering they have endured—particularly at the hands of other ethnonational groups—as a vital part of their own ethnonational history and heritage. The folk song 'O, My Nation!', translated as part of this work (in ch 8), serves as a good example of this heritage in the Kazakh case.

That brings me to the other angle from which my interests in these matters can be traced, namely the fact that since age 14 (1978) Martin Luther King, Jr. has been *and continues to be* a personal hero for me. I was *and remain* captivated by him and the cause of justice, equity and human dignity pursued in 'the Black Civil Rights Movement' which he led.[7] All because at age 14 I 'stumbled across' the six-hour three-day television movie (on NBC I believe) called simply 'King'. I was deeply impacted beyond all words and, as naive as it probably was, it became (for a good year or two) my youthful ambition to pick up where Dr. King had left off and lead the Black Civil Rights Movement forward 'when I grew up'. Since then I have read biographical accounts of Dr. King's life and have remained attentive, captivated and moved whenever the topic arises, including each year on what is now a rightful American national holiday, 'Martin Luther King, Jr. Day', when programs such as 'I Have a Dream', 'From Montgomery to Memphis' and 'Citizen King' (PBS) are aired annually on television in honor of his birthday. I have continued right down to the present day to check out various video series about his life and the movement from libraries or video rental shops and reflect again and again on that historic movement and all that it stands for. It was indeed an ethnonational movement concerned with the rights of not merely 'individual citizens', but the African-American 'ethnic nation' and its 'civil rights' within the political nation of the USA. In that regard, it took place within a particular socio-political and historic context. That context is not the same as Central Asia—in fact it is almost opposite—but the issues are closely connected. My reflections on that movement (and its relation with the ethnonational issues of Central Asia) were and still are stirred up whenever passing by Martin Luther King, Jr. Boulevard in greater Los Angeles, California, which has been my 'home away from home' since 1984 while living and working in both Kazakhstan as well as Japan with my Japanese (not Japanese-American) wife and visiting my family in the northeastern USA where I grew up.

The closely related problems of Apartheid in South Africa were brought to my attention in my later teenage years, though primarily through the musical bands and other performers on 'Saturday Night Live' during a time when my life had turned to less noble ambitions. A later return to my childhood Christian faith, with its concern for 'the nations'—a concern which Reverend King understood and employed in addressing issues of nationhood for his people in America—this also played an important part in opening my eyes to ethnonational issues both historically and presently across the globe.[8] However it all came about though, my sympathies and concerns run deep for these matters. I realize now that it was this foundational experience of 'King' which prepared in me from an early age a heart of concern for ethnonational peoples and their cause in the world. I herein write with that heart of concern and pray it will be of benefit not only to those nations, but to all nations and the common hope we share for a bright and peaceful tomorrow.

My heart has been shaped of course, not only by these kinds of personal experiences, but by my education, which includes bachelor's work in general liberal arts as well as religious (Christian) studies, an MA from Fuller Graduate Schools focusing on history, religion, culture and globalization and doctoral pursuits (May 2003 - April 2006) at Kazakh National University (KNU) in history, religion and culture. Apart from English language resources, my studies at KNU were all conducted in Kazakh, including conference speaking, the writing of articles and my dissertation, the latter of which was successfully defended in March of 2006. The topic assigned to me by my mentors was 'Cultural-Civilizational Foundations of Religious Processes in the Kazakh Nation'. 'Kazakh nationhood' is therefore very important to my personal studies as well as my broader interests.

This book is a product of my doctoral and masters level studies as well as my work as founder and chairman of the Central Asian Historical-Cultural Research Center (CAHCRC) in Almaty and Asia Research Associates (ARA) in Los Angeles (www.ara-cahcrc.com). I likewise have written a Kazakh version of this work which has been published in Kazakhstan via the CAHCRC (2005) under the title *Kazak pen ortaazialiktarding ulttigi men eldigin korgau* (see bibliography for English rendering). The Kazakh and English versions are not simple translations of one another. The Kazakh version actually represents section one of my dissertation. It is a good deal shorter than the English version, but the essential thrust and ideas are the same. This is accurately reflected in the 'Review Statements by Kazakh Scholars', i.e. those statements are based on the Kazakh, but nonetheless represent accurate appraisals of both the Kazakh and English versions.

To further clarify their relation, however, portions of the Kazakh have been directly translated from the English, but portions of the English have also been translated from the Kazakh. On top of that, both versions contain large sections where I wrote freely and independently in each language, of course bearing in mind the content of the other version at all times, though not restricting myself in any way to following it. Likewise, the material is not presented according to the same chapter scheme nor, for that matter, in the same order or even in the same chapters at times. Along with issues of time, etc, English and Kazakh audiences are simply not the same. For example, there are many details of Kazakh history that are not necessary to address for a Kazakh audience.

One thing to highlight though: While much of my critique of Olcott and the related discussion of DeLorme in chapter five appears (fortunately or unfortunately) in only the briefest, summarical fashion in the Kazakh version, most of the quotes from chapter four have been carefully, fully and accurately translated into Kazakh and incorporated into the Kazakh version. In this way, the Kazakhs themselves are presented with the actual primary material upon which I am basing my contentions.

On that note, I would like to clarify regarding both these versions that I have striven to conduct my critique with the utmost respect for all the scholars and materials with which I interact, albeit with straightforwardness and honesty regarding these very complex, delicate and vital issues. If I have fallen short in any way, I request grace in advance and also ask that it kindly be brought to my attention. One thing I would hope to avoid as much as possible is a repeat of Japanese history in Kazakhstan when "the West . . . presented Japan with numerous conflicting words of advice, which posed alternative models of national development. . . . And so the Japanese of the 1870s and 1880s faced not only the trauma of modernization . . . but also the necessity of deciding which features of Western life most deserved their emulation" (Hall 1970:288-89, *Japan: From Prehistory to Modern Times*). This is actually inevitable to some degree, but I take no delight nor do I have any desire to contribute to such a predicament, neither for the Kazakhs or any other ethnonational groups in Kazakhstan. I believe in and strive to practice genuine attentive dialogue which seeks to work toward resolution of issues, not engage in mere polemics for the sake of debate or proving others wrong and myself right.

Part of me does not want to publish this work because I never wished for my first book (in English) to be one which critiques Kazakh and Central Asian scholarship as though I were the long-time resident expert in the field. I do not feel this way at all. I have been engaged in Central Asian studies since the early 1990s, but like all of us, I have a great deal to learn, certainly more than others in many cases. I have already learned much of what I know about the Kazakhs and Central Asia from the very people I critique in this book and I look forward to learning much more from them in days and years to come. I remain, *together with* everyone, on a life-long journey of learning and adjusting my understanding when and where necessary. I will always need the help and interaction of friends and colleagues—Western, Asian and otherwise—within the global community. This work will be put to the same kind of critique to which it subjects other works, hopefully all in a spirit of mutual respect and cooperation. 'Iron sharpens iron'. Please send any such critiques directly to me and I will respond as best as possible (ca-nationhood@ara-cahcrc.com).

With that in view, it is not easy for me to release this work, but I believe I must. The stakes are very real and they are too high for me to simply remain silent, in Kazakh as well as English. I have to confess that I am somewhat disturbed in my heart and spirit by the manner of treatment, particularly some of the choices of phraseology (e.g. 'debris', 'ethno-engineering', etc), which appear in some of the Western sources. This is even reflected in my own choice of chapter and section titles as well as in the text. My personal disagreement with the 'Western modernist' paradigm of ethnicity, nations and (ethno)nationalism will be apparent enough. I respect that not everyone will share my views on the broader, theoretical aspects and approaches to such a complex subject and we can perhaps enjoy some engaging discussions to sharpen one another on those issues. But even more difficult is to see it actually applied to Kazakh and Central Asian ethnonational identity, especially the more radical versions. As reflected in the foreword and review statements, I am not the only one who is disturbed over this and I herein make an earnest appeal that we all give serious reconsideration to our manner of approach to these matters. We are dealing with real people struggling hard over very real and even painful aspects of human identity involving often painful events of ethnonational history. Whatever our theoretical views on ethnonational identity and its expressed aspirations in ethnonationalism as human social phenomena, let us at least strive to avoid adding insult to injury in communicating them. I can only hope that I myself have achieved such in spite of my sometimes pointed manner of speaking to the issues.

In the end, the destiny of Kazakhstan and Central Asia is not ours (i.e. Westerners, foreigners) to determine, but their own. That is one reason I felt justified in producing the Kazakh version, so that they can ultimately work through these issues themselves and respond in their own time and way because these Western (including Euroslavic) publications and their views are most assuredly affecting their world in profound ways. As for the West (i.e. English-based world), the more we can assist one another in sharpening our understanding and drawing nearer to agreement on these matters rather than farther away, the better off all of us will be, both us and them. That is the hope and spirit in which both versions of this book are released.

As a final note on the English version, Chapters 1-3 represent a condensed excerpt from a larger volume I am currently preparing entitled *A Closer Look at Ethnicity, Nations and Nationalism in the Kingdom of God and World History: Rethinking Western Approaches to Nationhood in the Modern Global Age*. Both works together represent six years of research and writing specifically on the topics in view. The larger volume should be out sometime in 2006 or 2007. It provides much broader and in-depth treatment of the core issues covered in this present work, though along more general as opposed to specifically Central Asian lines. I would certainly like to recommend it to readers, along with Anthony D. Smith's two works, *The Ethnic Origins of Nations* (1986) and *The Nation in History: Historiographical Debates About Ethnicity and Nationalism* (2001). Reading through these works would provide good next steps for pressing ahead with the challenge to properly understanding and responding to this vital topic which is now affecting nearly every discussion of history, religion, culture, society and politics in the modern global age and which, indeed, has profound consequences for the destiny of 'the nations' as well as the whole of humanity.

Acknowledgements

I am especially grateful to all those who have personally worked together with me during my time in Kazakhstan and who have made my research work, including this book, possible. While there are a number of dear friends, both national and expatriate, who could be named, I will limit it to just several. This would include first and foremost my wife, Yumiko, who has been a wonderful support not to mention one of the most important people, with her

---

Japanese heritage, in helping shape my understanding and view of ethnonational issues. The nearness of the Japanese and Kazakh worlds within the larger Altaic tradition has only enriched me personally not to mention, I hope, my ability to address these matters. Special thanks would also be due to my main mentor Garifolla Yesim, Dean of the Faculty of Philosophy and Political Science at KNU, my assistant mentor Tursin Hafizuhli Gabitov, professor of philosophy and culture, Nagima Baitenova, professor of philosophy and Aktolkin Kulsarieva, associate professor of philosophy and culture. All of these work at KNU and it has been my privilege and pleasure to study under them as well as produce this work with their assistance, including their kind reading of it and the foreword and reviews they provided. Beyond KNU would be Burkitbai Ayagan, doctor of history and current president of 'Kazakh Encyclopedia' who is also helping head up Kazakhstan's 'Cultural Heritage' program. He also read the Kazakh version and provided a review (i.e. the 'Introduction'). My wife and I both have the privilege, along with my doctoral studies at KNU and research work at the Central Asian Historical-Cultural Research Center (CAHCRC), to be working together with Dr. Ayagan and his staff in preparing translations of some of their material for publication in English.

On that note, permit me to advertise here that, as part of my work at the CAHCRC, I am also translating certain Kazakh materials into English. First is Garifolla Yesim, *An Insider's Critique of the Kazakh People and Nation: Abai Kunanbai-uhli and his writings, 1845-1904*. Second is the same author's article entitled "If Kazakhs are not ethnonationalists, then who?" No one should understand this man, by the way, as a 'hardcore, ardent Kazakh nationalist'. He is simply trying to recover from negative Soviet views and strike a fair balance in things. Third, then, is Tursin H. Gabitov and Aktolkin T. Kulsarieva, with contributions from Nagima Baitenova and Zhusip Mutalipov, *Kazakh Religion, Culture, Society and State in Historical Perspective*. Along with other materials and resources, selected portions from these works as well as updates on their progress will be maintained on the 'www.ara-cahcrc.com' website. All of these scholars have shown themselves very cordial, hospitable and able to widely embrace people of varying views, including foreigners such as myself. They have earned my deepest respect as well as appreciation.

Overview

This book explains in summary fashion the five main views of nationhood encountered among (especially Western, including Euroslavic) scholars (chs 1-3). It provides special focus upon the central debate between 'naturalists-perennialists' and 'western modernists'. It likewise explains the shift away from 'ethnicity' to the allegedly safer, non-political construct of 'culture' in Western modernism as part of the attempted Western solution to the problem of 'the separation of ethnicity and state'. As younger sister to the idea of 'the separation of religion and state' (whose foundations were worked out between the 17th and early 20th centuries in the West), the idea of 'the separation of ethnicity and state' has taken firm shape in the latter part of the 20th century and has become a cardinal dogma, an ethical imperative of most all Western scholarship treating the subject of ethnicity, nations and (ethno)nationalism in the post-WWII, post-Civil Rights, post-Apartheid era (i.e. since the 1950-60s). It has given rise to the now classic Western modernist insistence on the alleged distinction between 'ethnic nation' (cf. also 'cultural nation') and '(geo-)political nation'.

As the central focus of this work, a detailed critique (in chs 4-5) is offered of Western modernist writers treating the Kazakh and Central Asian nations. These writers insist upon the distinction between 'ethnic nation' and 'political nation', i.e. 'the separation of ethnicity and state', attributing the historical rise of ethnicity and statehood in Central Asia to the Russian Empire and/or the Soviets as an essentially artificial political fabrication of Russian "ethno-engineering." Through this, they allegedly demonstrate that today's nation-states in Central Asia are artificial constructs with no true or historic relation to the ethnic nations whose names they bear. Likewise, the concepts of 'Kazakh', 'Uzbek', etc, are treated by these scholars as having no real or *stable* historic depth or substance as part of their attempt to show that those 'ethnic nations' do not constitute legitimate bases for legitimate and *stable* 'political nationhood'. The Central Asians are conveniently (for Western modernists) left with no rightful historical or sociological claim as 'ethnic nations' to their own 'modern political nations'. This affects all discussion of international human rights, including ideas of 'national language, culture and history rights', 'national reconciliation', etc, both within and beyond the Central Asian 'nations'.

This approach, in its various forms and emphases, is encountered in Eickelman, Paksoy, Khalid, Roy, Brower, the trio of Allworth, Hambly and Sinor in Encyclopedia Britannica, the trio of King, Noble and Humphrey in Central Asia Lonely Planet, Akiner and others. It would also include Russian-Euroslavic scholars writing in English such as Slezkine, Shnirelman, Porkhomovsky, Prazauskas and others. A number of these writers explicitly seek to argue against any idea of special rights or privileges for native Central Asians and/or defend the rights of Russian-Euroslavic colonial descendents, both of whom now live together in the Central Asian nations. Other of these writers contribute to the same basic cause, whether intentionally or unintentionally, implicitly or otherwise. Their views and approach form a legacy of support for the old Russian colonial and communist policies of Russian language (and culture) as the 'common language (and culture)' among multiethnic Central Asia, not to mention 'equal' Russian political 'power-sharing', in the 'new' Central Asian states—only now they wield this support in the name of 'international human rights' in joint choral harmony with Western modernist scholars, effectively doubling the impact of international pressure upon these nations in the post-Soviet era and influencing a wide array of Western (and non-Western) readers.

In like manner, an in-depth critique (in ch 5) is given of M. B. Olcott and her historical treatment of Kazakh nationhood in her now classic work *The Kazakhs*. A response is then offered to her 2002 book entitled *Kazakhstan: Unfulfilled Promise* which politely accuses Kazakhstan based on allegations that as a 'modern nation-state' it (or at least its Kazakh constituency) is failing (among other things) to fulfill its alleged 'promise' to create a genuine multiethnic state. Her accusation is that "the Kazakh-dominated leadership" is pursuing "ethnic-based loyalty to the land of the Kazakhs" instead of "civic-based patriotism to a common homeland." In other words, in essential Leninist-Stalinist fashion still so fresh in their minds and hearts from yesterday, the Kazakhs are once again being accused as '(ethno)nationalists', only this time it comes from deep-seeded Western modernist convictions of multiethnic pluralistic democracy instead of in the name of 'the rapprochement of nations' hailed by Lenin and Stalin.

We then (in ch 6) pick up on an important theme which emerges near the end of chapter five and attempt to work further 'Towards Understanding the Dynamics of Internationalism, Pan-nationalism and Ethnonationalism in Kazakhstan and Central Asia'. Further critique of Western modernist attitudes and paradigms of 'the Central Asian conundrum' are offered amidst attempts to explain the delicate balance of these dynamics from more of a Central Asian view.

An important (though brief) comparison (in ch 7) of Kazakh with U.S. and South African national history is offered to demonstrate that the solutions for ethnicity and state worked out in those key Western historical contexts—which have given rise to the whole 'civil rights' and 'ethnic minority rights' agendas now undergirding 'international human rights' agendas as well as the related push for multiethnicity and pluralism, as the heir of the 'desegregation' policies arising from the Black Civil Rights and Anti-Apartheid movements, in 'the global age'—for the most part these do not apply and should not be applied to *the Central Asian context in light of its unique and almost opposite history.*

The final chapter (8) in the main discussion overviews Kazakh national history from a unified perspective of ethnonational-political identity showing that the ethnonational aspirations of the Kazakhs, including its political dimensions, remain strong throughout all stages and eras of their history. It reveals that the Kazakh 'ethnic nation' and 'political nation' have always 'naturally' gone hand-in-hand—before, during and after 'the coming of the Russians'. This means that Kazakh language, culture, history and statehood have been and still have the right to be woven together in the Kazakh nation, i.e. Kazakhstan—yesterday, today and tomorrow.

All of this is in demonstration of genuine humanistic-philanthropic commitment to and the concern of the one Creator for the Kazakhs and other Central Asian peoples and their ethnonational identity. This would include their well-being and international human rights—with '(ethno)national rights' worked out in proper historical perspective as an integral part of those human rights—in the modern global age.

—Chapter One—

THE DEBATE OVER ETHNIC VERSUS POLITICAL NATIONHOOD

The Debate Between the Organicist and Modernist Paradigms of 'Nations'

Walker Connor, "perhaps the leading student of the origins and dynamics of ethnonationalism" (1994:backcover), in a profound work on *Ethnonationalism: The Quest for Understanding*, made the following 'indictment':

> Scholars associated with theories of "nation-building" have tended to either ignore the question of ethnic diversity or to treat the matter of ethnic identity superficially as merely one of a number of minor impediments to effective state-integration. To the degree that ethnic identity is given recognition, it is apt to be as a somewhat unimportant and ephemeral nuisance that will unquestionably give way to a common identity uniting all the inhabitants of the state, regardless of ethnic heritage . . . It is not difficult to substantiate the charge that the leading theoreticians of "nation-building" have tended to slight, if not totally ignore, problems associated with ethnic diversity. A consultation of the table of contents and indices of books on "nation-building" will quickly convince the doubtful that the matter is seldom acknowledged, much less accorded serious consideration.[9]

Connor's 'indictment'—at least this particular one—was first put forth "at the Seventh World Congress of the International Sociological Association, held at Varna, Bulgaria, in September 1970" (1994:28), with his sentiments reiterated in an April 1972 article on "Nation-Building or Nation-Destroying?" appearing in *World Politics* (24:319-55). It has now been republished as part of his 1994 compendium of articles on *Ethnonationalism* (noted above). His indictment concerned what might be called 'people blindness', 'ethnic people blindness' that is. Indeed, Connor says elsewhere:

> Given the multitude of overt manifestations of ethnic nationalism throughout Africa and Asia (as well as elsewhere), it is difficult to reconcile its total absence or cursory treatment in so many studies on development. Even *in toto*, the preceding eleven considerations [given earlier of why it has been ignored] do not satisfactorily account for this failure to recognize the significance of the ethnic factor. *Eventually it is difficult to avoid the conclusion that the predispositions of the analyst are also involved; . . . that his passion has colored his perception so that he perceives those trends that he deems desirable as actually occurring, regardless of the factual situation. If the fact of ethnic nationalism is not compatible with his vision, it can thus be willed away.* A related factor is the fear that ethnic nationalism will feed on publicity. In either case, the treatment calls for the total disregard or cavalier dismissal of the undesired facts (1994:57; emphasis added).

Scholars may not ignore the subject of ethnicity as much as they did when Connor first issued his original indictment in the early 1970s. Perhaps he has had some impact. As we shall see though, whatever increase in measure there may or may not be, the treatment they do give to it remains less than optimal, even predominantly negative. In this sense, Connor's question of "Nation-Building or Nation-Destroying?" is still highly relevant. Likewise, much of the world still seems to suffer from the same essential 'people blindness', enough to warrant books like the 1995 release of *Unrepresented Nations and Peoples Organization.*[10]

All of this ultimately 'strikes' at the core of a major debate over just what a 'nation' *is* and even what it *should be*. And it is no small debate among theoreticians of 'nations' and 'nation-building'. There are two views which are at fundamental odds with and even 'diametrically opposed' to one another. With respect to understanding this debate, Anthony Smith—who in our own opinion and that of many others is, along with Walker Connor, one of the most important scholars of the last 40 years to address the issues of ethnicity, nations, and (ethno)nationalism—has bequeathed to us (among the many other works he has produced) at least two important books: *The Ethnic Origins of Nations* (1986) and *Nationalism and Modernism: A Critical Survey of Recent Theories of Nations and Nationalism* (1999). In both, he treats the clash between 'modernists' and 'organicists' (1986:7-13; 1999:18-24).[11] With our own modifications and clarifications added, Smith (1999:23) breaks the two primary views on 'nations' down into a comparative table in this way:

'NATIONS' are . . .	
Organicist Paradigm	*Modernist Paradigm*
An Ethno-Politico-Cultural Community	A Socio-Political, i.e. Civic and Legal, Community
Immemorial/Ancient	Strictly Modern (i.e. related to the Industrialization and Modernization Era)
Rooted within human society and History	Dependent on 'Modern' Economic-Political Conditions for Existence and Survival (i.e. 'on the surface of Human Society and History)
Natural/Organic (or Created)	Humanly Self-fabricated (i.e. Engineered via Socio-political Ideologies), Artificial/Mechanical
Qualitative (i.e. Naturally 'Being')	Human Resource-based (i.e. Functionally 'Doing')
Homogeneous and 'Seamless'	Integrated, Diverse, Heterogeneous
Based in Popular/Common Belief	Forged by Elite-Intellectualist Ideology
Ancestral/Kinship-based	Communication-/Technology-based

Smith himself notes importantly that this dualistic comparison has "deliberately magnified the differences, to bring out some of the antagonistic underlying assumptions" (1999:23). It nonetheless serves a very real and appropriate purpose. For the "underlying assumptions" of these two paradigms can, indeed, be rather "antagonistic" with regard to both historical as well as ethical interpretations and ideologies.[12] Elsewhere, then, Smith (1986:209) summarizes the difference between these two saying there are "two quite distinct conceptions of the nation and two routes to national status: the civic-territorial and the ethnic-genealogical."

'Nations and Nationalisms' in the Two Paradigms

Rather importantly then, these two primary paradigms of 'nations' yield correspondingly different views and theories of 'nationalism'. The modernist paradigm results in an economic-political version which may be referred to as 'civic nationalism'. And the organicist paradigm typically sees nationalism through the eyes of ethnicity, yielding 'ethnic nationalism' (i.e. ethnonationalism). A brief comparison of these two views may be set forth as follows:

- *The Organicist Paradigm of Nationalism*: A natural and voluntary self-assertion of ethnonational identity by the homogeneous group for purposes of protecting, reviving, and preserving their traditional, established identity and lifeways, including especially matters of land, language, and culture.
- *The (Western) Modernist Paradigm of Nationalism*: An intellectualist-elitist ideology of politicians and scholars designed to mobilize the social masses toward voluntary, patriotic love of and dedication to country (i.e. 'nation') as the means for building and sustaining economic-political nationhood and national life.

It is not as though the modernist and organicist paradigms have no recognition of, or view on, the 'nationalisms' of one another respectively. That is, the modernist paradigm recognizes, through its own 'rose-colored glasses', the existence of ethnic (or ethno-) nationalism. And organicists, likewise, recognize the existence of civic nationalism. If we set this out in a table once again, it will look like this:

RESPECTIVE VIEWS ON 'NATIONS' AND 'NATIONALISM' IN THE TWO MAJOR PARADIGMS OF 'NATIONS'	
Organicist Paradigm	*(Western) Modernist Paradigm*
Ethnic nations and nationalisms are primary. Nations are a natural outgrowth of organic human relations. Their nationalisms are a natural response of the people consisting of attempts to strengthen themselves or defend themselves in response to (perceived) threats against their nationhood.	Civic nations and nationalisms are primary. Nationalism is an intentional political ideology of elites for forging and building nations, thus making nationalism necessarily prior to, and not (naturally) flowing from, nationhood.
Civic nations and nationalisms are secondary. They are borrowed from the original form of 'nation' which was/is grounded in natural (i.e. organic) ethnonational ties and sentiments.	Ethnic nations and nationalisms are secondary by-products of civic nations. They are artificially constructed identities serving as a means for people to compete for resources in the state. They thus produce conflict and resistance to state integration and unity.

Rethinking the Alleged Dichotomy Between 'Ethnic Nations' and 'Political Nations'

Ultimately then, these two (i.e. the ethnic and political) aspects of 'nations and nationalism' are so intertwined and interrelated in human society and history, in national as well as international politics (including economic and religious matters), that no theory of either is complete without *sufficient* explanation of their relationship, given preferably in historical perspective. While *a distinction is recognizable*, ethnic 'nations' and nation-state 'nations', as well as their respective nationalisms, are so intertwined that in certain cases they (more or less) directly correspond to one another. That is, in cases like Japan and Korea, in spite of a small measure of ethnic diversity (which Western modernists are fond of emphasizing), the 'ethnic nation' remains the essential foundation and base for the political nation-state.[13] Likewise, as alluded to above, all of the new Central Asian nation-states are founded upon 'ethnic cores', each with unique claims of rights to the political state, which intimately involves language and other cultural rights issues, based upon claims of ethnic rights to their historic ancestral homelands. Not only these situations, however; even those nation-states whose ethnic foundations are not immediately visible participate in this close tie between ethnic nation and political nation. Smith (1986:214-5) lifts this important truth out for us in this way:

> . . . Modern conditions and trends have undoubtedly been responsible for spreading the idea and model of the nation as the sole legitimate political unit, but they needed the general inspiration of ethnicity as a model of socio-cultural organization and particular instances of strategic *ethnie*, to bring nations and nationalism into existence. . . . The means have quite patently changed. Formerly priests and scribes were the guardians and conduits of ethnic 'myth-symbol complexes', of ethnic memory from generation to generation. Now it is more likely to be intellectuals and professionals who rediscover and transmit to future generations the myths and symbols of modern nations, with the bourgeoisie and military replacing aristocracies as the power underpinning ethnic expansion and penetration. . . . So far, then, the modern nations simply extend, deepen, and streamline the ways in which members of *ethnie* associated and communicated. They do not introduce startlingly novel elements, or change the goals of human association and communication.

While many, as Smith (1986:209) points out, wish to emphasize "two quite distinct conceptions of the nation and two routes to national status: the civic-territorial and the ethnic-genealogical," we must realize that the 'ethnic-genealogical' conception also has a definite 'territorial' aspect which, as we shall see in time, involves the political while at the same time the civic-territorial has an ethnic aspect which very much involves 'kinship' relations and ideas of *father* or *mother*land. Ethnic nations and modern geo-political nations are not as polarized as they are alleged to be.

We simply cannot radically juxtapose a definition of 'ethnic nation' against, and detach it from, 'political nation' in an apparent vain effort to avoid the political question regarding ethnonational groups and their nationhood in the world order. The attempt to be 'apolitical' and only 'cultural', as if culture and politics had no genuine relationship in human affairs or history, is a misguided illusion. It may be possible in certain, limited circumstances, but it cannot be sustained across all time and boundaries, not even in the modern global age. If we believe we should speak out about other 'international human rights' issues such as religious freedom, women's and children's rights and the oppression of the poor, quite willing to take a political stance in these instances, then we should only be consistent and address the human rights of ethnonational groups in the international world order.

The attempt to juxtapose 'ethnic nations' against 'geo-political nations' is ultimately part of Western thinking that 'culture' can be conveniently 'privatized', separated from politics and related strictly to socio-cultural as opposed to socio-political issues. By taking this approach, when confronted with ethnonational issues in non-Western contexts, Westerners default to their own modernist socio-political ideals grounded in and shaped by their own historic experience in their own nation-states. They interpret and respond to issues of ethnonational *human* identity from the Western vantage point with the idea that their own views and convictions on these matters are the only appropriate interpretation, believing them to be universally valid and binding across the globe. Those who advocate the 'sacred marriage' between Christianity and democracy only wind up sacralizing Western socio-political ideals and values and then carrying them abroad to other nations in the name of the (essentially Western in this case) Christian God. But whichever route is taken, in the end, both Western secular and Western Christian approaches to nationhood in the modern age follow along similar lines.

Here we would express our agreement with Anthony Smith regarding one far-reaching implication of these truths, namely:

... No enduring world order can be created which ignores the ubiquitous yearnings of nations in search of roots in an ethnic past, and no study of nations and nationalism that completely ignores that past can bear fruit. . . . [T]he intense conflicts created by contemporary ethnic nationalisms will continue unabated until there is greater appreciation of the inner [ethnic] 'antiquity' of many modern nations (Smith 1986:5 and backcover).

Not only Smith, though; Graham Fuller, "a former vice chairman of the National Intelligence Council at the Central Intelligence Agency," makes a very similar point in his article on "Central Asia and American National Interests." There he urges that:

One of the paramount tasks *of the world* and the United Nations in this decade will be to try to evolve a series of alternative approaches and methods to handle . . . nationalist aspirations by small—or sometimes not so small—nations and peoples who seek fulfillment of ethnic aspirations (in Malik, ed., 1994:135; emphasis added).

"Clearly, ethnicity . . . has now become a central issue in the social and political life of every continent. The 'end of history', it seems, turns out to have ushered in the era of ethnicity."[14]

—Chapter Two—

FRAMEWORKS AND PARADIGMS IN THE BROADER DEBATE OVER NATIONHOOD

Toward Sociological and Geo-Political Paradigms of 'Nations and Nationalism'

As Anthony Smith himself recognizes however, the matter is not as simple as merely treating these two main paradigms (of organicism and modernism) and their respective relationship. There are actually five different paradigms regarding 'nations', each with their corresponding views on 'ethnicity' and 'nationalism'. And these all effect one's view of, and response to, ethnonational issues within the international-global world. Returning, then, to Smith's work on *Nationalism and Modernism* (1999), he overviews the entire field of scholarship on this subject for the last thirty years. In so doing, he offers abundant quotes from, and important discussions on, all the major contributors, explaining central matters of debate, and assessing strengths and weaknesses in each view. Of course, this is all from his own particular ('ethno-symbolist') vantage point. Nonetheless, his critique is valid and useful. He divides the study up into five major paradigms on 'nations', for which he offers a helpful summary in the conclusion. Based on his work, with significant reworking and modification calculated to include both 'descriptive' and 'prescriptive' angles, we offer the following overview of these five main paradigms.

Overview of the Five Main Paradigms of 'Nations'

1—**Postmodernist:** The 'nation' as well as the ethnic groups comprising them or within them are unique phenomena primarily related to the modern age (i.e.

post-Renaissance-Reformation). They are self-conceived and self-constructed social units, i.e. 'imagined communities' or 'invented traditions', which human beings themselves have chosen within a particular historical context (i.e. the modern period) as that which they deem best for their own benefit and welfare. In reality, however, these 'figments of their own imagination' often lead to strife, violence and tragedy. Neither of these constructs, 'ethnicity' or 'nation', have meaning or value beyond that which human beings themselves determine (cf. 'existentialism'). It does not ultimately matter whether human beings choose to order themselves according to 'nations' or 'ethnic groups' or not. Their benefit or detriment is entirely circumstantial and determined by each unique historical situation. However, their detriment with respect to divisiveness and violence appears to (far) outweigh their benefit and we would be better to 'deconstruct' these 'imagined communities' and 'invented traditions' in the post-modern age and reconstruct (i.e. 're-imagine') other more healthy and beneficial 'means' of organizing human society more in line with global identity in the post-modern era. (Note the 'instrumentalist-functionalist' base in this view).

2—**Idealistic Modernist:** The 'nation' as well as the ethnic groups comprising them or within them are unique phenomena related strictly to the modern age (i.e. post-Renaissance-Reformation, 'the age of nations and nationalism'). The 'nation' of today is essentially an artificial 'construct' which is 'engineered' by the intentional design of modern man as a socio-economic and socio-political ideology. It is an 'imagined community' or 'invented tradition' built by design for life in the modern, civilized world. The modern(ist) conception of 'nation' has no *real* or *significant* continuity with the past ideas of 'nation'. Former ideas of 'nation' (i.e. 'ethnos') were based primarily in quasi-tribal and ethnocultural-religious-linguistic groups and their ethnocultural-religious life. The 'nations' of the modern era are 'civic democratic'. They are not essential to the (global) human social order, but they are the best economico-socio-political unit for life in the modern world system. 'Ethnic groups' as related to them are 'self-imagined' cultural-religious groups who form based on *myths of common descent* as a means of vying for economic resources and political power. They are primarily negative and detrimental to the true goal of complete social integration, harmony, and individual equality at the levels of both the civic-democratic geo-political nation-state and international-global levels, especially if they manage to break away and form a socio-political community (i.e. ethnic-based 'nation') of their own. (Note the 'instrumentalist-functionalist' base in this view).

3—Pragmatic Modernist-Perennialist (i.e. Ethno-symbolist): The modern 'nation' is essentially a self-imagined and self-constructed community designed as a means of uniting individuals together in a social community and providing their basic needs and rights for life in the uniquely modern world. But it contains certain 'perennial' elements of past ethnocultural groups—themselves typically viewed as self-imagined and self-constructed social groups—whose fundamental identities have been intentionally taken over, 'revived' and revised, and incorporated into the foundation of the new civic-democratic 'nation'. Former 'ethnic' bases for 'nationhood' have been taken over and symbolically used but (entirely) reinterpreted along modernist civic-democratic lines. Both new and old exist together, therefore, in unique blend, having both continuity and discontinuity. The primary difference is that the modern nation has shifted from being a merely passive historical reality based in ethnic groups and their cultural-religious life and has moved toward becoming more an active 'construct' of 'elites' (i.e. scholars and politicians) by intentional ('instrumentalist, functionalist') design in the modern enlightenment era. This 'new' understanding of nation seeks to integrate various ethnic groups into new multi-ethnic 'nations' for socio-economico-political reasons. The modern 'nation', therefore, contains within it fundamental conflicts based in the ties between ancient ideas of 'ethnicity' and modern ideas of socio-political multiethnic community and these must be resolved in a meaningful way in order to abate ethnic tensions and establish social harmony at both national and global levels. That is, the ethnic foundations of modern nations must be recognized and appreciated in attempting to define and fulfill the nature and goals of those nations. (This is our own understanding of Anthony Smith's position in a 'nutshell').

4—Perennialist (i.e. Pragmatic Historical): 'Nations' are established (or at least modeled and, therefore, dependent) upon ethnic foundations. The distinction, therefore, between 'modern civic nations' and 'pre-modern ethnic nations' is not clear cut. Indeed, the two often overlap significantly with one another and even in rare cases generally correspond with one another. An ethnic core lying at the foundation of many 'modern civic nations' can easily be discerned. Likewise, the 'ethnic groups' making up multi-ethnic nations at times themselves become the basis for the formation of new 'nations'. 'Nations' and/or 'ethnic groups' are intimately bound together in ideas of 'nationhood'. This conception and reality of nationhood is perennial (i.e. 'of long, continuous and/or recurrent duration') throughout history. Such 'nations' have existed in the past and, generally, continue on with socio-political variations unique to each historical context. That is, in essence, the 'nations' and their foundational 'ethnic group(s)' of both past and present and most likely future will continue to have the same fundamental nature in spite of the varying political forms and structures or their precise social composition. However, the 'nation' does not exist or persist by any design (i.e. 'telos') or intention of some divine will or determining force of life. They do not have any 'natural' organic relationship to human society and its 'natural' social structure(s). They have existed throughout history, not by organic necessity, but more by chance. *They arise on 'the surface of history' as byproducts of (dialectical) historical circumstance as opposed to being rooted organically in human history and society*. In this way, they *appear* as the seemingly best way that humans *tend* to organize themselves. There *seems* something innate within us driven to these basic forms of organization, but these forms are not socially, ethically or biologically imposed upon us from outside ourselves; they are self-defined and self-constructed (i.e. self-imposed). They could fade on their own, be reconstructed or done away with and human society would still continue on without them. However, this is unlikely by virtue of their 'long duration' throughout history. The fact of their continuous and/or recurrent long duration throughout history makes them in the eyes of many perennialists important aspects of human society worth promoting and preserving while other perennialists view them as inescapable 'problem children' continually undergoing birth and death throughout historical cycles which must be 'tolerated' as part of the perhaps undesirable but nonetheless necessary reality of human existence.

5—Organicist-Creationist (i.e. Idealistic Sociological-Historical): The 'nation' is essentially rooted in 'ethnicity' so that ethno*national* groups provide the foundational core upon which the 'nation' has *typically* been built throughout history in most (though not all) cases. An ethnic core lying at the foundation of many 'modern civic nations' can easily be discerned. Likewise, the ethnic groups making up multi-ethnic nations at times themselves become the basis for the formation of new 'nations' because they have natural socio-political aspirations grounded in their own genuine and integral ethno*national* identity. Modern civic multi-ethnic nations cannot function or survive without the presence of ethnicity to undergird them and determine their course, whether existing within them or around them. Ethnicity and its close corollary of 'nation' have existed in the past and, generally, continue on into the present and future with variations unique to each historical context. The (ethno)national groups of past and present and future will continue to have the same fundamental 'ethnic' nature in spite of varying political forms and structures. The 'nation' is intrinsic to the 'natural' (created or evolved) human social order. It is an integral and essential part of the design and makeup of human society and *human identity*. This provides 'nations' with (ethno)national 'human rights' in the inter*national* human social order and establishes the basis upon which that nationhood and those rights can and should be promoted, safeguarded and defended. Ethnonational identity will not nor can it be removed from the human social order of this world without causing severe disruption to individual as well as corporate human social existence at both local and global levels. While genuine 'multi-ethnic nations' can be identified in humankind's past and present, attempts to establish such nations which ignore underlying ethnic foundations are destined to create or exacerbate *unnecessary* conflict and turmoil within human society, especially attempts to forbid ethnic-based nationhood on the premise of mandatory civic-territorial (i.e. 'idealist modernist') ideals of nationhood.

*   *   *

Just one year after *Nationalism and Modernism*, in yet another brilliant study entitled *The Nation in History: Historiographical Debates About Ethnicity and Nationalism*, A. D. Smith (2000) brings into still sharper focus the 'clash' between these various paradigms. In developing these 'clashes', he summarizes the matter (on pp 2-3) in this way:

> Three fundamental debates have structured and continue to define the historiography of nationalism:
>
> 1. The organicist versus the voluntarist understanding of the nation and the contemporary debates between primordialists and instrumentalists that stem from these understandings.
> 2. The perennialist versus the modernist approaches to nations and nationalism and the contemporary debates about the antiquity or modernity of nations.
> 3. The social constructionist versus the ethnosymbolic approaches to nations and nationalisms and the contemporary debates about the relationship of the past and present in the formation and future of nations.

Regarding 'primordialism' Smith notes (on p. 5) that "we can distinguish three broad strands or versions: an organicist, a sociobiological, and a cultural primordialism." The sociobiological version seems to be concerned with ideas of 'pure blood' and biological determinism. To clarify our own position here, then, we have no intention of affirming or promoting a sociobiological view in this work, associated as it correctly is with dangerous theories of 'pure blood' and 'pure race'. The distinction of 'organicist' as a particular strand here is unclear, but in our view it will be explained via our identification of 'ethnicity as kinship'. Our position incorporates ideas of flexibility so that we do not wind up with an overly naturalistic determinism based in some kind of rigid 'natural law' (whether of creation or evolution) strictly defining and governing human society while at the same time recognizing that ethnonational identity forms a genuine, 'organic', integral part of the social and psychological dimensions of human nature and identity. Regarding 'cultural primordialism', then, Smith remarks later (on p 19) that some voluntarist-modernist scholars assume "a secular trend from ethnic [organic] toward civic nationalism, with cultural nationalism as a kind of halfway house along the road." The strong belief in 'progress' in all aspects of human life which permeates this view is perhaps worth noting. In that regard, it has a ring of Marxist evolutionism to it. More importantly, though, we can discern here a (desire to) move away from ideas of organic kinship, based as they are in the 'organic nature' of human society itself, to an emphasis on detached cultural symbols as the locus for ethnonational identity and (ethno)nationalism. This marks an important shift of emphasis which seems very much to have affected all Western thinking regarding ethnonational identity. Indeed, for many modern scholars, especially in the West:

> One of the gravest problems for the twenty-first century is how we cope with the fears that cluster around *ethnicity*, the idea that keeps separating us from the Others while technology keeps bringing us all together. . . . *Culture* differentiates people. Sometimes it differentiates us so much that we forget that we are all members of the same species—we let it turn us into battling partisans, forgetting our common humanity. *Culture*, in other words, not only makes us what we are—it can kill us.[15]

Notice that 'ethnicity' and 'culture' are actually equated here. And for the author just quoted as well as many others of our day these two both become, as E. A. Aasland (2004:1) the provider of the quotes describes it, "public enemy number one." However much of an overstatement one feels this might be, let the basic point be well taken. And it holds true for 'ethnicity' more than 'culture' because 'culture' is the better alternative, 'the lesser of two evils' so to speak. It is made out to be—in the view of many Western anthropologists, sociologists, political scientists and theologians—a much 'safer' and 'non-political' construct. It can allegedly be detached from its grounding in organic human nature and then treated as a scientific 'object' or 'artifact' of observation, hypothesis and experimentation. It can be located in the 'traditional clothing', 'traditional foods' and the 'rituals, customs and traditions' of a people instead of in the people themselves. Meanwhile 'ethnicity' resides *in* people groups and their respective members, making it much more of a socio-political issue than many care to deal with, since after all it is the people, not their 'food, clothing, customs and traditions', who comprise the social groups and citizens of 'the nation'.[16]

Toward Philosophical and Ethical Paradigms of 'Nations and Nationalism'

One thing worth noting in the above scheme is the distinction between 'pragmatic' and 'idealistic' versions of certain paradigms. What this begins to point out is the important distinction between 'descriptive' versus 'prescriptive' aspects of nations in pursuing their study as well as in acting within and/or on their behalf. That is, a *description* ("was" or "is") of nations in world history and human society is not the same thing as a *prescription* ("ought" or "should be") of what nations should ideally have been or be in that world history and society.[17] We begin touching here into some age-old philosophical debates over the nature of reality, existence, and 'being' (i.e. 'ontology'). In the main, this includes the debate between 'Platonic' and 'Aristotelian' paradigms (i.e. 'ideal forms' versus 'particular manifestations') as well as between Parmenidian and Heraclitan paradigms (i.e. the static, unchanging versus the ever-flowing, changing).[18] These types of philosophical presuppositions surely underlie the various debates over nations and they should be studied further in relation to the subject as well as borne in mind during the course of inquiry.

Regardless, a distinction between the 'is' and the 'ought' is justifiable because one cannot even begin to discuss the subject of 'nations' unless there is some *idea* and *definition* of what 'nations' are, i.e. what 'nationhood' involves, in general (cf. a Platonic view). Indeed, this assumption is central to the debate between modernists and organicists as well as modernists and perennialists. It is to be observed in this respect that 'the international community' (e.g. the United Nations or even NATO, etc) must have some 'standard', some definition and qualities of 'nationhood' established in order to recognize and interact as 'nations'. If there are no set boundaries and ideas as to what constitutes a 'nation' and 'nationhood', then any grouping of human beings qualifies to be called a 'nation'. This, of course, would make the terms 'nation' and 'international' essentially meaningless and any and all attempts to discuss such subjects would become an exercise in futility. We do not need to become overly rigid or demanding in our definitions, but defining nationhood remains a crucial issue nonetheless.

Difficult matters of 'epistemology' (i.e. the source and basis of knowledge) come into play at this juncture. Noteworthy in this regard is that descriptive studies of nations in history provide much of the basis of discussion. As touched on above, this is important and helpful, even necessary and valid. But *description* itself cannot simply be transformed into *prescription*, otherwise this too is redundant and even dangerous in a world where nations are made up of 'less than perfect' (i.e. 'sinful'), even at times downright wicked human beings. Nations in history include 'the good, the bad and the ugly' as well as the beautiful. But unless the concepts of 'good', 'bad', 'ugly' and 'beautiful' with respect to nationhood are anchored in something other than the nations themselves and their histories, the entire matter becomes redundant and arbitrary and we are left with no way to determine when nations become 'good', 'bad', 'ugly' or 'beautiful'. Indeed, the whole question of whether there is anything good about nations and their nationhood could even be raised, as more than a few are surely doing against the backdrop of globalization. Then, of course, there is always the other path taken by radical extremist nationalists who feel that there can be nothing bad whatsoever about nations and their nationhood.

Humanity must be willing to look beyond itself for help and hope in the quest for answers to such a complex phenomenon as 'nationhood' so central to and profoundly affecting its entire history. We are thus driven back to the Creator of humankind as an ultimate ground for understanding our human world with its history and dilemmas, especially with respect to 'nationhood'. In this, the present writer, from his Christian worldview, and many scholars in the Central Asian context from their Muslim and/or Tengrist worldview, *share in common* a view of the basic created (cf. organic) nature of ethnonational identity as an integral and rightful part of genuine *human identity* in the inter*national* world.

Secular scholars might object to this, but we would note two things in passing: First, the choice to be 'secular' is itself a position; if we demand it of everyone as allegedly the only fair and impartial position possible, then we have become guilty of the same bias and exclusivity which 'religious' people have often been accused. Secularism constitutes a worldview which provides a framework for interpreting the world we live in. But as Paul Costello (1994:17) has clearly demonstrated in his insightful study of *World Historians and Their Goals: Twentieth Century Answers to Modernism*, ultimately "[t]here is no sharp dividing line between philosophies of history based upon a divine plan and those that emphasize a strictly secular progressivism." Actually there is a sharp dividing line and it is precisely in a view of ethnonational identity as created versus merely evolved as a 'natural' or, for others, unnatural byproduct of historical circumstance and/or human imagination. But Costello is right in so far as both approaches find themselves grappling to establish underpinnings for human origins, identity and destiny which provide genuine meaning for our existence, especially in this case for the existence of nations.

Whatever our basis of conviction however, we are ultimately confronted with matters of ethics and human rights in international relations with respect to nations and their 'national identity', including *ethno*national identity. No doubt an avoidance of neo-Nazi ideals of 'pure blood' (typically based in biological, evolutionary ideals) which lead to extreme and even horrendous acts of wickedness against other nations in the name of one's own nation (i.e. racism and ethnocentrism) are unacceptable. Extreme ideals not grounded in the reality of ultimate human unity, equality and brotherhood are simply dangerous.[19]

Yet, we find ourselves immediately ushered back to the critical tension and balance between human unity and genuine diversity as soon as we say such a thing. For claims of ethnocentrism and racism (cf. also 'separatist', 'divisiveness', 'anti-brotherhood', etc.) uttered against ethnic peoples and nations for an earnest desire, and even need in certain situations, to safeguard and nourish the uniqueness of their peoplehood and the foundations of their nationhood are not appropriate either. Attempts to condemn 'ethnic-based nationhood' by labeling it 'ethnocratic' are shallow and false. Likewise, '(ethno)nationalism' and 'ethnocentrism' (cf. also 'racism') are *not* the same thing and there is desperate need for discerning the difference between the two at this critical hour of world history. Indeed, if we are going to use terminology such as 'ethnocratic' and 'ethnocentric' then we must in all fairness begin employing terms such as 'international-cratic', 'international-centric', 'global-centric' and the like to distinguish between healthy and unhealthy forms and emphases with respect to *both* dimensions of our *inter-national* world, i.e. our world of genuinely interrelating nations. A truly 'international' world requires the preservation and ongoing existence of nations as well as the maintenance of their interrelating.

In this light, it is of no little significance that the United Nations proclaimed

---

the ten-year span of 1995-2004 "The International Decade of the World's Indigenous People" and its Commission on Human Rights has established an "inter-sessional working group" to research and draft a statement on the rights of 'Indigenous Peoples'.

> An objective of the Decade is the promotion and protection of the rights of indigenous people and their empowerment to make choices which enable them to retain their cultural identity while participating in political, economic and social life, with full respect for their cultural values, languages, traditions and forms of social organization.[20]

The ethnonational issues we are discussing here involve our view and interpretation of history from not only sociological and geo-political, but philosophical-theological and moral-ethical angles, both generally as well as specifically in relation to each event and circumstance. Broad sweeping generalizations are overly simplistic. Passively accepting all historical events and their outcomes as some kind of 'manifest destiny' for the nations is historical fatalism and confuses a true and proper view of the relation between God's sovereignty and human responsibility. Imperfect (i.e. sinful) humans who nonetheless retain the essence of God's image in their being are the actors and agents of history. Due sorrow over wrongs committed as well as confession, forgiveness, recompense, restitution and restoration are fundamental ideals involved in a healthy humanistic as well theistic perspective for righting wrongs of the past. 'Love your neighbor as yourself', in this case your ethnic neighbor, also stands at the forefront of ethical guidelines for human social affairs and behavior. The question of what our interpretations of history, including the application of our ethics to it, should mean for human beings as well as their actions and impact among 'the nations' must be answered in general terms and principles as well as in their application to each specific and unique set of historical circumstances.

Five Paradigms of the Relationship and Balance Between Ethnonational, International-Global and Individual Human Identity

As a small step along the path to finding resolutions to these kinds of ethical questions and issues, we offer, along with the above five paradigms of 'nations', the following five paradigms of the relationship and balance between ethnonational, international-global, and individual human identity. One can catch hints of ethical ideas in the words 'positive' and 'negative' in these titles and we have drawn from these two basic concepts in developing the following five paradigms.

The Paradigm of Negative Intolerance:
Modernist Civic Nationalism/Globalism

Ethnonational identity (or 'ethnicity') is essentially and ultimately negative because it is a group identity which suppresses individual identity and inhibits those individuals from being integrated fully and equally into a larger, corporate and unified identity. Ethnonational identity, as the basis for ethnonationalism and racism, is itself a primary source of human conflict and tragedy. It should, therefore, be dissolved and integrated into a larger, greater 'meta-national' identity. This meta-national identity is either the larger multi-ethnic civic nation-state within the international nation-state system or the one global unity of humankind which itself transcends and integrates all nation-states, and therefore, ethnic groups, into one global socio-political order.

The Paradigm of Negative Tolerance:
Modified Civic Nationalism/Globalism

Ethnonational identity has some good sides, but it is essentially and ultimately negative because it is a group identity which suppresses individual identity and inhibits those individuals from being integrated fully and equally into a larger, corporate and unified identity. Ethnonational identity, as the basis for ethnonationalism and racism, is itself a primary source of human conflict and tragedy. However, the mere persistence of ethnonational identity in human history demonstrates that it most likely will remain for many decades or even centuries to come as a phenomenon of human identity (at least until the nation-state system is replaced or transcended). It must, therefore, be tolerated and accepted within human society as a strictly non-political cultural construct, but it should not be permitted to take any precedence over the larger, greater 'meta-national' (i.e. multi-ethnic nation-state or global) identity or any of the other more important human identities, including basic individual ones and regional community ones. Thus, all ethnic groups must be held as tertiary or lesser identities in human society and all given equal treatment in every situation so that none can be favored over another or set in competition to one another. Restoration, preservation and/or strengthening of ethnonational identities do not deserve to be categorized as moral-ethical issues. Their priority status should remain low on the scale and should even be avoided in many cases because of their negative, dangerous, tertiary, and non-essential character. If ethnonational identities are weakened, dissolved, or done away with, it is merely the natural outcome of (amoral) historical processes and should not be of deep concern; it may even be for the better. However, in order to accommodate them in the present it is good to offer recognition of and appreciation for their uniqueness strictly at the cultural level in ways that maintain their proper distinction from any and all political identity or power.

The Paradigm of 'Perfect' Neutrality: Preferred Internationalism/Globalism

Ethnonational identity appears to be a recurring and enduring phenomenon throughout human history. However, it is entirely neutral and non-essential for ultimate human identity within human society. Its assets and deficits 'balance' or 'nullify' each other out so that ethnicity does not ultimately matter one way or the other. Thus, ethnonational identity can legitimately and genuinely be appreciated and celebrated for its cultural uniqueness and the way it adds color to human life. It can also help provide a framework for individuals to better understand themselves and function in society. This does not mean, however, that any real efforts need to be made to restore, preserve or strengthen such identities. They should not be treated as an ethical-moral issue. Ethnonational identity, as the basis for ethnonationalism, is often a source of social tension, strife, conflict, and even war through ethnocentrism and racism. If, therefore, a group's ethnic identity weakens, dissolves, or even disappears it should be accepted as a natural outcome of (amoral) historical processes. The more important identities for humanity are the civic national, international-global and the individual ones. *Ethnonational identities are primarily a means* to working toward, developing and strengthening these other identities.

The Paradigm of Positive Passivism: Popular Internationalism

Ethnonational identity appears to be a natural (or God-created), recurring and enduring phenomenon throughout human history. It can be negative, but it is generally positive and good, providing human beings with a genuine sense of their historic roots and social familial (i.e. kinship) identity within the larger kinship group of overall (i.e. global) human society. It, therefore, should be appreciated and even celebrated. But, it is strictly a tertiary identity and ultimately non-essential to the greater civic national, international-global as well as fundamentally more important individual identities of humanity. Thus, restoration, protection and/or preservation of ethnonational identity should not be counted a high priority and it should even be sacrificed whenever it conflicts with the building of civic national, international-global and/or individual identities. If ethnonational identities are altered, changed or even lost, whether through tragic circumstances or otherwise, the new resulting identities should still be accepted as the natural outcome of historical processes. The new identities should be treated as socially genuine and valid, without making attempts to undo history, and then used as a basis for incorporating individuals into the greater civic national, 'international/global' identity within the community of humankind.

The Paradigm of Positive Activism:
Nationalistic Internationalism

Ethnonational identity is a recurring and enduring phenomenon throughout human history. It can be negative, but it is generally positive and good, providing human beings with a genuine sense of their historic roots and social familial (i.e. kinship) identity within the larger kinship group of overall (i.e. global) human society. It is not logically necessary, but it is an organic (even God created) part of human society and is, therefore, existentially necessary as something naturally occurring within the human social order throughout history. Individual, ethnic, civic national and international-global identities are all genuine, good, and equally important in their own unique way as distinct facets of human identity. None should be given absolute priority over the others, but all should be held in balance and be emphasized in proper, though perhaps varying, degree in the various contexts of human life and history. True 'international' as well as individual human identity within human society as natural (even God-created and intended) phenomena, therefore, calls for the ongoing presence as well as restoration, sustenance and preservation of distinct ethnonational identities as much as is reasonably possible within the progression of sin-stained human history. There can be no true inter*national* world without its *national* component preserved and kept in tact. New ethnonational identities can be formed from pre-existing ones, and this can be a good, healthy and natural process. But the tearing apart, breaking down, or 'death' of an ethnonational group is, as a general rule, not to be desired or contributed to. A sincere and genuine effort, therefore, should be made to restore and preserve ethnonational identities while at the same time allowing for irreversible, necessary and/or dynamic change.

*   *   *

These five paradigms represent the range and flux of attitude and response in the search for balance between individual, (ethno)national and international-global human identities. If it has not become clear by now, this book takes the latter view, i.e. that of *Positive Activism: (Ethno)Nationalistic Internationalism*. Based in these convictions, our aim is *Rethinking Kazakh and Central Asian Nationhood* in hopes of helping all of us achieve balanced, just and fair resolution of the complex and delicate matters involved.

—Chapter Three—

WESTERN MODERNIST SCHOLARSHIP CONFRONTS 'THE UNIFIED ETHNONATIONAL COMPLEX'

Foundations of the Western Modernist View of Nations

The fact is that most people from the West (and perhaps the East) do not realize 'the clash of paradigms' which is taking place in the debates over ethnicity, nations and (ethno)nationalism. These debates and the various paradigms underlying them concern the proper nature, role and impact of ethnicity, nations and (ethno)nationalism *within* 'the larger frame of globalization', but also within and upon the continuing context of the international nation-state system. In spite of premonitions of its demise in the newly emerging 'global village', the international nation-state system remains largely in tact today. And its agenda has been set largely by the West[21] with its corresponding modernist paradigm.

This situation has developed *in special relation to* Western history, or perhaps world history as the West has experienced and responded to it, particularly since the Renaissance-Reformation. Two central issues—religion (i.e. 'church') and state as well as ethnicity and state—stand at the heart of that *uniquely Western* history. This history has been marked by the emergence and development of three parallel movements across Western Europe all dynamically interrelated with and reflexively shaping one another: 1) secular humanism of the Renaissance (and Enlightenment), 2) the formation of 'nations' breaking away from the 'Holy Roman Empire' and 3) the alignment of Christianity with those nations, especially the Protestant tradition which 'broke away' together, but also the Catholic tradition (as for example in Spain and France).

———

All of these in turn participated in the rising tide of European colonialism which gave birth to today's *Euro-American democracy-based* 'international' nation-state system. We should observe here then that Western European and North American approaches to nationhood have been profoundly impacted by both Renaissance humanism and Christian (especially Protestant) theology of 'nationhood'.

Against this background, we can highlight three primary stages or decisive 'revolutions' of Western ideology and praxis in the historical development of nationhood:

- There was an initial and parallel rise of humanist thought and Protestantism with the 'nations' of Western Europe in the 15-17th centuries as these 'nations' broke from and defined themselves in relation to the former declining 'Holy Roman Empire'. This established independent national sovereignty for non-Roman-Italian *Christian* peoples based especially in ethno-cultural-linguistic domains (cf. 'the bible in *the language of the people* as a primary Reformation cry). There was no idea of separation of Church and State nor of Ethnicity and State in this period. Rather, there was a strong tie between Church and Nation (-State) *with both based primarily in ethnonational identities.*

- In consequence of the often *religiously* fueled political wars between these newly formed 'nations' and the devastation which they wreaked on Europe during this period, there arose (the attempt at) a clear break in the 17th to early 20th centuries between 'Church and State'. On the one hand was the (allegedly) 'secular-civic-public non-religious political state' and, on the other, 'private religion and religious freedom'. This was exemplified in the American (1776) and French (1789) Revolutions, which marked the 'revolution of democracy' (i.e. strictly democratic-based nationhood) and the intense concern in democracy for 'religious freedom' (which was initially concerned only with 'religious freedom' *within Christianity*, but after the 20th century with broader 'religious pluralism'). From this, it established a predominantly negative view of 'religious nationalism' which has profoundly affected the right and ability of religion to speak to issues of nationhood. *But there was no real concern for separation of 'Ethnicity and State' during this period.*

- In consequence of European 'white supremacy'-based colonialism-imperialism and its oppression of non-Caucasian (i.e. 'non-white') ethnonational groups came (the attempt at) a clear break between 'Ethnicity and State'. The three main historical events which convinced *the Western democratic world* of the need for this break to be made an ethical imperative of democracy were World War II (i.e. WWII) and the problem of especially Nazi German (but also Italian and Japanese) *ethnopolitical nationalism* (1940-50s), the Black Civil Rights Movement in the USA (1950-60s) and the closely related problem of Apartheid in South Africa (1970-90s). This gave rise to emphatic concern for a 'secular, civic *multi-ethnic* political state', forbidding all claims of unique or 'pre-eminent' right to political authority in the nation-state by any one, particular ethnic (i.e. core ethnonational) group. It also fueled a predominantly negative view of 'nationalism', particularly any form of ethnic nationalism (i.e. 'ethnonationalism'). The latter became associated almost exclusively with 'ethnopolitics' and condemned as an essentially negative and inherently dangerous phenomenon. It also gave rise to the false dichotomy between 'patriotism' as that which is positive and related to civic democratic nationhood versus '(ethno)nationalism' as that which is negative and related to 'ethnocratic' (or religious-based) nationhood. *It is this third stage which marks the rise and development of the 'Western modernist' position.*

The establishment of nations in East Europe and Central Asia is closely associated with Euroslavic (i.e. East European) colonialism and their unique developments affected by later Marxist ideas of nationhood. Those developments have likewise played a vital role in the formation of the international nation-state system. We will return to treat those developments soon. For now we can note that nations and their corresponding ideals of *democratic* nationhood in the Western Euro-American tradition arose in the Renaissance-Reformation era and have then taken their shape across the last several centuries. This would include their establishment across Africa as well as West Asia (i.e. the Middle East), South and East Asia via Western European colonialism. It is this tradition of *democratic* nationhood which stands behind and beneath the modern international nation-state system. Here the remarks of Charles Tilley should be carefully reflected upon when he observes that:

> . . . the study of European state-making has at least one point of relevance to the politics of the contemporary world: Europeans played the major part in creating the contemporary international

state-system, and presumably left the imprints of their peculiar political institutions on it. It is probably even true . . . that a state which has adopted western forms of organization will have an easier time in the international system; after all, the system grew up in conjunction with those forms.[22]

The international nation-state system has of course developed within the course of 'modern' world history. The importance of one's view of ethnicity, nations and (ethno)nationalism in properly understanding and interpreting world history can be seen, for example, in the work of the very esteemed world historian, William McNeill. Although McNeill's work should be left to ultimately speak for itself—and it is certainly a worthy read—we will again draw from another esteemed scholar, A. Smith, to help us understand this vital relation of one's paradigm of 'nations' and world history in McNeill's work. Smith (2001:60) explains that:

> For McNeill, human history is marked by three stages. The first, premodern epoch, was marked by polyethnic hierarchies of skilled labor. These hierarchies created the great civilizations out of their much-sought-out skills, and civilized communities were accordingly polyglot polyethnic. In the second stage, from 1750 to 1914, a unique combination of factors nourished the age of nations; the classicism of the intelligentsia, the new conscript armies, the new reading publics, and the ability to replenish from an ethnically homogeneous countryside labor skills depleted by disease. Together, these factors fed the dream of national unity and cultural homogeneity (McNeill 1986, chaps 1-2). But by the mid-twentieth century their power had waned, and the dream of national unity, which in any case was largely a mirage, faded. Now we are once again returning to looser transnational economies and cultures based on the old polyethnic hierarchies of skill. As NcNeill sums it up: "Polyethnic hierarchy is on the rise, everywhere." Like the cultural critic Homi Bhabha and the historian of India, Partha Chatterjee, McNeill envisages a much more fragmented and hybridized society as we move into a postnational era, largely as a result of large-scale immigration and mass communications. The contemporary scene is essentially fragmented and cosmopolitan;

it has no place for communities of devotion and purpose, for
the moral community or the sacred community of the nation
(McNeill 1986, 82 . . .)."

Smith's appraisal of McNeill agrees with that of Paul Costello, who includes
McNeill, along with H.G. Wells, Oswald Spengler, Arnold Toynbee, Piritirm
Sorokin and Lewis Mumford, among those 20th century world historians
pursuing a goal of 'world unity'. In pursuing that goal, he notes, for instance,
how "[t]he utopias and anti-utopian societies of [H.G.] Wellsian fiction serve
either as guiding ideals or as warnings of possible dehumanization . . . if
certain *negative trends* in the present are not reversed and if historically residual
patterns and practices from *nationalism* and factory specialization to class
differentiation are not left behind" (1994:23; emphasis added). We begin to
glimpse here in Well's thinking the close relation between nationalism and
industrialization in 20th century Western modernist thinking, an influence of
Marxian interpretations regarding the rise of 'nationhood' in the Marxist
economic version of world history.

But even such a great writer as Christopher Dawson—for all his profound
insight into the *Dynamics of World History* and *Religion and World History*
(which are the titles of two key compilations of his writings) drawn from his
own Catholic tradition—still turns out to be one of these same 20th century
world historians treated by Costello who sees the rise of nations and
"nationalism" in Europe as a primary "source," together with Luther and the
Protestant Reformation, of what "destroyed the unity of Christendom and
split Europe asunder."[23] (The quote is drawn from Dawson's own writings, by
the way, not Costello's assessment of him.) Thus Dawson seeks 'world unity'
via a return to "the unity of Christendom," in its Catholic form of course, and
its necessary corollary of a return to European unity.

These pursuits of 'world unity' in 20th century historians represent a basic
framework for understanding the origin, development and role of 'nations'
and 'nationalism' in world history in one major school of modernist
interpretation. The main point of distinction between the two main schools
would be whether 'nations' (in the sense that modernist scholars understand
them) will continue on or will fade into the sunset of globalization (cf. e.g.
Mittleman 2000:20, *The Globalization Syndrome*). Regardless, they all argue
that 'nations and nationalism' *as we know them today* emerged at a unique
point in human history due to peculiar historical circumstances related to the
'modern age' and its industrialization (or 'modernization') in the face of

declining feudalism. 'Nations', therefore, in the 'modern age' have little or no continuity with any ideas of 'cultural' or 'ethnic nations' of the 'pre-modern period'.

For example, in McNeill's scheme, we see that it is in "the second stage, from 1750 to 1914" that "a unique combination of factors nourished the age of nations." The exact dating of this 'age of nations' varies from modernist scholar to modernist scholar. Some take it as far back as 1648 and the Treaty of Westphalia, others suggest 1776 or 1789 in connection with the American and French Revolutions respectively, while still others offer 1830 as the crucial starting point. The national(ist) 'Revolutions of 1848' in France, Italy, the Austrian Empire and Germany are also important in the overall scheme. Regardless of its starting point though, WWI (1914-17) serves as an important point of closure to this major critical period of 'nations and nationalism' in all modern, including modern*ist*, studies. But the point at which 'nations and nationalism' allegedly peak in modernist thinking would vary as much as the point of origin, at least for those who believe they have peaked or will peak. Some see it with the closure of WWI in 1917. Some see it with the end of WW2 in 1945. Others see it with the rise of globalism beginning sometime in the 80s or 90s of the 20th century. Whatever the points of origin and closure, however, central in the modernist view is this 'age of nations' and its unique tie to the 'modern' era.[24]

This paradigm of 'nationhood' identified here as 'Western modernism' has emerged from and been largely shaped by its initial reactions to several major 20th century events: World War I and, then, in particular to Nazism (as well as Japanese and Italian 'fascism') in World War II, the Black Civil Rights in America in the 1950-60s and anti-Apartheid efforts in South Africa between 1970-90. At the heart of this paradigm is its cardinal distinction between 'ethnic nation' and '(geo-)political nation' which again represent "two quite distinct conceptions of the nation and two routes to national status: the civic-territorial and the ethnic-[organic]" (Smith 1986:209). Kazakh scholars are certainly aware of this proposed dichotomy, as for example Tursin Gabitov, who notes in his treatment of "The National Idea of the Kazakhs as a Problem of Cultural Study" that:

> In modern literature the word "national" is characterized by dichotomization: [first,] its ethical interpretation, where civic features are being put in the foreground, rather than ethnic ones. By *nation* some scholars imply a state and civic community

based on human rights. From their point of view national identification involves a civic mentality which is characterized by a realization and appreciation of an individual and his\her belonging to a unified civic community, i.e. the state. . . the second interpretation of national idea comes from seeing it as an ethnic idea, where ethnos itself is defined as 'a group of people who speak the same language, acknowledge their common origin, have a set of customs and a life-style that is preserved and sanctified by tradition'.[25]

The Western modernist paradigm took a strong turn toward the civic-territorial model of nationhood in the 1960s and 70s as an intentional effort to resolve the ethnonational issues which had arisen out of the key 20th century events just noted above. In the course of doing so, it became and still remains inherently opposed and calculated, quite often with a 'religious' passion, to work against ideas of ethnic-based statehood (including ethnic-based appeals to rights of political autonomy and/or independence) in the late 20th, early 21st century. "Autonomy" of course is different than complete 'independence'. It is also different than one particular ethnic group within a multi-ethnic nation-state claiming unique preeminence in political rights within the national state, which are inseparably bound up with language and culture rights, as is the case for example with the Central Asian nation-states in the post-Soviet period. But these issues are intricately and inseparably related to and flow out of the same well-spring of ethical ideals and values which pertain to ethnic groups in 'multiethnic nation-states'. And these ideals and values have become standards for the international nation-state system in the 'world community', primarily through strong Western influence coming from governments as well as powerful 'human rights' lobby groups which enjoy rich financial and political backing, not to mention Western NGOs, missionaries and other Western citizens living and working abroad. They are profoundly affecting all discourse and debate concerning politics, language, culture and other ethnonational *human rights* in the modern global age.

'The Unified Ethnonational Complex'
In developing an understanding of 'the unified ethnonational complex' which underlies Kazakh and Central Asian nationhood in the modern global age, we will first turn our attentions to a view of ethnonational identity and being which is rooted in the monotheistic tradition of West Asia (i.e. 'the

Near-Middle East') as well as Central Asia. Judeo-Christian and Muslim thinking on nationhood are closely interrelated and have been an integral and vital part of and, indeed, had a profound impact upon the entire tradition of nationhood in both West and East. In the West this includes the later secular versions, which have often taken over the Judeo-Christian tradition and recast it in secular terms with a 'religious' passion all their own—albeit it a 'religious' passion which prefers to exclude God from the mix. And here the comparison of Western modernist with Marxist ideas of nationhood come to the fore again.

Eastern ideas of nationhood are intermingled in the aspirations of 'nationhood' in the Turkic Muslim Jadidist movement across Central Asia.[26] Interrelation of the Judeo-Christian and Muslim traditions surfaces in the comparisons to be drawn between the Protestant and Jadid reformers in their views, approaches and responses to national identity, politics, religious traditionalism, education, economy and more.[27] This does not mean that the Turkic Muslim Jadid reformers simply 'mimicked' or directly borrowed from the Reformers. But they did intentionally "borrow" from European culture— which included both Christian as well as humanistic contributions—to *enhance* and *reform* their own *pre-existing* ideas and traditions. Included in that borrowing were certainly ideas *connected with* 'nationhood', though it cannot be said that they simply tookover the European idea of nationhood as something entirely new to them. Perhaps worth noting here though, these borrowings occurred *before* the later 20th century Western shift aimed at dissociating ethnicity from political nationhood. The Turkic (including Kazakh) Jadids had no concept of or aim to separate ethnic from political nationhood. But we will return to give more in-depth attention to these issues and the debate about nationhood surrounding them soon enough.

With respect, then, to the West (and Central) Asian tradition in relation to 'the unified ethnonational complex', historically speaking we find its clearest, most succinct expression in 'The Table of Nations and Tower of Babel' narrative which occurs in Genesis 10-11 within the larger context of Genesis 9-12. There are many complex issues arising from out of this whole paradigm, especially questions regarding the abusive application of these passages in Nazi Germany as well as Euro-American enslavement of Black African peoples and the later problems of Segregation and Apartheid which arose therefrom. All these deeper issues have been properly addressed in our work entitled *A Closer Look at Ethnicity, Nations and Nationalism in the Kingdom of God and World History: Rethinking Western Approaches to Nationhood in the Modern Global*

Era. Here we must limit ourselves to a passing glimpse at the quintessence of nationhood within this West Asian paradigm.

The foundational essence and attributes of 'ethnos' are defined in the West Asian tradition primarily in terms of kinship groups incorporating flexibility through defined, *non-mythical* "mechanisms for transforming non-kin to kin" (Bastug in Erturk 1999:77), who have territorial (i.e. land), and linguistic *identities* and associations. That is, *ethnic-kinship groups are given socio-political rights of land and language as the primary, foundational attributes of their 'nationhood'.* This is based on the fact that Genesis 10 repeats three times (with slight variation of order) that the peoples of the earth "were separated into *their lands,* everyone according to *his language,* according to *their families,* into *their nations.*"[28]

Importantly here, these summaries reflect the foundation-stone of the broader West (and Central) Asian understanding of ethnicity and nations as well as their nationhood. This is confirmed by Daniel I. Block in his work on *The Gods of the Nations: Studies in Ancient Near Eastern National Theology.* He concludes that "several different elements contributed to ancient Near Eastern feelings of national unity (common genealogical descent, a shared history, a unifying language, occupation of an identifiable geographical territory, etc.) . . ." ([1988] 2000:149; cf. D.J. Wiseman[29]). This again would reflect the Islamic part of that world as well.

Central to our point, this view essentially continues down to the present, as seen for example when Connor says:

> Indeed, very few scholars have directly addressed the matter of the nature of the ethnonational bond. A common empirical approach of those who did so during the first half of this century was to ask the question: "What makes a nation?" Among the scholarly giants who raised this question were Carlton Hayes and Hans Kohn. They addressed themselves to what was necessary or unnecessary for a nation to exist. *The typical response was a common language, a common religion, a common territory, and the like.* Stalin's 1913 definition of a nation, which still exerts a massive influence upon Marxist-Leninist scholarship, was very much in this tradition: "*A nation is a historically evolved, stable community of people, formed on the basis of a common language, territory,* economic life, and psychological make-up manifested in a common culture" (1994:73; emphasis added).

Of course, Stalin's definition was influenced not only by communist ideology, but by the realities of ethnonational identity which confronted him and the Soviets in their efforts to establish the 'Union'. This reality was there before Stalin and the Soviets engaged in their efforts to resolve 'the national question' and it has survived in the collapse of those efforts. This reality of nationhood is reflected, for example, in what Akseleu Seidimbek has to say on the subject of 'ethnos' in relation to his own people and nation, the Kazakhs, amidst their present struggle to rebuild their nation of Kazakhstan in the post-Soviet era. He says:

> We can summarize the meaning of the word "ethnos" in current scholarly usage (lit. 'circulation') in this way: An "ethnos" is said to be a group (lit. 'ecclesia') of people who have historically grown and multiplied in a familiar/known territory, which has a common and established language, culture, and psyche of its own, and in like manner, who both can characteristically identify its own structural unity and who have a developed consciousness that recognizes its own uniqueness from others [i.e. self-awareness].[30]

Seidimbek's definition reflects Stalin's, but does not merely mimic it. It properly reflects the Kazakh reality. He has surveyed, quite commendably, the scholarly field respecting the meaning and usage of "ethnos." In the end what we find is that he has essentially incorporated and applied the idea of self-awareness[31] to the description of a 'nation' given in Genesis 10. Ultimately, then, in Seidimbek's definition, *an ethnonational group is a group of people who share a self-awareness of having their own land, language, culture, character, and ethnosocial ancestral (i.e. kinship) relations.*

Following directly on the heels of all this, note that a primary, burning issue of our day is that of "**Vanishing Cultures**: Indigenous peoples have become the human equivalent of endangered species. Now many battle to save *the things that define them: their lifeway [i.e. culture], their language, and their land.*"[32] Thus, "a more aggressive stance taken recently by a number of indigenous groups has prompted a growing global recognition of their rights to keep *their lands, their languages, and their cultural identities.*"[33] This same emphasis on *kinship groups bound together and identified primarily by their language, land, and culture* lies also at the heart of James Geary's article (July 1997) on "Speaking in Tongues" in an international edition of *Time* entitled "Back to Babel."

What all of this means is that there is a flexible, dynamic and durable, yet complexly integrated, singular and unified ethnonational being and identity which is grounded in the ethnosocial kinship group who then gives *personal* life to all components of its ethnonational identity. This integrated and unified 'ethnonational complex' of being and identity thus consists of *social, political, linguistic, cultural, religious, and historical* (not to mention economic) dimensions which are all integrated and inter-related in and through the 'ethnos' (i.e. 'ethnonational people group'). *Ethnonational identity is necessarily a group, not an individual, matter.* If the ethnonational group does not share a common heritage and identity as a community, then there is no ethnonational group or ethnonational identity of which to speak. The ethnonational group forms a genuine, integral whole whose components should not be confused, compartmentalized or cut-off from one another and/or ignored *in spite of the recognition* that other ethnonational groups share certain measures of culture, religion, etc. (i.e. 'pan-groups' or 'civilizations') as well as the recognition that various individuals and 'sub-groups' within the ethnonational group emphasize (or 'negotiate') certain of these dimensions more than others at given times and in given situations and sometimes even in *internal* opposition to one another. The idea of 'ethnonational group' also remains valid in spite of the fact that the elements, components, dimensions, and aspects which make up ethnonational groups are not found in equal measure or importance or balance among each group.

To set all this in plain relation to 'ethnonationalism', past and present, the succinct description of Deryck C.T. Sheriffs, in his intriguing article "'A Tale of Two Cities'—Nationalism in Zion and Babylon," is well worth consulting. There he says: "'Nationalism' is an ideology, that is a set of ideas used to express a nation's aspirations by an influential group within it. It may draw on feelings of *ancestry, kinship, shared history, language, homeland, and a sense of destiny.*"[34]

Sheriffs' comments, along with the above descriptions of ethnonationalisms of our day, help make clear that the common understanding of ethnonational identity among ancient as well as modern 'indigenous' people, as well as a number of scholars past and present, consists of the same basic elements. *And these very elements have been and continue to be the heartbeat of ethnonationalist concern (in varying degrees of measure and intensity) over the span of nearly 5000 years of human history. And through it all, we find that the ethnokinship, ethnocultural and ethnolinguistic aspects of 'ethnic nations' can never be detached from the ethnopolitical.* Indeed, the words of Hans Kohn still carry significant truth for our day when he says:

Such factors as language, territory, traditions—such sentiments as attachment to the native soil, the *Heimat,* and to one's kin and kind—assume different positions in the scale of values as communal psychology changes. Nationalism is an idea, an *idée-force,* which fills man's brain and heart with new thoughts and new sentiments, and drives him to translate his consciousness into deeds of organized action. Nationality is therefore not only a group held together and animated by common consciousness; but it is also a group seeking to find expression in what it regards as the highest form of organized activity, a sovereign state. As long as a nationality is not able to attain this consummation, it satisfies itself with some form of autonomy or pre-state organization, which, however, always tends at a given moment, the moment of 'liberation', to develop into a sovereign state. Nationalism demands the nation-state; the creation of the nation-state strengthens nationalism. Here, as elsewhere in history, we find continuous interdependence and interaction.[35]

Kohn himself may have had modernist ideas in mind, especially of nationalism being merely a mental construct preceding instead of following from nationhood. But there remains a close connection between 'cultural (i.e. ethnic) nation' and 'political nation' in both his description as well as in the real world of today.

In developing this "interdependence and interaction" of which Kohn speaks, nationalism—and specifically ethnonationalism in this case—may be defined in its simplest terms as any action or effort which contributes to the establishment, affirmation, strengthening, promotion, protection and/or restoration of one's 'nation', with the idea of 'nation' in this case being based in one's ethnonational identity. Since this identity is based primarily in kinship relations which personifies itself through the *personal* cultural elements of *national* language, homeland, customs and traditions (including religious traditions, national calendar, and the like) and their shared history, it means that the spokespersons, media, and heroes of ethnonationalism are any and all of those who participate in this establishment, affirmation, strengthening, promotion, protection and/or restoration. Ultimately, then, all books, songs, poems, epics and epic heroes, newspapers and newspaper articles, journals, news broadcasts and other TV programs, museum exhibits, and the like which affirm, promote, and strengthen ethnonational identity in one way or another, and the producers and writers as well as viewers and readers who patronize those materials—whether these be official or non-official peoples, academic, political, or common—these all make up the spokespersons, media, and heroes of the ethnonational movement.[36] And they all contribute through both intentional and unintentional dynamic interaction with one another in dialectic relationship as well as in further dynamic relationship with 'other' group identities which can be both complementary or competing and threatening.

To repeat ourselves here, then, we simply cannot nor should we attempt to 'neatly' separate ethnolinguistic, ethnocultural and ethnosocial identity from ideas of (ethnic-based) political nationhood. Likewise, we cannot nor should we attempt to neatly separate the aims and aspirations of the masses from those of the 'elites'. They each have their own unique distinctions, but they cannot be radically separated from and juxtaposed against one another. As one of the Kazakh ethnonationalist writers himself puts it:

> It is doubtless that with the appealing ideas of liberty and freedom [come] *the founding of a national state at the very base of our national people* who soar on wings [like eagles]. For that, of course, we must be established as a whole people who have an integral national essence-and-solidarity; that is to say, it is necessary that our forefathers' traditions, manners and customs be firmly set in place in daily life. This itself is directly connected with a national consciousness. But, national consciousness is established upon a national worldview. And 'when all is said and done', a national worldview is found to be the golden treasure of establishing a national state. Until we admit this, it is futile to say that 'we will be renewed-[and]-restored', that 'we will once again discover our national character, and will lay hold on success along the road of progress'; [instead] we will [only] remain in our darkened, hybrid state of the past. Now is the time that our national consciousness, which though birthed long ago has not lost its worth, though running headlong into misfortune its heights have not disappeared, must become the spiritual riches of every person [in our nation].[37]

The Crucial Question:
Can Ethnic (Cultural) Nations Become Political Nations?

All such ideas of 'a unified ethnonational complex' coming to fruition in political statehood sound an urgent alarm for Western modernist scholarship. It leads scholars like Andre Liebich to write articles asking, "Must Nations Become States?" With a view to distinguishing *'nations'* "as cultural units" (i.e. 'cultural or ethnic *nations*') from 'political *states*', the following excerpt from the article abstract reveals the writer's central concern. It tells us that:

A world in which every [ethnocultural] nation has become a state, that is, a world in which cultural and political units coincide, would be a very different world from the one we know. There are now close to 200 political units recognized as states in the international system. *Nations, understood as cultural units, are not as easily identified . . . . The claim that cultural nations must become political states thus presumes strongly on present-day reality and has deep implications for the future . . . .* Though resisted by many jurists and other scholars, the thesis that nationhood, understood in a cultural sense, must . . . entail political statehood continues to advance in public consciousness. After the end of decolonization, where state creation was dictated by unique considerations, we have continued to witness a rise in the number of recognized states and, even more so, in the number of struggling independence movements. Debate focuses on procedural issues, such as modes of separation from existing states, rather than on the fundamental premises underlying and legitimizing the acquisition of statehood. In this paper I propose first to examine three sorts of arguments invoked to justify the claim that cultural nations must—in the different senses of that term—become political states. These are arguments that can be described as definitional, causal or functional, and moral. The definitional argument makes a case based on linguistic coherence in the use of terms. The causal or functional argument founds itself on a sociology of modernity which posits the interdependence of culture and politics. The moral argument is rooted in an ethics of autonomy and self-rule, recognition and identity.[38]

First of all, Liebich's framing of the issue as "a world in which . . . [ethno]cultural nations must . . . become political states" is misleading from the start. The issue is not whether they "must" become political states. It is whether, in principle, ethnic nations *can*, that is, whether they *should have the right*, i.e. *be permitted* to become political nations or not. That is, does the international nation-state system have room to *officially* recognize and facilitate geo-political nations which are built upon ethnic bases? Why or why not?

Secondly, Liebich's framing of the issue as "[a] world in which every [ethnocultural] nation has become a state" is also very misleading. No one is pushing for such a world. Likewise, it is false and misleading for Liebich to assume that it will automatically happen and then argue his whole case based on that assumption. The question, if properly asked, of whether ethnic nations *can* become political states would naturally lead to the question of whether "every [ethnocultural] nation . . . must become a political state," but that question is secondary. It is an improbable thesis. It certainly cannot be used as grounds for precluding the idea, in principle, of ethnic nations *somehow* coinciding with and/or underlying 'geo-political nations', nor of their right to do so. Besides, Anthony Smith, in his 1986 work on *The Ethnic Origins of Nations*, long ago addressed this particular concern of Liebich, namely the idea of 'a world of small nations' (pp 209ff).

But 'a world of small nations' is not the only concern Liebich has. He is again concerned with a matter of principle, even though his manner of framing it has greatly clouded the issue. The fundamental issue is the proper relation of ethnicity to political state. This fundamental question is separate from the question of how large or small or how numerous or scarce the ethnic or political nations may be. Here we should also bear in mind the proper distinctions between (ethno)national political autonomy versus (ethno)national independence as well as the distinction between 'ethnicity' *completely* coinciding with a political 'nation', which is rare, versus the idea of one particular ethnic group functioning as the core foundation of a political state, which would usually mean such an ethnic group has or claims to have unique preeminence with respect to political, cultural, language and/or other ethnonational rights within a geo-political nation-state containing more than one ethnonational group. The latter situation is far more common and is an integral, even central, part of the issue being debated in the international world, particularly Central Asia.

But no matter how we 'slice the pie', Liebich is obviously trying to mark a clear distinction here between '(ethno)cultural nation' and 'geo-political state'. And this certainly 'rings a bell', that is, the hallmark bell of Western modernist scholarship. Whatever Liebich's own ultimate convictions and conclusions are, it is clear he believes that the claims of 'cultural or ethnic nations' to political nationhood "presume strongly on present-day reality" because "cultural units are not as easily identified." This too is a hallmark of Western modernist scholarship, that is, the effort to undermine ethnonational claims to nationhood by questioning the very foundations of ethnonational identity itself.

Here we find it valuable to consult Anthony Smith again, who points out regarding the modernist paradigm that:

> The main theories in question, those of Eric Hobsbawm and Benedict Anderson, can be regarded both as Marxian varieties of classical modernism, but also moving beyond some of the assumptions of that paradigm. Their respective traditions of the 'invented traditions' and the 'imagined communities' of the nation have provided the seedbed for more radical 'postmodernist' developments in which *the idea of national identity is treated as inherently problematic and broken down into its component narratives* (1999:5-6; emphasis added).

"Component narratives" refers to all the various social relationships that each individual is involved in, producing in each case a unique 'dialectic relationship' and therefore an allegedly 'new' identity in each 'new' relationship, a fact in our opinion which is over-stressed, especially in reference to 'globalization', in order to make the idea of consistent, stable ethnocultural identities appear "inherently problematic."[39] In this respect, we are reminded of Smith's warning that a good portion of "the current interest in the concept of globalisation . . . reasserts the Western and modernist bias . . ." (1999:12). Essentially, there is an attempt to write off ethnicity as questionable at best, if not a downright illusion or 'myth', i.e. an 'imagined community' or 'invented tradition', with no genuine foundations in 'objective' reality. Once this is accomplished, the argument against 'ethnic nations' functioning as viable, *stable* foundations for 'political nations' is essentially a foregone conclusion, which is precisely why the view that ethnonational identity is "inherently problematic" and the view that 'ethnicity cannot and should not function as a base for political nationhood' go hand in hand in Western modernist scholarship. These are the prevailing views of Western scholarship in the modern global age.

—Chapter Four—

THE WESTERN ALLIANCE AGAINST ETHNIC-BASED NATIONHOOD IN CENTRAL ASIA

In starting off this chapter we should first note that, while the term 'Western modernist' is broadly applied to the writers treated herein, they do not all hold precisely the same views or follow the same approaches to the issue of Kazakh and Central Asian nationhood. Many of them provide stimulating discussions and thought-provoking insights. Each deserves our respect in their own right and a reading of their respective works, each on its own terms in its own context, is ultimately merited. But the essential harmony and impact of their thought on the issues at hand is clear and this provides justification for seeing them as part of one broad school which, for convenience sake, can be labeled 'Western modernist'.

In accordance with their established convictions based in late 20th century Western ideals of multiethnic pluralistic democracy, scholars holding critical Western modernist views continue to advance arguments against the ethnic and national identity of the peoples of Central Asia. Whether openly and explicitly or more subtly and implicitly, their views work against the idea of any one ethnic group asserting priority in language, culture or land rights in relation to a political state. Instead, they offer support for the political idea that the 'nation' should be a multiethnic pluralistic 'nation'. In this view, giving special recognition and priority of rights to any one particular ethnic group of a political state, 'indigenous' or otherwise, is a violation of multiethnic, pluralistic ideals.

With support from scholars and politicians in their political 'fatherlands', Euroslavic (and particularly Russian) groups now identifying themselves as

---

'ethnic minorities' in the post-colonial world of Central Asia claim that they are discriminated against or underprivileged in that political context and, from that vantage, also appeal to Western modernist ideals because these ideals work for their own socio-political advantage. This appeal in turn garners support from Western modernists so as to effectively double the pressure from the (Western-based) 'international community' in their push to conform the Central Asian nations to their own allegedly 'fair and just' ideals of (Western and/or post-Soviet 'union' style) democratic nationhood.

As part of their effort to conform the Central Asian nations to their ideals, Western modernist (as well as Soviet-trained Euroslavic) scholars insist upon the separation of 'ethnic nation' and 'political nation', i.e. 'the separation of ethnicity and state', attributing the historical rise of ethnicity and statehood in Central Asia to the Russian Empire and/or the Soviets as an essentially artificial political fabrication of Russian Tsarist ethnography and/or Soviet "ethno-engineering." Through this, they allegedly demonstrate that today's nation-states in Central Asia are artificial constructs with no true or historic relation to the ethnic nations whose names they bear. Likewise, the concepts of 'Kazakh', 'Uzbek', etc, are treated by these scholars as having no real or *stable* historic depth or substance as part of their attempt to show that those 'ethnic nations' do not constitute legitimate bases for legitimate and *stable* 'political nationhood'. The Central Asians are conveniently (for Western modernists) left with no rightful historical or sociological claim as 'ethnic nations' to their own 'modern political nations'. This affects all discussion of international human rights, including ideas of 'national language, culture and history rights', 'national reconciliation', etc, both within and beyond the Central Asian 'nations'.

The "Academic Wars" of Eickelman, Shnirelman, Poliakov, Porkhomovsky and Prazauskas

This approach with its corresponding convictions and values can be seen, for example, in Dale Eickelman's treatment of *The Middle East and Central Asia: An Anthropological Perspective*. Section III is entitled "Constructed Meanings." In that section, he begins his discussion of "Ethnicity and Cultural Identity" with these thoughts:

> *Notions of ethnicity are cultural constructions, although in popular usage, especially in the form of ethnogenesis in Central Asia, it is sometimes assumed to be . . . the basis for national identity.* In Russia

and Central Asia, ethnogenesis is understood as "a lengthy and continuous process of development of the main characteristics of an ethnic community, including the physical characteristics of its members, language, and other cultural features," *and it is used to create national ideologies and "lay claim to scarce resources, whether they be political, social, economic, or demographic." Thus even the past can be claimed to support contemporary boundary disputes or the favouring of one people over another"* ([1981] 1996:199; emphasis added).

The title of the book which he quotes from in this (above) passage reveals his radical modernist (or post-modernist) paradigm of ethnicity and national identity rather clearly. He borrows much of what he says from the work of a Euroslavic scholar, Victor A. Shnirelman, *Who Gets the Past? Competition for Ancestors Among Non-Russian Intellectuals in Russia.* In a footnote, Eickelman clarifies and even praises Shnirelman's perspective while at the same time adding reference to another critical Soviet work. The footnote reads as follows:

Shnirelman offers an excellent analysis of the "re-imagination" of identities following the Soviet collapse and an account of the rise and fall of Soviet theories and practice concerning ethnicity and nationalism. For scathing, even patronizing, comments on Central Asian intelligentsia efforts to "construct" national identities independent of the approved Soviet ones, see Poliakov, *Everyday Islam . . .* (p 199).[40]

Thus both Eickelman and Shnirelman, as well as Poliakov, believe that the ethnic and national identities of modern Central Asians are "(re-)imagined," "created" and/or "constructed" by either the Central Asian peoples themselves, or by the Soviets who offered them official "constructed" and "approved" ethnonational identities, or perhaps a combination of both. And very importantly, they believe such identities are mere political 'tools' which are "used to create national ideologies and 'lay claim to scarce resources, whether they be political, social, economic, or demographic'. . . to support contemporary boundary disputes or the favouring of one people over another."

Victor Ya. Porkhomovsky views the matter in a similar fashion. In his chapter on "Historical Origins of Interethnic Conflicts in Central Asia and Transcaucasia," he says:

Apart from the general policy of protectionism toward the titular nations, an important place here undoubtedly belongs to the ethno-tribal and ethno-territorial groupings playing a paramount role in the sociopolitical life of all Central Asian republics and *certainly providing obvious advantages to the members of the titular ethnoses.*

The disparity between the new and the past ethno-political realities is easy to see in the widespread attempts to interpret the history of culture in extrapolation to the past. This results in "academic wars" for national attribution of outstanding monuments of ancient culture and architecture, masterpieces of medieval literature and their authors, and so forth. Such attempts are hard to correlate with the fact that none of the contemporary literary languages of Central Asia is a continuation of the medieval written and literary languages, which had *a pronounced transethnic or even non-ethnic character and were poles apart from the spoken ethnic dialects. Besides, the ethnic situation of the Middle Ages, including ethnonyms, cannot be superimposed on the contemporary.*[41]

It is clear that the author, apparently himself of Euroslavic descent, is unhappy about the allegedly "obvious advantages to the members of the titular ethnoses" of Central Asia. He wishes to oppose the grounds for such advantages by attempting to expose what he feels are "widespread attempts to interpret the history of culture in extrapolation to the past." He thus claims that the pre-existing historical situation was one of "transethnic or non-ethnic character" which therefore, in his view, has no legitimate connection to today's "titular ethnoses." Especially apparent is his concern for the language issue. He is clearly opposed to the use of the 'national languages' of the 'titular ethnoses' as 'national languages' of the Central Asian nation-states. The same would follow with respect to questions of 'national culture' as well as 'national history'. The intimate relation here between national language and culture issues in today's Central Asian nations with historiographical (re)interpretations of ethnicity and statehood should not be missed.

Algis Prazauskas, Head of the Department of Political Science of the Institute of Oriental Studies at the Russian Academy of Sciences in Moscow, shares the same basic convictions. He contributes a chapter to a collection of articles entitled *Ethnic Challenges Beyond Borders: Chinese and Russian Perspectives of the Central Asian Conundrum* (edited by Yongjin Zhang and

Rouben Azizian, 1998). And he indeed takes a "Russian perspective of the Central Asian conundrum" in his chapter entitled "Ethnopolitical Issues and the Emergence of Nation-States in Central Asia." There he argues strongly against any geo-political nation-state in Central Asia in which ". . . a single ethnic community is both politically and demographically prevalent, and ethnic minorities, if any, are bound to accept the culture and language of the majority as normative" (p 51). He notes that such an approach to nationhood is "rejected outright by minority leaders and many liberal (not to mention Communist) social scientists" (p 52). In order to undermine the basis for all such situations, he insists in Marxist and Western modernist fashion that: "Much as in the former colonies of Western powers, the emergence of states in Central Asia precedes the formation of ethno-nations as fairly homogeneous sociocultural and sociopolitical formations of a modern type" (ibid 52-53). Essentially we have here the view that both the statehood and the allegedly subsequent "formation" of homogeneous ethnonational groups arose out of "the former colonies of [Russian] powers" as 'creations' of those colonial powers. Together with this view, we also have the idea that the founding of political nation-states "precedes the formation of ethno-nations" (i.e. ethnicity). This is part of the Western modernist choral refrain regarding the alleged "rise of the nation-state" and the subsequent "imagination" or "invention of ethnicity." This view has a definite socio-political aim of achieving 'multiethnic nations' as the only conceived means (in Western civic democratic or post-Soviet Russian eyes) for attaining true ethnic 'equality'.

Khalid and 'New, Imagined' Nations in 'The Politics of Muslim Cultural Reform'

Another writer taking a Western modernist approach, though himself not technically a 'Westerner', is Adeeb Khalid. His treatment is worth examining in greater detail since he places his own variety of modernism in contrast to other major modernist views involved in the whole debate. In his rather popular 1999 work on *The Politics of Muslim Cultural Reform: Jadidism in Central Asia* he explicitly follows (with minor qualifications) Benedict Anderson's (1991) view of nations as *Imagined Communities* (with its subtitle: *Reflections on the Origin and Spread of Nationalism*). Indeed, the chapter (six) title under which Khalid covers this issue is borrowed directly from Anderson: "Imagining the Nation." In perfect accord with his title and convictions, Khalid asserts forthrightly that "all nations are imagined, but they may be imagined in a number of ways" (p 187). He emphasizes that the ethnonational identities (i.e. 'nations') of Turkic Central Asia, which according to his view did not emerge until the late 19th or early 20th century, were "something new . . . all of them were modern" (p 184). That is, they were clearly modernist conceptions of nationhood in which "new understandings of the world engendered new notions of identity" (p 184). They had no real historical continuity nor foundations in any previous Turkic Central Asian 'national' identities.

In contrast to his own understanding of these 'new nations', Khalid identifies and classifies three different views of Central Asian Turkic nationhood commonly encountered in scholarly treatments. These include two non-Soviet foreign views: One holds that the Turks were comprised of various distinct national entities (i.e. Turkic nations, plural) and the other that there was only one single 'pan-Turkic nation' (with its corollary of 'pan-Islamism' in restricted connection to all the Turkic 'Muslims of Russia'). He quite correctly notes that "[b]oth these views see the emergence of distinct nations in the 1920s as the result of imperial fiat, a classic case of divide and rule, imposed by an omnipotent regime on a helpless victimized population. They both also share the view that Central Asian identities were focused elsewhere and that Central Asians were only passive participants in larger dramas being played out elsewhere" (p 185).

His own modernist conception of these nations as 'imagined' with its clearly Andersonian roots and veins, however, do not offer great improvement to this motley pair of options. Indeed, they are all in the end, including his own, modernist visions of Turkic Central Asian nationhood which "share the view that Central Asian identities [themselves] were focused elsewhere." We see this in Khalid's own insistence that "[t]raditional Central Asian visions of history had revolved around dynasties or tribes" in direct contrast to the allegedly "new understandings" of 'nation' which emerged in the late 19th and early 20th century. The 'dynasties' he speaks of are typically interpreted as multiethnic confederations and his emphasis on 'tribes' betrays the classic modernist view of Kazakh nationhood, for example, which juxtaposes a unified national identity against disunified tribal identity, as though the two were mutually exclusive. The only real difference in Khalid's view is that he properly rescues the Central Asian Turkic peoples from being mere "passive participants in larger dramas." But he still considers their 'nations' to be 'imagined', they are just 'self-imagined' by the Jadid reformers them*selves* instead of 'Soviet imagined'—though even this 'self-imagining' was borrowed from the Russians in the Empire period.

This brings us to the third view described by Khalid, namely what he calls the Soviet view. He says that it "asserted the 'objective' existence of nations since time immemorial. History was the process of the elaboration and refinement of these national identities through processes such as ethnogenesis" (p 186). This, however, is somewhat odd, for we have here a perennialist view of nations being ascribed to the Soviets. Indeed, his explanation at this point becomes even more perplexing because, in the midst of treating the Soviet view, he brings the two "non-Soviet views" back into the discussion and asserts for them a similar belief in "the ontological existence of nations, the assumption that nations are 'sociohistorical organisms', sharing common origins ('ethnogenesis') and united by common 'historical destinies'" (p 186). This also carries the strong aroma of a perennialist view, one which does not fit neatly (at least in our mind) with the idea previously ascribed to these views of "imperial fiat" which "imposed" ethnonational identity on "passive participants." If, in this light, we were to accept his ascription of one and the same type of "ethnogenesis" to both the Soviet and the non-Soviet views, then it seems the author should have recognized the shared assumptions in all three of the views he is treating or else somehow made clearer their shared features and their precise distinctions.

Regardless, he calls this alleged Soviet belief in "the 'objective' existence of nations since time immemorial" an "obviously romantic idea" which "from the beginning, formed the basis of Bolshevik (and hence Soviet) understanding of the 'national question'" (p 186). This take on Soviet interpretations of nationhood contradicts the classic Marxist-Leninist-Stalinist approach (which itself was actually a forerunner to Khalid's own modernist convictions regarding the humanly self-constructed, i.e. the 'imagined', nature of nationhood). This is why, based faithfully on Marxist teaching, Lenin, Stalin and company made primary use of the term 'national consciousness', locating nationhood strictly in the self-imagined psychological consciousness, i.e. the mind, and feelings-emotions of people, not in "the 'objective' existence of nations since time immemorial." Indeed, both Marxist and Leninist-Stalinist understandings of nations saw them as strictly modern, self-imagined communities which emerged as byproducts of 'the dialectic of history' (cf. Hegel). In this sense, Khalid is correct in saying that the Soviet view of nations believed "[h]istory was the process of the elaboration and refinement of these national identities." But they did not view this historic process of nation formation as going back to "time immemorial." It was certainly not located by Marx in the stage of feudalism, which according to him, immediately preceded capitalism. Thus it could go back no farther than 'the modern period' marked (in both the Marxist and Western modernist view) by 'the rise of the nation-state', and with it ethnicity, in the European capitalist system. And in perfect keeping with this, communism saw the ultimate demise of nations in the triumph of itself as the end to which the entire dialectic of mankind's economic history was headed. 'Nations' were, for the communists, only fleeting 'imaginations' of humanity. They appeared only briefly on the stage of humankind's long history, having their rise and fall with the coming and going of the capitalist era. Communism, therefore, not only envisioned but strategically aimed for the demise of nations through pursuit of the complete 'union' of peoples void of all class, ethnic and other 'distinctions' which allegedly served as the basis for competition, conflict and exploitation in the capitalist system. Here again the close tie between Marxian and Western modern views is exposed.

In one sense though, Khalid is correct in ascribing this view of "the 'objective' existence of nations since time immemorial" to the Soviets, for "[i]n his 1913 tract, *Marxism and the National Question*, Stalin had defined a nation as '*a historically evolved, stable community of people*, formed on the basis of a common language, territory, economic life, and psychological make-up manifested in a common culture'."[42] It was a definition which did then and "still exerts a massive influence upon Marxist-Leninist scholarship."[43] Of course, Stalin himself was actually a Georgian whose real name was Dzhughashvili, so perhaps he, like many Russians in regard to their own deep historic national heritage, found it hard to fully embrace a Marxist-Leninist view (Connor 1984:567). We should also recall the influence of German 'romantic' scholars who were hired by Peter I (i.e. 'the Great') and who thus influenced the subsequent development of Tsarist Russian ethnography.[44] This might explain Khalid's description of this view as an "obviously romantic idea" (since 'romanticism' is typically linked by historical scholars with 18th-19th century Germany).

In spite of this however, the Marxist-Leninist view was the foundation of Soviet thinking, whether it be about nationhood or any other Soviet policy and practice. Lenin himself, as a good Marxian communist, was determined to hold onto his conviction that socialism would prove more significant than the power of national ideals for his vision of the Union. As Connor (1994:156-7; *Ethnonationalism: The Quest for Understanding*) points out, however, he was eventually forced to bend the knee before the power of 'national consciousness', for:

> As Lenin discovered during World War I, Emerson's definition
> [of the nation as "the largest community, which when the chips

are down, effectively commands men's loyalty, overriding the claims of both lesser communities within it and those which cut across it or potentially enfold it within a still greater society"] indeed holds true when the chips are down. Forced to choose between their proletarian consciousness and ethnonationalism, the working class of France and Germany elected to fight as Frenchmen and Germans. Indeed, nationalism even pervaded the proletariat's vanguard, an apostasy which Lenin would describe following the war as "the despicable betrayal of Socialism by the majority of the leaders of the proletariat of the oppressing nations in 1914-19." With this harshly learned lesson concerning the relative strength of class-loyalty versus ethnonational loyalty behind them, Lenin et al decided that it was strategically advisable to give the appearance of allying themselves with national causes, and the most blatant appeals to ethnonational aspirations thereafter became a staple in Marxist-Leninist propaganda.

Lenin et al were likewise forced to negotiate compromise in the face of (ethno)national cultural-political aspirations in the struggles commenced with the February and October Revolutions. From 1917-20 they found various 'nations' of Central Asia calling for their own cultural-political autonomy (or independence) in the interim period between collapsed Tsarist rule and the still undecided struggle between 'white' (former Tsarist) Russian armies versus 'red' Russian communists. Thus, the Kazakh scholar K. Nurpeisov notes in his article on "The Alash Party's Role and Its Place in the Social and Political Life of Kazakhstan" that: "The Soviet leadership in Moscow, taking into account the complex military-political situation in the national regions, came to the conclusion that it would be necessary to pursue the intensification of national State building reforms, which meant the formation of national autonomies in Tataria, Bashkiria and Kazakhstan, as quickly as possible."[45]

But this call for cultural-political autonomy was nothing new. It certainly was not a 'Soviet invention'. As another Kazakh scholar, Sabit Shildebai, points out in his profound 2002 work on *Turkic Nationalism and the Ethnonational Independence Movement in Kazakhstan*, it formed the entire historical background to Lenin's efforts to establish his glorious Marxian socialist union, for:

> In the process of development of the Turkic nationalist movement the founding of "The Union of Autonomous Nations,"[46] whose

aim was to bring ever closer together estranged nations in the struggle for independence, was an important undertaking for the Turkic peoples also. . . . On November 19, 1905 a convocation was held which was organized by "The Union of Autonomous Nations" in which 83 representatives participated from Azerbaizhan, Armenia, Gruznia [i.e. Georgia], Poland, Latvia, Ukraine, Kazakh[stan], Tatar[stan] and others from among the ethnonationally oppressed nations. In the gathering, which was called the convocation of autonomous nations, the resolution was put forth that all ethnonational peoples should mutually participate as republics in establishing Russia's empire; 'hands off' with respect to the rights of the ethnonational peoples; Russia's government should be in a form which does not have [everyone] harshly subjected to one center, [but rather] every ethnonational people should receive autonomy in which they run their own affairs (p 72).

Here we should not fail to recognize, by the way, that *ethno*national identities *and their political aspirations* were clearly alive and well among not only the Central Asians, but most of the 'nations' which were to eventually be founded as 'Soviet Socialist Republics' in the Union *before the Soviets ever came to power*. Indeed, it was this *already pre-existing (ethno)national identity* teeming among the nations themselves that guided Stalin as he drafted his influential definition of 'nation' for employment in all communist negotiations with those nations.

As Connor points out, then, in his penetrating 1984 analysis of *The National Question in Marxist-Leninist Theory and Strategy*, Lenin, Stalin and company held contradictory views and aims with respect to the whole 'national question'. Indeed, whatever significance might be assigned to Stalin's 1913 definition of nationhood, it cannot be forgotten that it was Stalin himself who became the most ardent persecutor of anything and everything that even hinted of 'nationalism'. For the most part, all of the Soviets, including Stalin, followed a predominantly communist view and agenda which merely used Stalin's definition of 'nation' as a means for exploiting ethnonational sentiments and gaining the allegiance of the various nations to the Soviet Union. Thus:

In time [the] policy of promoting pluralism came to be known as "the flourishing of the nations." Lenin reasoned that as the policy of equality dissipated the antagonisms and mistrust that had previously estranged nations, those human units would naturally move closer together, a process that became known in the official Marxist lexicon as "the rapprochement" or "coming together" of nations. . . .

To Lenin, language and other overt manifestations of national uniqueness were construed, on balance, as conveyors of the messages emanating from the party. In and by themselves they were merely forms. It was the party, acting through the state, which would give them content. Forms did, nevertheless, have an important role to play in enhancing the receptivity accorded the messages. Lenin and his successors believed that sovietization would not be resisted by minorities as an alien program identified with the state's dominant ethnic element if it came dressed in the local tongue and other appropriate national attire. Employing the individualized national forms would convince the people that Marxism-Leninism was not just a new guise for assimilation by the dominant group. In 1925 Stalin would confer upon this entire approach to the national question the official, abbreviated title of "national in form, socialist in content" (Connor 1984:201-2).

In this way, in the words of the Tenth Session of the Russian Communist Party, they could promise "the right of national minorities to free national development" which allegedly had been "ensured by the very nature of the Soviet system."[47] As the Kazakh scholar Nagima Baitenova notes however in her treatment of "The Philosophy of Ethnos," the Leninist-Stalinist approach to ethnicity and nationhood "in its own turn brought numerous negative, even politically harmful effects crashing down upon [ethnonational peoples]: It stripped them of their right to declare their own distinct path, their opportunities to establish political state structures," i.e. their right to self-determination of nationhood and the development thereof.[48] Baitenova immediately thereafter says rather accurately and profoundly: "We must draw attention [to the fact] that this same understanding of ethnonational identity has found a place in the West as well." Indeed it has.

In the end then, the lack of willingness of Lenin, Stalin and company to come through on these promises, based in their exploitational approach, precipitated the ultimate collapse of the whole Union. Thus, "Carrere d'Encausse (1979, 1988, 1990) argued that Soviet ethnic identities were strong and on this basis prophesied the collapse of the USSR a decade in advance . . ." (Privratsky 2001:8). Connor had done much the same in his 1984 work on 'The National Question'.

Be that as it may, Khalid considers it rather unfortunate that "[t]he collapse of the Soviet Union has done little to challenge the belief in the reality of the nation among intellectual and political elites in formerly Soviet lands" (pp 184-7). In this, he reveals again his Andersonian modernist convictions regarding the essential nature of nationhood and nationalism as that which is grounded in and flowing forth from, not the peoples themselves and their historic objective identity, but the imagination of intellectuals and political elites who stir up the imagination of national ideals in the masses for their own socio-political agendas. He regrets that no "challenge" can be found to "the belief in the reality of the nation," particularly when those nations are built upon the foundations of ethnic identity.

Brower, Slezkine and Paksoy: Central Asian Nationhood as Russian Ethnographic Debris

With that, we come to Daniel Brower's treatment of "Islam and Ethnicity: Russian Colonial Policy in Turkestan" contained within the collection of articles edited by himself and Edward Lazzerini. That collection is entitled *Russia's Orient: Imperial Borderlands and Peoples, 1700-1917*. The book is highly useful for understanding the complex historical background of the period. Alas though, Brower explains the entire emergence of ethnicity in Central Asia as a product of the Tsarist Russian "imperial ethnographic crusade" in which "[e]thnicity was to become a servant of . . . colonial rule" (p 123). This was based in the conviction that "[e]thnic differences constituted meaningful bases for imperial rule" (p 131). "After all, these basic social categories constituted a tangible reality that in many respects shaped their relations with their subjects" (p 129). But one should not take Brower's statement that "these social categories constituted a tangible reality" too literally, for his own perspective on this idea shines through: they "constituted a tangible reality" strictly in the minds of the imperial powers, including their ethnographic representations, only to be, in Khalid's words, "imposed by an omnipotent regime on a helpless victimized population." Thus, Brower emphasizes the "colossal confusion" created by these efforts. "Peoples *often* did not produce a neat set of ethnic features all distinct from other groups; *frequently* they used multiple and contradictory names to describe themselves" (p 128, emphasis added). This resulted in the need for others to come along, "[s]weeping away the debris of the ethnographers" in their attempts to find better means to categorize their subjects and rule over them (p 128). Indeed, it seems that Brower himself is amongst those coming along to try to "sweep away the debris."

Bearing in mind that *Russian* Soviet and *Russian* Tsarist ethnography cannot be neatly cut off from one another, Brower's view here can be compared, for example, with that of Svat Soucek (*A History of Inner Asia*), who notes that "the scientists, in this instance Russian linguists, anthropologists, and politicians, had done fairly competent work," so much so that they "correctly identified principal nationalities" (2000:225, 238). Here again we are reminded of Stalin himself and his drafting of his 1913 definition of 'nation'. He too had, in general, "correctly identified" the essence of national identity so alive and well among the peoples of the Russian Empire, both in its Tsarist and Communist eras as well as in between.

Regardless, Brower, like Khalid, makes clear that he lays the foundations for his primary understanding and study of ethnicity in Benedict Anderson's idea of *Imagined Communities*. In Brower's opening paragraph (p 115) we read how:

> Benedict Anderson has stressed the importance attributed to ethnic naming of subject peoples by European colonial administrators, and to the impact of ethnic classification on the emergence of national identity among these peoples. Ethnicity in this perspective is a social invention with enormous cultural and political consequences.

It should be of no surprise then that Khalid himself has contributed a chapter to this same volume with its view of ethnicity as a "social invention."

Yuri Slezkine, apparently of Euroslavic descent, has also contributed a chapter to this volume. His contribution is entitled "Naturalists versus Nations: Eighteenth Century Russian Scholars Confront Ethnic Diversity." There he points out the German influence upon Tsarist Russian ethnography via Peter I and would very much seem to share (Brower and) Khalid's notion of the "obviously romantic idea" of ethnicity in both German and Tsarist Russian scholarship. Indeed, the very ideas reflected in his choice of title, i.e. that naturalists are somehow engaged in some kind of competition *against* nations and that scholarship "confronts" ethnic diversity, betray a view which sees ethnicity and nationhood themselves as inherently problematic, phenomena riddled by "diversity" and inconsistency as opposed to any kind of stability. While his article as well as the whole book and even Khalid's book reviewed above are all very important and make challenging contributions to the study of ethnicity and nationhood, Slezkine seems eager to stress throughout his entire span of treatment that "[t]he new world discovered by academic ethnographers appeared pluralistic, decentered and relativist" (pp 36-7). Thus the title phrase "ethnic *diversity*" is proven apt. This would accord with Brower's treatment so that both Slezkine and Brower come out taking an approach which is ultimately in agreement with Liebich's conviction that notions of ethnicity "presume strongly on present-day reality," a reality in which "cultural units are not as easily identified" as political states and therefore do not serve as legitimate bases for the establishment of such states. Certainly all of them, like B. Anderson, are vitally aware that ethnicity has "enormous cultural and political consequences."

Of course, as the editors of the volume note, their "rethinking of the empire's history is not the product of one conceptual paradigm" (p xv). The "new tools and methods" (backcover) which the writers contributing to this volume ground their work in not only embrace this essential paradigm of Anderson, they are grounded and centered in "an understanding of ethnicity as a *socially constructed* bond of group identification" (p xv, emphasis added). For Fredrik Barth, a key contributor to this paradigm, this means that: "The critical focus of investigation . . . becomes the ethnic boundary that defines the group, not the cultural stuff it encloses."[49] "These boundaries are permeable" (Brower and Lazzerini, eds., 1997:xv), which of course might be fair enough to say. We ourselves affirm that 'the unified ethnonational complex' involves "a flexible, dynamic and durable" nature. The problem is how far we choose to push these "boundaries," i.e. how "permeable" or "flexible" we envision and then treat them to be. The authors of this volume, at least those we have read and critiqued here, apparently feel they are so highly fluid and permeable that they have little stability or grounding in reality and, thus, have little need for affirmation, encouragement, preservation and/or protection. But this again is what the spirit of the Western modernist age calls for, so much so that ethnonational identity is "broken down into its component narratives and treated as inherently problematic" (A.D. Smith 1999:5-6). It thus offers no "cultural stuff" to build a strong, healthy and vibrant ethnonational identity upon nor to build a stable, political nation upon. Quite to the contrary, it holds that: "Imperial conquest and rule of subject peoples elevated ethnicity to a position of political prominence in modern history" (Brower and Lazzerini, eds., 1997:xv).

Finally here then, we may turn our gaze briefly upon H. B. Paksoy, who, in his article on "Nationality or Religion? Views of Central Asian Islam," holds the same basic perspective as Brower and friends. He argues that:

> The designation "Altai," as Ozbek and Kazakh, are primarily geographical, tribal or confederation names, not ethnonyms. Those appellations were mistakenly or deliberately turned into "ethnic" or "political" classifications by early explorers or intelligence agents arriving in those lands ahead of the Russian armies and bureaucrats. . . . Only since the Soviet language "reforms," especially of the 1930s, have the dialects been asserted to be "individual and unrelated Central Asian languages."[50]

Together with the "dialects," of course, come the ethnonational groups themselves, which Paksoy denies as having actually existed prior to Russian "explorers or intelligence agents . . . turning them into 'ethnic' or 'political' classifications." Of course, Paksoy does not even attempt to deal with the etymology, for instance, of the ethnonym 'Kazakh'. He certainly provides nothing by way of response to or interaction with Central Asian scholarship, as for example A. Abdakimuhli (1997:54-5), who offers a list of at least seven historical evidences tracing the earliest possible occurrences of the term back to the 10-11th century, long before Tsarist colonial ethnographers were ever born (see actual list in ch 8).

Allworth, Hambly and Sinor:
The 'Ingenious Soviet Strategy' for
'Creating New Nations' via 'Ethno-engineering'

In like manner, Edward Allworth, Gavin R.G. Hambly and Denis Sinor, in their *Encyclopedia Britannica* article on "Central Asia, history of," build off of this same basic paradigm. But they assign its ultimate achievement to the Soviets, not Tsarist Russia. Near the end of the article, we read that:

> *Eventually the Soviets developed an ingenious strategy* for neutralizing the two common denominators most likely to unite Central Asians against continuing control from Moscow: Islamic culture and Turkish ethnicity. After a protracted period of trial and error, their ultimate solution was the *creation* of five Soviet socialist republics in the region: the Kazakh S.S.R. (now Kazakhstan) in

1936, the Kirgiz S.S.R. (now Kyrgyzstan) in 1936, the Tadzhik
S.S.R. (now Tajikistan) in 1929, the Turkmen S.S.R. (now
Turkmenistan) in 1924, and the Uzbek S.S.R. (now Uzbekistan)
in 1924. The plan was to will into being five new nations whose
separate development under close surveillance and firm tutelage
from Moscow would preempt the emergence of a "Turkestani"
national identity and such concomitant ideologies as Pan-
Turkism or Pan-Islamism. To some extent, this *ethno-engineering*
reflected colonial conceptions of the peoples of Central Asia dating
back to tsarist times.[51]

Here we can see the almost convincing attempt by these well-known and
respected scholars to explain the whole thing as entirely emerging from and
dependent upon the pan-Islamic and pan-Turkist movement(s). That is, the
"ingenious strategy" for "creating" these "new nations" with their "separate
development" via Soviet "ethno-engineering" was all Moscow's doing as a
political solution to undermining pan-Islamism and its corollary of pan-Turkism
in Central Asia. As we have glimpsed above, however, the Turkic peoples
themselves already had clear, pre-existing ethno*national* identities, with
corresponding territories, which they themselves sought to save from being
swallowed up in the smothering embrace of a single pan-Turkism. This would
include the Kazakhs and their demands for being part of a "democratic federal
republic" as an "independent state" governed by their own "Kazakh political
party" (i.e. 'Alash party'). It would also include the Tatars, Bashkorts (or
'Bashkirs') and the many others mentioned by Shildebai (see above) who were
involved in similar efforts to secure cultural-political autonomy. These were
the pre-existing ethnonational groups with their already self-established identities
who forced Lenin, Stalin and company "to pursue the intensification of *national*
State building reforms, which meant the formation of *national* autonomies in
Tataria, Bashkiria and Kazakhstan, as quickly as possible" (see ref above; emphasis
added). The Tatars had been know to the Russians since the 13-14th century, a
knowledge which included battles between the two over 'national territories',
autonomy and independence.

'Pan-Turkism' and the Underlying Debate Revisited
Beyond even this though, we should recall that Khalid considered the
pan-Turkic view of nationhood to be not only a "non-Soviet" view, but a non-
Turkic view. And with this we begin to uncover an underlying debate regarding

the actual origins of pan-Turkism itself, a debate which then affects one's entire understanding and interpretation of the emergence and significance of Central Asian ethnonational identity. Paksoy would agree with Khalid it seems in calling 'pan-Turkism' a non-Soviet as well as non-Turkic view. He declares outright that: "In fact, this 'Pan' movement has no historical ideological precedent among Turks and has been documented to be a creation of the Westerners. Around the time of the occupation of Tashkent by Russian troops in 1865, the doctrine called 'Pan-Turkism' appeared in a work by Hungarian Orientalist Arminius Vambery."[52] It should be called to mind that Paksoy also argued for the 'creation' of the various Central Asian ethnic identities by Tsarist Russian ethnographers. Thus, in his view, we wind up with Tsarist Russians apparently creating the distinct ethnonational identities as a strategy to undermine a foreign constructed pan-Turkic 'movement' whose origins were not the Turks themselves at all, but the Hungarians and their orientalist scholars. Who knows, perhaps Paksoy would argue that in the face of Russia's advance toward eastern Europe in the 1850-60s the Hungarians and Tsarist Russians were engaged in a struggle for control of Central Asia and that out of this struggle arose two artificially and foreign created 'Turkic' identities—one pan-Turkic and another multiple distinct Turkic—which were both, to borrow Khalid's words again, "imposed by [two] omnipotent regime[s] on a helpless victimized population."

In direct relation to this idea of the alleged foreign origin of pan-Turkism is the idea of the alleged foreign origin of pan-Islamism. Shildebai (2002:74-5, *Turkic Nationalism*), tells us that "[i]f one said 'you are a Muslim', it was closer to [the heart of] a child of the Turks in the beginning of the 20th century than saying 'you are a Turk'." He then goes on a few lines later to tell how:

> Coming along in this situation 'pan-Islamism', which was counted as an enemy by the government of the Tsar, emerged. In the meeting of the State Duma [Assembly] which took place on March 13, 1912, the deputy Sadriddin Maksudi came to tell how there had never been [any] 'pan-Islamism' among the Turkic intelligentsia. He came saying: "Pan-Islamism, gentlemen, this is a myth. The product of this enemy fantasy, this has been given birth by politicized missionaries [of Russia]. Pan-Islamism has never existed any where other than the articles and books of the principle enemies of Muslims, the politicized missionaries, and it never will. Gentlemen, you may now ask where the idea of pan-Islamism came from," and [then he proceeded] to give

an answer to where it came from. . . . The representatives of the Turkic nationalist movement in the documents of the Tsar's administration are found at one time to be 'Jadidists' as well as 'pan-Islamists' and 'pan-Turkists'.

This must be the general context and intent of the passing statement by a top Kazakh scholar, Garifolla Yesim, dean of the philosophy and political science department at Kazakh National University, who says in speaking of "Independence and Islam" in Kazakhstan: "All of us remember how only yesterday there were the fake politics known as pan-Islamism."[53] Regardless, we should note here that Shildebai (like Yesim) is concerned in the broader context of this section to dissociate '(pan)-Turkic nationalism' with political fundamentalist movements typically associated with Islamic revivalism, especially those calling for the radical overthrow of governments. While this is entirely fair with respect to Jadidism, Shildebai himself directly associates the Turkic nationalist movement with "all Russia's Muslims." Whatever technical term we wish to apply, this in the end is nothing other than 'pan-Islamism', albeit restricted within the broader Muslim world to its panoramic embrace of "all Russia's Muslims," who are also referred to as 'all Russia's Turkic peoples'. And certainly, as both Shildebai himself and Serif Mardin (in Erturk, ed., 1999:117) note, Islam in its Jadidist form was indeed a rally cry for 'all Russia's Turkic peoples'. Indeed, only a few sentences before telling us that "[i]f one said 'you are a Muslim', it was closer to [the heart of] a child of the Turks," Shildebai speaks about the "efforts to form [one] group [out] of the Turkic peoples . . . via the unity of Islam." Whatever Russia's "politicized missionaries" may have meant by the term in their own technical sense then, the general idea of some kind of 'pan-Islamism' as a unifying force among "all Russia's Turkic Muslims" is not without foundations in the corresponding reality, neither then nor now.

With that in view, we can turn our attentions to Aydin Cecen, who writes as a Turk himself contributing to Korkut A. Erturk's 1999 work which aims at *Rethinking Central Asia: Non-Eurocentric Studies in History, Social Structure and Identity*. In his article on "Uzbekistan Between Central Asia and the Middle East: Another Perspective," Cecen argues (p 143) that:

. . . the genesis of ethnonationalism among the Turkic peoples of Russia should be sought, not in the legacy of the converging pan-Islamist and pan-Turkic ideologies, but in the official Soviet nationality policy and the concomitant federalist, cultural-autonomist framework which replaced, in practice, the right to self-determination.

In other words, pan-Turkism is a genuine organic phenomenon originating from the inner world of the Turkic people(s) themselves, but it has little or nothing to do with the emergence of distinct ethnonational identities or their ethnonationalisms among Turkic peoples. Such identities, Cecen alleges, were a creation of the Soviets to divide the one unified Turkic (or rather in his view 'Turkish') people. Shildebai comes close to this view, whether in relation to the Tsarists or Soviets, when he makes a passing comment about "the Turkic peoples who had descended into colonialist oppression in a situation where they were becoming divorced from historical consciousness and being formed as separate, distinct ethnonational peoples." At the same time, however, he is supportive of the participation of the various Turkic ethnonational peoples in the "Union of Autonomous Nations" and its resolution that "every ethnonational people should receive autonomy in which they run their own affairs" (2002:72). We will return to this 'both/and' tension just below. For now, note that Cecen goes so far as to pit the "autonomist framework" against "the right to self-determination" of nationhood, an alleged dichotomy which wishes to attribute '*self*-determination' of nationhood to the single Turkic 'nation' which he envisions in opposition to the idea of self-determination of autonomous nationhood, as if those seeking autonomous nationhood were not doing it them*selves*.

Note here that Erturk (1999:6), in the "Introduction" to this volume, says: "It appears that the consolidation of power by the Bolsheviks in the 1920s interrupted various national movements in the Soviet Union . . ." The question would be whether Erturk has in mind various Turkic national movements for autonomy (cf. also independence) or a single Turkic national movement as part of the larger context of national movements involving Poland, Ukraine and others (cf. Shildebai 2002:72; see above). It would seem he, like Shildebai, takes a view to the various Turkic national movements among the Tatars, Bashkorts, Kazakhs and others. From this vantage point, "the consolidation of power by the Bolsheviks in the 1920s [which] interrupted various national movements in the Soviet Union" would implicitly recognize the fact that "various national movements" among the Turkic peoples were *already* under way *before* the Soviets came along and "interrupted" them. Instead of the alleged external and artificial Soviet 'creation' of those nations and their national movements then, we would have more properly the 'interruption' of those internal and natural movements.

Whatever his exact views on the artificial or natural emergence of ethnonational identity in Central Asia, another Turkish scholar pressing a pan-Turkist agenda for Central Asia today is Orhan Soylemez. In his 1995 dissertation entitled *Preserving Kazak Cultural Identity After 1980* he brings his work to a climax in his final chapter on "Shifting from National to Supra-National Identity." In this chapter, Soylemez is "Projecting the future of Kazakstan." There he suggests that "[t]he completion of the process of nation-building may even force Kazak intellectuals to take one further step into [a] supra-national identity process which has already shown some signs in Kazakstan and other states in the region" (p 199). He stresses that "because of historical, linguistic, cultural, and, most important, religious ties, their new geopolitical conditions have pushed them closer to one another. Some analysts believe that from the economic, political and geo-political perspectives these newly independent republics would be better off if they created some type of economic, political union . . ." (pp 200-1). In reference to the article by Ahad Andican, "From Central Asian Turkic Republics to the United Turkistan: socio-political analysis of a historical must,"[54] Soylemez notes (p 201) that: "One former Central Asian scholar, in Turkey at the present time, argues that it would be much better for the Central Asian republics to get together and form a single 'Turkistan' rather than to remain separate. In this, he revives the cultural and political idea espoused by the Central Asian reformers (Jadids) before and after 1917." He likewise notes (p 202) that . . .

> . . . some contemporary, educated Kazaks, particularly after 1991, have constantly stressed the evident kinship between the Kazak and the other Turkic languages, using the inclusive name 'Turki', rather than Kazak, to describe both the language and literature. Not only do Kazak intellectuals raise the question of their own languages and their own people, but they also concern themselves with links between the Turkic languages and the Turkic people.

All of this accords well with his previous chapter on "Filling the Blank Pages in History" where he takes the common view that internal tribal disunity "prevented the Kazaks from emerging as a Kazak state or a nation until" at least the mid-18th century, i.e. after the Russians came along and began to colonize their land, if not sometime afterward. The history of Kazakh nationhood therefore, in his view, is late in coming and closely related to Russian colonialism. This would naturally call for Kazakhs and others to "not only . . . raise the question of their own languages and their own people, but . . . also concern themselves with links between the Turkic languages and Turkic people" since the colonial power which imposed its visions of nationhood upon them is now gone.

Soylemez and Cecen would therefore appear to be among the neo-pan-Turkists who argue that the Tsarist and/or Soviet Russian Empire was responsible for 'creating' the political national identities of the various Central Asian 'nations'. If so, these neo-pan-Turkists would be in agreement with scholars like Allworth, Hambly and Sinor. It perhaps is not coincidental that Allworth was the main advisor for Soylemez (pp v-vi). But whatever likeness or relation there may be, where these neo-pan-Turkist scholars would seem to differ from the majority Western view is in their interpretation of the consequences of this alleged historical 'fact' of Tsarist or Soviet 'creation' of Central Asian nationhood. Whereas most Western scholars would use this idea as a basis to argue for retaining the current nation-states, but insisting that they should be transformed into 'multiethnic' nations in late 20th century civic democratic fashion, Cecen and the neo-pan-Turkists would argue from their "non-Eurocentric" vantage point that the Soviet 'creation' of nations and national identities in Central Asia divided up the once unified Turkic world, cutting the Turks off from one another. With the passing of this era, *the Turks should now restore their former organic unity and establish a single pan-Turkic state.*

Without necessarily attributing this view to Shildebai himself, we might recall here his reference to "awakening the Turkic consciousness and establishing a new Turkic State" as the only "living and vital" option in the post-Ottoman era (2002:77). Indeed, the neo-pan-Turkist view can be explained by reference to the previous struggle between the Turkish Ottoman and Russian Empires (cf. Shildebai 2002:77). It is attributed to Turks (centered especially in Turkey) who still wish to revive the former glories of the *Turkish* (dimensions of the) Ottoman Empire and finally achieve its long sought after dream of wrestling control of the Turkic domains of Central Asia from Russian domination and bringing them into the fold of one united Turkish empire.

It should perhaps be noted here that Gaspirali, whose home was among the Crimean Tatars, came along as 'the father of pan-Turkism' with his call for "unity of language, of thought, and of action (dilde, fikirde, iste birlik)" just after the most intense period of struggle over the Crimea between the Ottomans and Russians had peaked in the early 1860s. But it should also be noted how Zeki Velidi, following Ismail Gaspirali, held a pan-Turkist vision "covering all Turkic Muslims, explaining their history as one of gradual differentiation within the framework of a foundational Turkish 'nation' taking in a number of Central Asian collectivities. The implication was that this common Turkic trunk showed sufficient cultural uniformity to merit being revived" (Mardin in Erturk, ed., 1999:121). We see here allowance for a 'both/and' view, i.e. "gradual differentiation" of distinct ethnonational identities as historically 'natural' yet which, in his mind, is "within the framework of a foundational Turkish 'nation'." Mardin's accentuation of 'nation' with single quotes is worth noting; he may be alluding to this type of 'both-and' flexibility. Whatever the particular accentuation of that term means in this context however, we must call to mind the fact that Velidi ultimately allowed the title of his book on "Turkish History" to be modified by the Kazan publishers to "Turkish-Tatar History" because "[t]he opposite of 'Turkism', 'Tatarism' had been nourished by Qayyum Nasiri's uncompromising stand on 'Tatar' as a distinct language and his followers opposed the 'Turkist' position of Gaspirali Ismail" (ibid). Even beyond the title though, it is doubtful the Tatars, for one, would have agreed to publish a book representing their history if it did not recognize their distinct Tatar identity within the larger framework of Turkic identity.

This remains true among various Turkic peoples of Central Asia today. For example, we find the Kazakh scholar, Tursin Hafizuhli Gabitov, quoting from another Kazakh scholar to demonstrate that:

> The space of Turkic civilization which was formed from ancient times as one whole unit consisting of a rich, wide territory, was cut off from some of its land since (the beginning of) the modern era by its imperialist neighbors. It is certainly possible to say that this is the reason why the territory of the State of Turkey, that is, the only state from this supercivilization that preserved its independence down to the end of the 20th century, did not maintain its direct connection with the territories of its kindred nations. The (tie) between Siberia and Central Asia, the (common) center of the Volga region and the lands of other Turkic peoples, the (connection) between Europe and Asia— these were all tossed asunder as a result of the expansionism of the colonialists of Russia. "Certainly,"—writes M. Tatimov,— "such an injustice could not last for ever. Justice had triumphed;

the Soviet Union which had brutally oppressed the Turkic peoples has collapsed; Central Asia and Kazakhstan, receiving independence, have established their own states. Conditions and opportunities have developed for restoration of Turkic unity (through the healing of) broken relations as well as for its development on a level with today's world civilization."[55]

Note here that Gabitov, as a Kazakh speaking *from within* the Central Asian context, clearly affirms that "Central Asia and Kazakhstan, having gained independence, established their own states." As with most other Kazakhs including Shildebai, Gabitov would not argue for giving up political independent sovereignty for Kazakhstan in order to create a single political Turkic empire. Likewise, very few if any Kazakhs could be found who would argue that the Russians—Tsarist or Soviet—'created' Kazakh ethnonational identity either in its cultural or political dimensions. Here we should note that Gabitov is affirming the view of Tatimov when he speaks of "the Soviet Union which had brutally oppressed the Turkic peoples." That is, the *already pre-existing* "Turkic peoples" were not 'created' by the Russians, but were rather "brutally oppressed" by them. Indeed, Gabitov expresses this view near the end of his chapter on "The Origins of *Kazakh* Culture" (emphasis added), which he traces all the way back to the Turkic Khaganate and even beyond it to the first nomadic peoples of the Eurasian Steppe. While he affirms from this basis the common trunk of 'Turkic-ness', he nonetheless recognizes multiple "Turkic peoples." He therefore, like many other Turks in Central Asia, seems to hold a 'both-and' view, i.e. both overall Turkic ethnonational unity which cooperates culturally, religiously, economically and politically in some kind of 'Turkic Union' (cf. the 'European Union'), yet which retains the distinct ethnonational-cultural as well as political identities of the various Turkic peoples in Central Asia, including their nation-states.[56]

In the end, there are Turkic pan-Turkists who see both a singular pan-Turkic national identity as well as distinct "Turkic peoples" as deriving naturally from the inner world of the Turks, not as outwardly imposed artificial 'creations' of foreign intellectual, political powers. There are clearly grounds here for comparison with the view of Kashgari, Balasaguni and other Turks of the 11th century who saw "the Turks" as one overall people group ordained even by God himself via a hadith of Muhammed (see Soucek 2000:91), yet who recognized linguistic, cultural and even political distinctions among various Turkic groups, as Kashgari certainly did.

While this comparison with the Turkic world of the Middle Ages is appropriate and valid however, we know of no efforts made by Gaspirali or other pan-Turkic leaders in his day to explicitly ground their ideas in these former streams. From a chronological perspective then, it must be admitted that Gaspirali and Velidi developed their ideas *after* the Hungarian orientalist Arminius Vambery. But mere chronological order does not establish causal connections so we cannot conclude from this mere fact that Vambery was the source of Gaspirali's ideas. Indeed, Alexandre Bennigsen and Fanny E. Bryan, in their treatment of "The Jadid Renaissance" in their article on "Islam in the Caucasus and the Middle Volga," note that:

> The movement began in the early nineteenth century with an attempt by Tatar 'ulama', educated in Bukhara, to break with the conservative Central Asian traditionalists who had dominated the spiritual life of Russian Muslims. The first to challenge their scholasticism was Abu Nasr Kursavi (1783-1814), a young Tatar teacher in a Bukhara madrasah. Accused of impiety by the emir of Bukhara and by the mufti of Orenburg, he was obliged to flee to Turkey.[57]

It seems then that Vambery may actually have gotten his ideas from the Tatar Jadidists educated in Bukhara. We should remember, therefore, that while pan-Turkic as well as various distinct Turkic ethnonational identities may ultimately have been politically manipulated by Tsarist and Soviet Russians, Hungarians and even other foreigners, they are both part of the real 'inner antiquity' of the Turks and their long, rich history going back to the Turk khaganate (see ch 8). The only question which remains is the proper relation between their 'ethnic-cultural nationhood' and their 'political nationhood'. It is an issue that even the Turks themselves have struggled and continue to struggle over, though whether they emphasize pan-Turkic (cf. also 'Turkish') nationalism or distinct Turkic identities, they do not conclude that their ethnonational identity is 'imagined' or 'invented' nor, likewise, that 'ethnic-cultural nation' and 'political nation' must be cut off from one another and left to their abandoned state.

Olivier Roy, Lonely Planet and Dru Gladney: Central Asian Nationhood as a Soviet Political Fabrication

And with that, we turn to another Western modernist writer who follows a Soviet 'imperial fiat' view similar to that held by Allworth, Hambly and

Sinor, namely Olivier Roy. His book is entitled *The New Central Asia: The Creation of Nations*. The description offered by the publisher summarizes his thesis in this way:

> During the anti-Gorbachev coup in August 1991 most communist leaders from Soviet Central Asia backed the plotters. Within weeks of the coup's collapse, those same leaders—now transformed into ardent nationalists—proclaimed the independence of their nations, adopted new flags and new slogans, and discovered a new patriotism. *How were these new nations built, among peoples without any traditionalist nationalist heritage and no history of independent governance?* Olivier Roy argues that Soviet practice had always been to build on local institutions and promote local elites, and that Soviet administration—as opposed to Soviet rhetoric—was always surprisingly decentralized in the far-flung corners of the empire. Thus, with home-grown political leaders and administrative institutions, *national identities in Central Asia emerged almost by stealth [i.e. secret].*[58]

Along with this, Roy (2000:vii-viii) himself makes clear what his view is of the whole situation when he says on the first page of the book that:

> There was no historical memory of a nation lost, nor had there been nationalist movements preparing the ground, as there had been in Armenia, Georgia and the Baltic countries. The Muslim republics of the ex-USSR were the creation of decrees that were issues between 1924 and 1936, which determined not only their frontiers, but also their names, their re-invented pasts, the definition of the ethnic groups that they were reckoned to embody, and even their language. . . . Unbeknownst to itself, the Soviet Union was a formidable mechanism for the manufacture of nations in Central Asia.

Clearly Roy believes that the native Central Asian peoples of today are "peoples without any traditionalist nationalist heritage and no history of independent governance." Thus, "[t]here was no historical memory of a nation lost, nor had there been nationalist movements preparing the ground" for the emergence of *The New Central Asia* and *The Creation of Nations* therein. This again sounds very much like the old Soviet view (borrowed from Hegel) with their talk of 'historyless' and 'cultureless peoples' whose ethnicity was 'invented' in direct connection with and *after* the 'rise of the nation-state'. Roy locates, in classic modernist fashion, the emergence of national identity in the promotion of "political elites" by the Soviets. He thus declares that: "The Muslim republics of the ex-USSR were the creation of decrees that were issues between 1924 and 1936, which determined not only their frontiers, but also their names, their re-invented pasts, the definition of the ethnic groups that they were reckoned to embody, and even their language." He writes off today's Central Asian nations as nothing else than "artificiality," saying: "This artificiality led many observers to predict that the fall of the USSR would see the return of supra-national identities (for instance pan-Islamism, pan-Turkism or pan-Turanianism, and even a return to Sovietism reincarnated in the Commonwealth of Independent States)" (pp. vii-viii). We of course have just finished addressing such views in relation to Allworth and company. Regardless, for those following Roy there is no other conclusion to come to except that the Central Asian people of today have no grounds, other than very weak and shaky ones, for making any claim to a priority of language, culture or other political rights in the 'new' Central Asian nations because, according to him, their national identities are politically fabricated identities of Soviet-trained elites. They have no *genuine* historical (i.e. no pre-existing and thus pre-established) connection to those 'new' nations.

The perspective offered in Lonely Planet's *Central Asia* guide book (1996 edition) is clear. It, too, follows the standard Western modernist approach when discussing the "Construction of Nationalities" in its section on "Facts About the Region—History." The authors allege that, "starting about 1924, nations were *invented*: Kazak, Kyrgyz, Tajik, Turkmen, Uzbek. Each was *given* its own distinct ethnic profile, language, history and territory. Where *an existing language or history did not exist* or was not suitably distinct from others, these were *supplied and disseminated*."[59]

This same type of perspective, applied in this case to the ethnic world of China, is also encountered in the work of Dru C. Gladney, *Muslim Chinese: Ethnic Nationalism in the People's Republic*. Along with his primary focus on the 'Hui' people, his study deals with the Kazakh, Kyrgyz, and Uighur peoples and their respective 'nations'. He follows Ernest Gellner in positing "The Rise of the Nation-State and the Invention of Ethnicity" (pp 79-80). In accordance with standard Western modernist convictions, the order of these two phenomena in his title are not coincidental: 'the invention of ethnicity' historically *follows* 'the rise of the nation-state', that is, nationalism as an ideology precedes the nation and gives rise to the 'imagined' formation or 'invention' of 'ethnic identities' within and from out of the modern political nation-state context. In Gellner's view, he sees this being done from out of previously existing 'lower (primitive) cultural identities' in the transition of human society from pre-modern to modern. In the view of Gladney and others of our day, the emphasis on 'lower (primitive)' may be significantly downsized or even dropped, but the '(ethno)national identities' of the 'Muslim Chinese' (and others), along with their 'ethnic nationalisms', ultimately arise and take shape from out of the intentional and strategic manipulation, fabrication and "invention of ethnicity" for political purposes relating to the ideals and goals of the nation-state (or 'empire', as in China's case).

Western Modernism and the 'Frankenstein' of the Post-Colonial, Post-Modern World

And so, through all of this, Western modernism insists that it was "[i]mperial conquest and rule of subject peoples [which] elevated ethnicity to a position of political prominence in modern history" (Brower and Lazzerini, eds., 1997:xv). "Ethnicity in this perspective is a social invention with enormous cultural and political consequences" (Brower in ibid, p 115). Indeed, the "enormous cultural and political consequences" involve, in Western modernist eyes, the unfortunate and mistaken association of 'ethnic nationhood' with 'political nationhood' and one is left with the impression that this, for them, is the 'Frankenstein' of the post-colonial post-modern world—a Frankenstein who must now be put to death using 'new tools and methods' in the scholarly arsenal employed in the cause of 'a new approach' in the West to denying ethnonational peoples in our world their cultural, social and political rights. In this, they continue the Western (including Russian) imperial-colonial legacy of denying and even cutting ethnonational peoples off from their genuine and integral ethnonational *human identities*, including their ethnonational cultures, languages, histories and the like. It is all part of the "academic wars" (cf. Porkhomovsky) which Western modernist and post-Soviet scholars seem to be waging in joint choral harmony against ethnonational identity and its burning aspirations in Central Asia, the former Soviet Union and, indeed, the entire modern(ist) world.[60]

—Chapter Five—

AKINER AND OLCOTT: 'THE KAZAKHS' AND THEIR 'UNFULFILLED PROMISE' IN KAZAKHSTAN

In the face of the kind of repeated treatment by Western modernist scholars witnessed in the previous chapter, we can only wonder which path writers like Peter B. Golden (1992), *An Introduction to the History of the Turkic Peoples: Ethnogenesis and State-Formation in Medieval and Early Modern Eurasia and the Middle East*, and Steven Sabol (2003), *Russian Colonization of Central Asia and the Genesis of Kazak National Conscious* have taken.[61] When the opportunity to read these works comes, will they prove any different? One can only hope. For now, we might at least note that, according to Michael Rouland's review of Sabol's work (in "A New Kazakstan: Four Books Reconceptualize the History of the Kazak Steppe"), "Sabol avoids the pitfalls of the nation and empire debate . . . by presenting a historical narrative outline of the Kazak intellectuals who emerged just before the Bolshevik revolution."[62] Rouland closes out his review though by alleging that "as the Soviet idea of nation evolved, a new Kazak idea of autonomy and a sense of culture were translated into a new socialist type of nationalism" (p 238). Whether this is Rouland's own idea or whether he is attributing it to Sabol is unclear however. How active versus passive the Kazakh intelligentsia were in the 'translation' of this idea is also unclear. Are they as well as their "new" idea of nationhood viewed as 'Russian created' or are they viewed as actively pursuing their own course of plan and action in dynamic interaction with as well as against Russian ideas and efforts? Relatedly, just what connection is posited between this "new Kazakh idea of autonomy" and former ideas of autonomy and/or nationhood? Here again we should recall the fact that the Kazak intellectuals were actively

---

involved by their own initiative in movements to achieve national autonomy well before the Soviet's came along, and the ideas and aims of those movements were contrary and opposed to Russian colonial aims and ideas (Shildebai 2002:72).

Also to be pointed out here, Rouland asserts that "[t]he disconnect between intellectuals of varying persuasions and the general populace was significant across the Russian Empire" (p 237). Once again though, whether this is his own view or he is attributing it to Sabol is unclear. Regardless, we can only call to mind that, however true it may or may not be, this take on things is standard in Western modernist thinking. That is, the 'intelligentsia' and the 'common masses' are separated off from one another so that the intelligentsia can be portrayed as developing ideas of nationhood which were previously non-existent among the masses and, thus, essentially foreign to them, from whence they commence to promote their 'elite' nationalism among the masses so that 'nations' are self-imagined and created out of the nationalist ideology of elites (see comparative chart in ch 1). This theory does not square well with reality, however, since *the ideas of elite nationalists must be grounded in the perception of national history and identity shared by the masses and must, on those grounds, resonate in the hearts of the masses in order for them to gain sufficient and sustainable allegiance to their cause.* In this light, the continual, enduring and widespread occurrence of (ethno)nationalism among elites and commoners alike, indeed in mutual cooperation with one another, throughout the long duration of human history stands against such theoretical approaches to nations and (ethno)nationalism.[63] That said, until the chance for a firsthand reading, Sabol's view on these issues remains unclear, but they will certainly prove important in the overall debate regarding the destiny of the Kazakhs and modern Kazakhstan.

In focusing our attentions here on the Kazakh nation and its history in relation to the modern nation-state of Kazakhstan, we can draw one final point of importance from Rouland. Namely, he notes the following:

> we can see ... that two predominant North American schools of Kazak history are developing. The first sees the Kazaks as yet another nationality case in the Soviet experience through the limiting lens of Russian history. Although their sources often engage Kazakstan from the grassroots, these scholars tend to pursue questions that confirm dialogues in Soviet historiography. The second moves away from Soviet centrism to present

Kazakstan within its own context rather than as a case study of the Russian Empire or Soviet cultural hegemony. Moreover, scholars in this school use new methods to describe the historical experience of the Kazak steppe by utilizing Kazak-language sources. Whether the objective of the study is to participate in Soviet historical discourse or to explore new territory, all of these monographs present a view of the colonized and elucidate the relationship of Kazaks with state-enforced ideology (p 234).

Akiner and the 'Vulnerability of the Kazakhs to Soviet Ethno-engineering'

Whichever of Rouland's two categories her work may fall under, Shirin Akiner (1995), *The Formation of Kazakh Identity: From Tribe to Nation-State*, surely presents us with another example of Western modernism's take on Kazakh history and nationhood. After offering generally fair coverage of pre-Soviet Kazakh history, she almost 'out of the blue' attempts to make a radical break between Kazakh (ethno)national identity in the pre-Soviet (i.e. Russian Tsarist) and Soviet era, alleging that:

> The Kazakhs, still at a comparatively early stage in the transition from a traditional existence (i.e. nomadic pastoralism and an orally transmitted culture) to sedentarization and literacy, were *especially vulnerable to Soviet ethnic engineering*. The boundaries—physical, metaphorical and *imaginary*—that were staked out at this time to differentiate the Kazakhs from their neighbors, thereby to give sharper articulation to *the formulaic Marxist-Leninist concept of national identity, were thoroughly internalized; consequently, they acquired an emotional validity that largely outweighed traditional ties and even objective historical realities*. Thus, the parameters of modern Kazakh nationhood which were established and consolidated over the ensuing seventy-odd years, and which continue to exist today, were *essentially a Soviet creation*" (1995:34; emphasis added).

Here is perhaps the epitome of Western modernist approaches to Kazakh (and Central Asian) nationhood. Akiner lays the foundation for her view in the idea that Kazakh ethnonational identity was 'weak' and in an unstable "stage" of transition which made them "especially vulnerable to Soviet ethnic engineering." Regardless of how she achieves it though, she, like all the others, believes that

"Kazakh nationhood" was "a Soviet creation" artificially manufactured through, again, "Soviet ethnic engineering." "The boundaries," both geo-politically and ethnically, were intentionally and artificially "staked out" by the Soviets as part of their 'divide and rule' strategy which was built upon calculated application of "the formulaic Marxist-Leninist concept of national identity . . . to differentiate the Kazakhs from their neighbors." Until that point, it seems in her view there was no *real* difference between the Kazakhs and their Turkic Central Asian neighbors, even though she spends the first part of her book discussing 'the Kazakhs'. With that in the past though, she now, like Khalid, laments to think that "[t]he collapse of the Soviet Union has done little to challenge the belief in the reality of the nation" among Kazakhs today (Khalid 1999:184-7). That is, in her own words, Kazakh ethnonational identity today has "acquired an emotional validity that largely outweigh[s] traditional ties and even objective historical realities." Modern Kazakh ethnonational identity, in Akiner's view, is *not* an "objective historical reality." The implication, as with the others, is that a genuine and healthy political nation cannot be and, indeed, has no right to be built upon such artificially constructed (ethno)national identity because, in the end, it is not a genuine, organic "tangible reality" with any true depth of historic continuity to today's geo-political nation of Kazakhstan.

Olcott on the Origins and End of the Old Ethnic-based Kazakh State

We come last but not least in our long two-chapter list of secular scholars to Martha Brill Olcott, one of the most well-known *Western* scholars of Kazakh-Kazakhstan studies in our day. Referencing Barthol'd's *Four Studies on the History of Central Asia* (1962:V3:129), Olcott affirms in her now classic work on *The Kazakhs* that: "The term Kazakh came into use by residents of the area possibly as early as the end of the fifteenth century and certainly by the mid-sixteenth century" so that "[b]y the mid-sixteenth century these people . . . were calling themselves Kazakhs . . ."[64] Observe here that while Abdakimuhli and other Kazakh scholars have traced the use of the ethnonym 'Kazakh' back as far as the 10th century (see previous as well as 8th chapter), we at least have here in Olcott the rather early *self-naming* of the Kazakh people. In this, she seems to spare us the view that their fundamental identity as 'Kazakhs' was 'created' by the 'imagination' of Tsarist Russian ethnographers or Soviet ethno-engineers and then imposed upon them. Indeed, she notes later in relation to the Alash Orda movement that "[t]he very name *Qazaq* was . . . the Kazakhs' own name for themselves as opposed to the Russian misnomer "Kirgiz" (p 118).

In similar fashion, she recognizes the establishment of the Uzbek khanate in 1420 AD and "the common use" of 'Uzbek' "to designate the Turki[c] tribes" inhabiting the region (p 7). While some might place the distinction earlier, Olcott takes the view that it was "[f]rom the reign of Qasim Khan on" that "Uzbeks and Kazakhs lived side by side, but they never again considered themselves one people" (p 9). Note here by the way 'the right of *self-determination* of nationhood' operating in this ancient historical period.

In connection to this emergence of the Kazakhs as a distinct Kazakh people *and nation*, Olcott deals faithfully in noting: "The consensus is that the Kazakh people or Kazakh nation was formed in the mid-fifteenth century . . ." (p 3).[65] This 'formation' was in direct relation to the founding of 'the Kazakh khanate' under the khans Kerei (1458-73) and Zhanibek (1473-80) (or as per Olcott "Kirai and Janibek") and "their attempt to create a unified Turkic state in the Kazakh steppe" in or around 1466 (p 22).[66] In spite of "their attempt" however, Olcott tells us that "Qasim Khan [or Kasim khan, 1511-1523] is generally credited with the creation of a centralized and unified Kazakh khanate" (p 9). The Kazakh scholar B. Kumekov, in his article on "Problems of Kazak[h] Statehood," would seem to agree on this account, saying: "The Kazak khanate reached its greatest power in the years of ruling of Zhanibek's son Kasym khan . . . For the first time after the Mongolian invasion almost all the Kazak clans and tribes in Kazakstan were united in one state."[67] The only thing to bear in mind here is that Kasim's credit came via the bank of unity which Kerei and Zhanibek as well as their successor Burunduk Khan (1480-1511) had built up before Kasim ascended the throne.

Regardless, with respect to Kasim's era and the 'uniting' of various Turkic tribes under him in the Kazakh khanate, Olcott tells us that now "[i]t was possible for the first time to consider the Kazakhs a people: they were approximately one million strong, spoke the same Turki[c] language, utilized the same type of livestock breeding, and shared a culture and a form of social organization. Under Qasim, political unity was established as well . . ." (p 9). While again one could debate whether it was at this precise point, under Kasim, that "[i]t was possible for the first time to consider the Kazakhs a people," Olcott is still kind and conservative to date this recognition so early, i.e. only 50 years give or take beyond the founding of the khanate in (roughly) 1466, *though she views ethnic formation largely following instead of actually preceding state formation* (cf. Ismagulov in Kozibaev, ed, 1998:50).

After Qasim, however, his "successors were unable to maintain the unity he had achieved" so that "a single, unified Kazakh state as such did not then exist. However, one of the [three] khans generally functioned as the pre-eminent authority or military commander for the whole Kazakh nation" (p 24). Here, of course, we must bear in mind that differences of emphasis will be placed by different authors upon the measures of unity versus disunity in 'the Kazakh nation' at any given time and, relatedly, difference of opinion will be held as to whether "a single, unified Kazakh state as such did not" or did "then exist." And these differences often stand in direct relation to the debate over the question of 'nationhood', both in its ethnic as well as political dimensions. Olcott's focus is on the political here. And in that focus, Kazakh political unity and, with it, statehood does not seem to exist for very long. She is still willing to use the language like "the whole Kazakh nation" at this time. In similar fashion, she tells us earlier that: "Despite the division into three hordes, the Kazakhs were one people, with a common language, culture, and economy. . . . Although the Russians [later] dealt with the Kazakhs as separate hordes, *the Kazakhs continued to view themselves as one people* . . ." (pp 11-12; emphasis added). The latter italicized phrase is marked out as being of obvious significance because it highlights the Kazakh view of "themselves as one people," a view which is located *in the later Russian colonial era.*

Olcott does seem to view Kazakh nationhood as somewhat weak as well as lacking longevity and depth, however, when she suggests that: "In the first century and a half that the Kazakhs were emerging as a distinct people, . . . the survival of a culturally distinct Kazakh people was always in doubt" (p 23). She offers fair historical circumstances for raising such a question, but the issue continues to be in the choice of wording and the perspective which it communicates. Is it really fair to say "always in doubt" as opposed to expressing it as 'at times in doubt', 'periodically threatened' or the like. Regardless, "[t]he first century and a half" would of course be approximately 1470-1620, i.e. the late-middle 15th to early 17th centuries. From there she tells us that "although the Kazakhs were able to remain a distinct people, the history of the seventeenth and early eighteenth centuries records the defeat and destruction of the Kazakh khanate" (1995:23). This would be the era of the Zhungarian (called also Jungarian, Oyrat and related Kalmyk) attacks (ca. 1690-1758), which the Russians also viewed from the distance as a threat to their own welfare and agenda. Against this background, Olcott tells us that:

> . . . in 1731 Abu'l Khayr, with his sons and deputies, swore their loyalty to the Russian empress. This action marked the end of an independent Kazakh state. . . the Kazakhs emerged

during the khanate as a distinct ethnic group. The end of the Kazakh khanate did not mark the end of the Kazakh people, however; instead, it introduced them to a life of conquest and colonial rule (pp 26-7).

Something important to note at this juncture would be Olcott's equation (throughout her treatment of "The Origins of the Kazakhs") of the terms the "Kazakh people" and the "Kazakh nation" (p 3). Later she declares: "The Kazakh khanate and the Kazakh people were synonymous" (p 10), thus equating all three terms. She also uses the term "the (early) Kazakh state" (as well as "Turkic state") on numerous occasions in reference to and/or as synonymous with "the Kazakh khanate" (pp 14, 19, 23, 24, 27). We must ask: Do we not have here the essential equation of 'ethnic nation' with 'political nation' in her treatment? The answer, in case we are wondering, is a resounding 'yes'. And with that we are dangling on the edge of confusion over just what difference there is between 'the Kazakh political nation (or state or nation-state)' in *past* Kazakh history and the modern political nation (or state or nation-state) of 'Kazakhstan'. Indeed, "Kazakh nation" would be the precise English translation of the Kazakh term (i.e. 'Kazakh eli') used by most Kazakhs today in reference to Kazakhstan. But, as we glimpse in Liebich above, it is precisely this interchanging of 'nation' and 'state' and the compound 'nation-state' derived from both which creates problems, particularly for Western modernists who wish to insist on the alleged radical distinction between 'ethnic *nation*' and 'political *state*', both historically and ideologically.

The crucial issue is this: If 'the Kazakh khanate' is identified as a political 'nation' or 'state' and then intimately associated with the 'Kazakh ethnic nation', we begin running into troubled waters, at least as far as Western modernist scholars are concerned. Why? Because if 'the modern political nation or state' of Kazakhstan is viewed as essentially a continuation of the 'perennial' (i.e. ongoing, enduring) history of that former 'political nation or state', then we wind up with the sticky problem of a 'Kazakh State' on our hands, i.e. political statehood woven together with and founded upon ethnic nationhood, which would mean the no-no of 'ethnopolitics' in today's Central Asia. And this would raise all kinds of linguistic, cultural and even political rights issues in what Western modernist (including Euroslavic) scholars want desperately to be, and even insist by way of ethical imperative should be, 'multiethnic nations' (according to Western defined ideals and standards).

Olcott on the Russian Creation of
a Kazakh Nationalist Elite
and Late 19th Century Conversion to Islam

Amidst all her affirmations of the Kazakh people's oneness as "a distinct people," Olcott presents us with a Kazakh political state which only seems to achieve genuine "political unity" under Kasim (or Qasim) khan but which thereafter cannot be viewed as "a single, unified Kazakh state." A century and one-half later she rounds out her treatment of "The Origins of the Kazakhs" by heralding "[t]he end of the Kazakh khanate," i.e. the end of the old 'Kazakh political nation (or state)'. She draws a distinction, however, adding that this "did not mark the end of the Kazakh people." It seems, in all fairness, that her main emphasis throughout this treatment is not on the recognition of "a single, unified Kazakh state," though she certainly affirms it in varying degrees along the way. Rather, her primary emphasis seems to be on the idea that "the Kazakhs emerged during the khanate as a distinct ethnic group." Although "in the first century and a half" it was "always in doubt," she is ultimately much clearer in her affirmation of "the survival of a culturally distinct Kazakh people."

Here then we come to an important crossroads in our interpretations of the history of 'the Kazakhs' and 'Kazakhstan'. Are we dealing with essentially two histories of two distinct 'political nations': one 'pre-modern' and closely associated, even equated, with 'the ethnic nation' and the other 'modern' with the ethnic association significantly distanced and/or somehow redefined? Or are both viewed as part of fundamentally one and the same history of 'political nationhood' in unique relation to one ethnonational group? And when standing at that crossroads, in direct relation to her discussion of the late 19th-early 20th century Alash Orda movement, Olcott tells us that:

> During these decades straddling the turn of the century, the Kazakhs increasingly thought and acted as a homogeneous community. This was partly because of the Russian policy of secular education, which led to the development of a self-aware Kazakh elite, and partly a product of the spread of Islam, which introduced another definition of community and provided a literate clergy who could maintain a communication network throughout the steppe (pp 112-3).

First note here that whatever confidence she had in the idea that "the Kazakhs were one people" in the previous khanate era, her language in this above quote indicates that she sees something lacking at "the turn of the [19th-20th] century" in "the Kazakhs . . . as a homogeneous community." What has happened in between is that "Tsarist colonial policies had weakened the traditional authority structure in the Kazakh community" so that "[b]y the beginning of the 19th century, . . . [t]he internal rule of the khans had all but disintegrated. As Levshin describes it, Kazakh self-government was nothing more than an 'archaic combination of despotism with freedom for every individual'" (pp 100 and 57 respectively). According to this interpretation then, we have come to a period in Kazakh history which parallels the period in ancient Israel when, "in those days, there was no king in Israel; everyone did what was right in his own eyes" (Jdg 17:6; 21:25).

Regardless of how accurate that description may or may not be in relation to the period of Kazakh history in question, another question still arises: How closely does she associate the former 'pre-modern Kazakh nation' of the khanate with the now emerging 'modern nation' of this 'new' period? Does she see a strand of continuous 'Kazakh nationhood' running through the entire history? Or do we somehow find (or create) a 'break point' which can serve to distinguish or separate the 'two nations' from one another? To draw a brief parallel from ancient Israel, the biblical writers saw the history of Israel as the history of a single, continuous nation spanning across this *temporary* period of national disunity in spite of the fact that the period in question covered some 300-400 years. But the history of *ancient* Israel is not complicated by the fact, as in the Kazakh case, that this transitional period is precisely the transitional period which the Western modernist paradigm sees as the critical transition between ancient-medieval and modern forms of nationhood (cf. ch 3).

Whatever the case, in connection to Kazakh history, the most important event prior to the Alash Orda movement which serves as an indicator of perspectives on this question is the 'uprising' or 'independence movement' under Kenesari Kasimuhli (or, as per Olcott, Kenesary Qasimov), 1837-47. We might first note that, while there are surely *some* Kazakhs, we would question Olcott's idea that Kenesari "is regarded by *many* Kazakhs today as the first Kazakh nationalist" (p 65; emphasis added). All of the khans noted above in connection with the founding and building of the Kazakh khanate, along with the 'batir' (warrior 'heroes'), Kenesari's grandfather Abilai Khan, and others who were involved in defending the Kazakh *nation* against the Zhungarian invasions—these are all 'regarded by many Kazakhs today' as 'Kazakh nationalists'. So are all others involved in the founding, preservation and defense of the nation (which means that 'Kazakh nationalist' or 'nationalism' should not be taken in a negative sense).

In spite of the fact, however, that Kenesari is noted by Olcott as being a Kazakh nationalist, he oddly enough as a 'nationalist' does not seem to be credited with having even aimed for, yet alone achieved any true sense of Kazakh nationhood in her view—and that is the crucial question. Instead, she speaks only of "the large followings achieved by Kenesary Qasimov in the Middle Horde" (p 58), thus assigning his aims and efforts as well as popularity and support to the Middle Horde and little else (cf. pp 65-67). Meanwhile, most Kazakh scholars today, including the new, official *Kazakhstan National Encyclopedia* and secondary school textbooks, understand the 1841 election of Kenesari as an election to be khan not only of the Middle Horde, but the entire Kazakh nation.[68] Of course, Olcott bases her treatment of Kenesari and the movement on one lone Russian source from the communist era, namely E. Bekmakhanov (1947), *Kazakhstan in the 20-40s of the 19th Century*,[69] which, in spite of its having been attacked by the communists and subsequently revised in 1957, still does not provide us with a sure, solid footing and certainly not a Kazakh tested and affirmed one for understanding and interpreting Kenesari and the 'independence movement' through non-communist eyes.

Here we should turn to the 'Foreword' of Olcott's work to highlight one further thing: "The most important questions in this connection are interpretations of the historical significance of the Kazakh submission to Russian rule and the significance of the Kazakh anti-Russian movements" (Vucinich in Olcott 1987:xvi). Indeed, what is the significance of certain Kazakh leaders "swearing their loyalty to the Russian empress" in 1731, an action which Olcott says "marked the end of an independent Kazakh state"? Did they essentially give up on their political nationhood, turn it over to the Russians and forfeit all rights to it for all days to come? At least Olcott notes in this regard that a good deal of this was done "without the knowledge or support of the Kazakh people" (p 31). Nonetheless, she seems to paint a picture moving from original, general acceptance of the conditions of surrendered statehood toward one in which "[t]he Kazakhs had grown increasingly unhappy with Russian policies in the steppe until discontent climaxed in the 1916 uprising" (p 100). This would include "a change in attitude" which "no longer approved the Russian administration uncritically" (p 107).

Here again we seem to find an important difference in Olcott's manner of presentation with that encountered in Kazakh sources. In the Kazakh sources, it is a forced choice between the lesser of two evils. The Kazakhs were forced to turn to Russia for 'assistance' in order to withstand the Zhungarian attacks, a situation which Russia took advantage of by subjugating the Kazakhs and 'stealing away' their statehood. While the Kazakhs definitely 'enjoyed' certain benefits from Russian rule and while periods of 'peace' can be found *in between* their resistance efforts, they were never really content with having Russia take over their political destiny as a nation and, thus, always retained the aspiration for *recovering* political power from the Russians and *regaining* control of an independent Kazakh state. Thus uprisings and resistance movements are encountered throughout the entire era of Russian colonial rule, some on more local levels and others larger, with Kenesari's movement representing and even temporarily achieving the aim and desire which resided in the Kazakh heart from start to end of 'the Russian imperial era'.

On top of this however, the view among more than a few Kazakh scholars is that the Kazakh treaties with the Russians between 1731-42 were overall of little significance. The well-known Kazakh historian, Burkitbai Ayagan, notes that it was only a matter of a decade or so before the Zhungarians were wiped out by the Chinese (1758). Thus, the need for Russian assistance in protecting the Kazakh homeland against the Zhungarians was no longer there. Likewise, he notes that apart from the limited military outposts along the far northern borders, no significant Russian presence was sent into Kazakhstan, i.e. 'the land of the Kazakhs', until the early or middle 1800s.[70] On this score, it should be observed that G. Yesim, in the foreword to this book, says: "The Kazakh people who had been associated with the Kazakh State established in 1466 were cut off from their nationhood through the official resolution of the Russian Empire in 1822." He thus places "the end of the Kazakh State" almost a century later than Olcott. In similar manner, though placing the emphasis on slightly later events and actions instead of on the "official resolution" itself, the Kazakh historian A. Abdakimuhli (1997:113) says that is was especially between 1867-68 in Zhetisu, Sirdaria, Orinbor and Western Siberia that "legal rights were given like smoke into the hands of the Russians who were carrying out—with respect to government, military, economy, and religion—the entire matter of oppressive lordship over the traditional [Kazakh] system of oversight." In fact, these actions immediately followed strong intensification of Russian military action and occupation of Kazakhstan and Uzbekistan in the 1860s which reached to Tashkent by 1865.

All this accords with Shildebai's (2002, ch 1) division of Russian Tsarist occupation into three major periods or phases: 1731-1822, 1822-1867 and 1867-1891. The first period (1731-1822) is considered somewhat insignificant with respect to the actual carrying out of colonial-imperial policy in Central Asia. Thus, it is in the second period or phase that the brunt of colonial force came in, actually 'transforming' Kazakhstan from an 'independent nation' into a 'colonial nation'. With respect to the third period, along with Abdakimuhli's comments just above, he adds a few lines later that: "In 1868 the founding of the "Nomadic Committee" opened the way for the intensifying of missionary service [among the nomads]. . . . The Nomadic Committee carried out the policy of russification by combining it with what they called the "Chamber of Russification."[71]

Whatever position she has taken on the precise dating, however, Olcott has nonetheless pronounced "the end" of the old Kazakh *political* nation and we can only wonder how she views the tie between that 'old' Kazakh political nation and the later political nation which arises in Kazakh(stan) history. In direct connection then to the question of submission to Russian rule, what is the significance of 'the independence movement' lead by Kenesari? If it was simply a regional 'uprising' of temporal discontent vented against certain mistreatment by the new Russian overlords, then no *national aspirations or interests* can be assigned to such events. If, however, it was (the expression of and attempt at) a *national independence movement*, especially one embracing the entire *nation*, then we have here *sustained* aspirations and efforts to break free from Russian rule and *re*-establish "an independent Kazakh state."

Even if we do grant 'national status' to Kenesari's movement, however, another question still remains. Namely, whether we should view Kenesari as aiming at the *re*-establishment of the former state or the establishment of a new state. This question is directly tied to the stream of Kazakh nationalism and the Kazakh nationalists who champion its cause. If Kenesari is really "the first Kazakh nationalist," then we are essentially talking about ideas of nationhood which begin with Kenesari under and perhaps by influence of Russian colonialism and its vision for Kazakh nationhood. Given that the modernist view generally assigns 'the age of nations' and, with it, the rise of 'nationalism' to the period "from 1750 to 1914" (cf. McNeill above), and this likewise is the precise period of alleged transition between the previous Kazakh nation and later Kazakh nation which we are dealing with here, it is quite reasonable to ask whether the modernist view is a dynamic somehow influencing, however strongly, the interpretation of Kenesari as "the first Kazakh nationalist." The fact that the Marxist view of 'the rise of nations and nationalism' is essentially the same as the Western modernist view only makes the question doubly important. The Soviets were very desirous to demonstrate that Kazakh history revealed a clear movement from a feudal stage to a modern national stage in attempting to convince the Kazakhs that they were on a path of historical development which would ultimately culminate in post-national communism. Here again, while the primary source which Olcott is relying on for her interpretation was revised to come more in line with the communist view, it was not entirely condemned and thrown out. It thus conformed sufficiently to that view to merit its simply being revised as opposed to discarded.

But the same question of the Marxist as well as modernist view of the crucial period of transition between old and new forms of nationhood in human society and history and the measure of influence which this view may be exerting on various interpretations of Kazakh history at this critical stage— this same question applies not only to interpretations of the nationalist Kenesari, but to any interpretation of Kazakh nationalism and Kazakh nationalists in this transitional period. Therefore, whatever Olcott's precise view on the 'uprising' or 'independence movement' under Kenesari and its significance for Kazakh nationhood at this mid-19th century juncture, she ultimately sees a significant move toward Kazakh national unity (i.e. homogeneity) at "the turn of the [19th-20th] century" in direct relation to the emergence of a Kazakh nationalist 'elite'. Let us return, therefore, to that crucial crossroads.

First here we can highlight the fact that Olcott attributes this move toward greater national unity (i.e. homogeneity) to two sources: "the Russian policy of secular education" and "the spread of Islam." In the first of these two sources, her approach in treating the matter of "the Russian policy of secular education" certainly has the 'ring' of the standard Western modernist view. This is seen not only in the quote above, but in her earlier section and its title "The Creation of Secular Elites" (pp. 104-6), which describes the process she is referring to in the quote. In that earlier section, her explanation is that "[t]he Russians saw" the opportunity and need "for the creation of a loyal, peaceful Kazakh population. They intended the graduates of the Russian-Kazakh schools to serve the colonial administration . . ." To this end, "[t]he Russians . . . encouraged" various Kazakhs ("particularly . . . aristocratic families," cf. 'elite') to attend the schools which they, the Russians, established for their own political aims and ends. Those Kazakhs who then studied in those schools "formed a new secular elite."

Afterwards, "[t]his first secular elite . . . helped shape the attitude of the Kazakh intellectuals who came to maturity just before the revolution" (w/ phrase order inverted). This 'second secular elite' would be those behind the Alash Orda movement with its aims, aspirations and efforts in achieving autonomous Kazakh nationhood. And here we come to the crucial question hanging over the whole interpretation of that movement: Were those aims, aspirations and efforts something essentially 'new' and 'different' from ideas of 'Kazakh nationhood' in the past or are they more properly viewed as a continuation of that past nationhood, as a 'restoration' and/or 'reform' movement *arising from out of and within the flow of one continuous Kazakh national history*?

In Olcott's view, Russian socio-political aims and ambitions carried out through "secular education" were responsible for the "development" or "creation" of "a self-aware Kazakh elite." Or to put it in her own words again: "the Russian policy of secular education . . . led to the development [cf. again "creation"] of a self-aware Kazakh elite." Note here, by the way, that the idea of being 'self-aware' is crucial in the entire nationhood debate because recognition (or 'awareness') of nationhood is not granted by *others* until the people them*selves* are not only '*self*-aware', but then, based in that self-awareness, declare themselves to be a 'people' or 'nation'. Indeed, this concept is behind the whole idea of 'the right to *self*-determination of nationhood' which results in nations established 'by the people, for the people'. Olcott's idea that Abai, as one of these 'first Russian-created Kazakh elites', "began to criticize the traditional Kazakh way of life" would fit well within this whole scheme.

Likewise, note here that Olcott represents this 'first new Kazakh secular elite' as being primarily cut off from the main Kazakh population, saying: "This first secular elite had only slight contact with the Kazakh community . . ." (p 105). This effectively detaches from the rest of the *old* 'Kazakh nation' the new ideas of 'Kazakh nationhood' that were apparently beginning to brew in the new "self-aware Kazakh elite's" mind—placed there as they apparently were by "the Russian policy of secular education." From these detached 'first elite' then arise "[t]he second generation, . . . [who] were committed to restructuring the authority relationships within the Kazakh community." That is, they were committed to a new form of government and, presumably with it, a new form of nationhood. The juxtaposition of this new form and structure of political nationhood against "the passing of Kazakh pastoral nomadism and urg[ing of] economic reforms . . . by more secular Kazakhs" should not be missed (p 109). We are indeed hanging on the edge of an interpretation which, despite its uniqueness and greater depth, is essentially in line with that of Akiner (or rather vice versa since Olcott 1987 precedes Akiner 1995 historically).

Thus, Olcott's idea of the "creation" of "a self-aware Kazakh elite" through Russian political aims and efforts at this late stage of Kazakh history is implying rather strongly the idea of an 'awakening' of these elites to their identity as a (new type of modern) 'Kazakh nation'. While distinctions certainly exist, this interpretation is uncomfortably close to the view of Olivier Roy and others who attribute the origins of Central Asian 'elite nationalists'—and with them, the origins of 'modern' Central Asian nationhood—to the Russians and their political strategies and efforts. This is also the interpretation given by some scholars to the sense of Mirzhakip Dulatuhli's poem-song of 1909, 'Awake, Kazakh!', which served as a 'battle-cry', a 'national anthem' of sorts, for the Alash movement. The interpretation is that until the Alash elites themselves were 'awakened' to become 'self-aware' of their own identity as a (new type of modern) 'Kazakh nation', and they in turn then 'awakened' the 'old, pre-modern cultural nation' of the Kazakhs to this 'new, modern' idea of 'nation', the Kazakhs were all asleep, blissfully 'unaware' of their own identity and destiny as 'a modern political nation'. As Olivier Roy puts it, "[t]here was no historical memory of a nation lost," there was only an 'awakening', an 'enlightenment' a coming to 'self-awareness' at this late hour of history of an (allegedly) new type of 'modern political nation' which had never existed before in the 'collective memory' of their national conscious. Here again we can only wonder what view Steven Sabol (2003), *Russian Colonization of Central Asia and the Genesis of Kazak National Conscious* has in mind regarding this crucial question. Is there no "genesis" of Kazakh national conscious before this?

In moving towards answers, first Olcott notes that "Kazakh nationalism was not an abstract issue in the 1920s; at stake was the development and advancement of a Kazakh nation" in which "the Kazakh leaders struggled to insure their own participation in the development of their own republic and in defining the program of social and economic reform to be applied to the Kazakh population" (p. 210). We certainly have here *self*-initiative in "the development and advancement of a Kazakh nation,"[72] but it does not answer the question of the *genesis* of this conscious effort and, through it, the nation which is being 'developed and advanced'. We might actually wonder whether she is using the term "development . . . of a Kazakh nation" here in the sense of 'create' as she does in connection with the "development" or "creation" of the elite who are behind it.

Regardless, before attempting to answer that question, let us point out that immediately after saying "at stake was the development and advancement of a Kazakh nation," Olcott emphasizes that ". . . there was little agreement among the Kazakh elite about the desired end or the road to achieve it . . . the Kazakh elite . . . were not only a minority in their party but also a divided one" (p. 210). She apparently has a very short-lived idea of 'the Kazakhs increasingly thinking and acting as a homogeneous community' in view. But that is not the main issue on the table at this moment.

In attempting to deal with the main issue, i.e. the question of the 'genesis' of this "Kazakh nation" which is surely "at stake," Olcott notes something of importance in regard to the Alash Orda movement and one its mouthpieces, the *Qazaq* newspaper. She tells us:

> The editors of *Qazaq* [newspaper] had as their primary goal the preservation of a distinct Kazakh people with a consciously political purpose: they claimed that the Kazakhs were entitled to political as well as cultural concessions. They understood their 'Kazakhness' as a form of national identity, . . . Baitursunov and his co-editors were trying to preserve their language, culture, and history, fight the assimilationists among them, and argue that one could be Kazakh and speak Kazakh while still being progressive, modern. They maintained that the Kazakhs could achieve economic parity with the Russians through technical education in the steppe and the subsequent spread of modern (that is, Russian) agricultural and livestock-breeding techniques. All this could be achieved without becoming Russified, whereas assimilation would buy modernization only at the price of national identity (p 118).

She at least recognizes here the "primary goal" of those involved with this newspaper as being "the preservation of a distinct Kazakh people with a consciously political purpose." We actually come close here to a view which *might* be interpreted *in connection with prior notions* of "a distinct Kazakh people with a consciously political purpose." But Olcott's assignment of the "creation" of this elite and their education to the Russians still leaves a question mark hanging over any such interpretation, at least within her scheme. We are still left wondering whether this "consciously political purpose" is ultimately a *modern* one of Russian and not of Kazakh origins and one which traces its roots back no further than somewhere near "the turn of the [19th-20th] century." Indeed, she clarifies her view of "modern (that is, Russian)" within the text. She also highlights that "[t]hey understood their 'Kazakhness' as a form of national identity." Indeed, they did. But what is the significance of this in Olcott's view? She long ago detached 'Kazakhness' from political identity with "the end of the Kazakh khanate" and left it only as an ethnic-cultural identity, i.e. an 'ethnic' or 'cultural nation'. Thus a new association of Kazakhness with political identity has taken place somewhere along the way and there is no other place to locate it within Olcott's scheme except in the Russian 'creation of a Kazakh secular elite' who were raised up to handle local administrative, i.e. political governmental tasks for the Kazakh steppe region as part of the Russian Empire.

Here then let us turn to the very last page of her original 1987 edition, where we find her bringing together her view of these "early Kazakh secular nationalists" with those undergirding modern Kazakhstan. She says:

> . . . the early Kazakh secular nationalists . . . chose to modify and adopt their culture, and so they have managed to survive as a culturally distinct people, able even to compete with the Russians for control of their social and, to a lesser extent, political life. This choice was reaffirmed by the nationalists' descendents as well. The present Kazakh intellectual elite seems committed to this same strategy of cultural adaptation, first to attain cultural survival and ultimately to achieve full control (1987:256).

Note first that "[t]he present Kazakh intellectual elite" are "the . . . descendents" of "the early Kazakh secular nationalists." The direct correlation between elites, nationalists and nationalism should not be missed here by the way, for it is part of the standard Western modernist view (cf. chs 1 and 2). Regardless, "[t]he present Kazakh intellectual elite" are actually those of 1987 (when the edition we are quoting was published). This was two years before Nazarbaev came to power. Nonetheless, Nazarbaev and other 'secular Kazakh elite' from that period are the ones who, like their "early Kazakh secular nationalist" 'ancestors', were trained up by and served the Russian administration—only in the case of the "early" ones it was the Russian Empire whereas in the current case it was the Soviets. And it was these "nationalists' descendents" who came to power and 'laid the foundations' of modern independent Kazakhstan. We should therefore observe here the likeness between these "early Kazakh secular nationalists" and their "descendents" in the desire which both have to take their Russian training and political experience and use it to "compete with the Russians for control of their social and . . . political life." This is precisely the sense of both this quote and the one above it regarding "the editors of *Qazaq*." With respect to "the early Kazakh secular nationalists," the political ambitions were "to a lesser extent," seemingly because they were on a downhill slide, i.e. fighting a loosing battle in their day. In the case of their 'descendents', we find that their aim is "ultimately to achieve full control." (Olcott has almost 'predicted' here, in 1987, the independence of 1991, even though she had no idea it would come about within five years; cf. 'Preface' to 1995 ed.)

Here then we have Russian trained Kazakh secular nationalists behind both the 'earlier' and 'later' periods of the *modern* national development of Kazakhstan. It is one national history, i.e. the history of one "developing and advancing" *modern* nation. Its "early" period, i.e. its origins, are traced back no further than the late 19th century, i.e. the time when "[s]ince the 1880s an ever-increasing Kazakh intelligentsia had expounded its views . . . ," most of whom "were graduates of the [Russian] state schools" (p 100-1). And with this, it seems that here, with Khalid (see ch 4), is where she locates the beginning of a new and different type of modern Kazakh nation. Likewise, in classic Western modernist fashion, she grounds "the development and advancement" of this modern nation in an 'intellectual elitist' view of nationalism (cf. table in ch. 1), one which sees it ultimately, like Olivier Roy and others, as a 'new' ideological construct learned from (i.e. "created" by) the Russians and then functioning as an intentional ideological "strategy" employed by "elites" to "achieve full control" of the nation.

If we are truly dealing with a standard Western modernist interpretation here in Olcott—and it seems we are—then these 'secular nationalist elites' are the ones who inculcate the 'common masses' and 'cultivate' in them *political* nationalist sentiment. Such sentiment, according to the Western modernist view, does not exist among the masses prior to the elites stirring it up in them. This is part of why the modernist view holds that nationalism precedes nationhood and not vice versa so that whatever form of nationhood emerges as a result of nationalist ideology, it cannot be traced back and connected with ideas and forms of nationhood existing beforehand. Likewise, in that view, it mainly serves to fulfill the socio-political aims of the elites themselves and not the masses. This view will essentially be confirmed when we return later to discuss Olcott's belief that "the Kazakh-dominated leadership" of today's Kazakhstan is essentially responsible for ongoing "ethnic-based loyalty to the land of the Kazakhs," a view expressed in her 2002 work entitled *Kazakhstan: Unfulfilled Promise.*

Not only in relation to "the Russian policy of secular education" and "the development of a [new] self-aware Kazakh elite" however, Olcott attributes the move toward Kazakh national unity (i.e. homogeneity) "at the turn of the

---

century" to a second source. As quoted earlier, she says it was also "partly a product of the spread of Islam, which introduced another definition of community and provided a literate clergy who could maintain a communication network throughout the steppe" (pp 112-3). She actually gives fuller expression to this view earlier in the same chapter, saying:

> The last half of the nineteenth century witnessed one other major change in Kazakh society: the spread of Islam among the Kazakh masses and the emergence of Islam as a major social and moral force in Kazakh society. By the last quarter of the century there were a large number of Kazakh intellectuals who had been educated in Muslim schools in the steppe and were committed to the merging of Kazakh culture and Islam (p 101).

Here again we must point out Western modernist ideas and approaches underpinning her whole presentation. First, what she has in mind regarding "the spread of Islam" is the sending of Tatar missionaries to the Kazakh Steppe by Catherine II in the late 18th-early 19th century in an effort to help 'civilize' and bring the illiterate nomadic Kazakhs under Russian imperial control. According to Olcott, Catherine's efforts could be called successful in the sense that "[t]he Kazakhs became Muslims; . . ." (p. 102). This idea, however, of a 19th century conversion of the Kazakhs to Islam, which is fairly standard in Western (including Russian) interpretations, has been quite sufficiently answered by Devin Deweese as well as Bruce Privratsky.[73] Both scholars, not to mention a good number of Kazakh Muslim scholars (e.g. Bulutai 2000 and Nurtazina 2002), trace the "spread of Islam" among the Kazakhs back to even the pre-Kazakh era.

Of course, even Olcott notes that "the Turki[c] nomads of the Kazakh steppe nominally embraced Islam in 1043" (pp 18-19). But key in her interpretation is the word 'nominal', which is essentially the 'veneer theory' of Islam among the Kazakhs (cf. Gabitov 2001:287-8). This is why Olcott insists that, in that earlier period, ". . . the pastoral nomads (the Kazakh masses and most of the Kazakh nobility) had only the sketchiest knowledge of Muslim tenets and practices. . . . The self-sufficient nomads did not have much contact with the Muslim centers of the Tatars to the northwest or the Chagatai to the south" (p 19).

The primary force in "the spread of Islam" among the Kazakhs was the sufi saint of Turkic ancestry, Kozha Akmet Yasawi (1094-1167)—himself a disciple of Aristan Bab—and Yasawi's disciples such as Suleimen Bakirgani

(1104-1186). This was in the pre-Kazakh Kipchak era of the Steppe. Yasawi's mausoleum in the city of Turkistan, where he lived out his latter days, marks the most sacred spot on Kazakh (and even much of Central Asian) soil today and *helps* create, along with the tombs of the ancestors, a genuine valuation of Kazakh soil as their 'ancestral homeland'. But whenever exactly one wishes to commence the history of Islam among the Kazakhs, it begins well before the Kazakh khanate came into being in the mid-15th century and was quite sufficiently established among the Kazakhs throughout most if not all of the history of that khanate. Even Olcott notes that "... by the end of the seventeenth century, Kazakh oral literature included poems venerating Allah and Muhammad. The code of Tauke also shows that the Kazakhs had accepted some of the principles of *Shari'a* law by the end of the seventeenth century" (p 19). The fact that the code of Tauke khan (1680-1718) incorporated "principles of *Shari'a* law" shows more than just "some" acceptance of Islam by this time; it shows the significant impact of Islam, indeed enough of an impact for it to serve as a source for an entire nation's legal code. While *Shari'a* law cannot be detached from Sufism, note here as well that the focus on *Shari'a* law represents the path of Islam which "the Muslim centers of the Tatars to the northwest or the Chagatai to the south" followed. Likewise, with respect to the historical depth of Islam among the (larger masses of) Kazakh people, the tradition of "venerating Allah and Muhammad" in Turkic and "Kazakh oral literature" clearly goes back beyond "the end of the seventeenth century" to, again, Yasawi and his *Diwani khikmet* (*Book of Wisdom*) in the Kazakh-Turkic steppe (cf. Yesim 2002a:140-1).

Certainly changes occurred through both internal and external stimuli in the course of the history of Islam among the Kazakhs; all religions undergo such dynamic development throughout their respective histories. But such changes in no way constitute the initial "spread of Islam" among the Kazakhs. Neither do they not warrant the conclusion that it was through Catherine's socio-political efforts in sending Tatar missionaries that "[t]he Kazakhs became Muslims." Neither, therefore, was there any 'introduction' of "another definition of community" at this time, as if we might be able to locate the *solidifying* of a Kazakh "homogeneous community" (i.e. national unity and identity) to such an alleged 'introduction' of Islam at this late hour of Kazakh history. Such would only echo the view of Akiner, simply adding Islam into the mix with the Russian impact.

This has enormous consequences for anyone, including Olcott, who takes such a view. It means that whatever measure of 'increase in the Kazakhs thinking and acting as a homogeneous (cf. national) community' which is attributed to Islam, it must be applied further back, much further back, into Kazakh history. Indeed, Islam has certainly contributed to Kazakh ethnonational solidarity through its concept of the 'ummah'. And we would do well here to remember that this concept had strong tribal foundations in 'the Arab nation' from whence it arose (cf. the *nation* of ancient Israel as well, the Arabs' West Asian neighbor and even 'brother'). This idea of 'community' fit very well within 'the Kazakh nation' to which it came and even the earlier 'Turkic nations'. Olcott herself even takes the view that: "Although they were Muslims, these [Kazakh] writers venerated the values and teachings of Islam primarily because they preserved and strengthened most Kazakh cultural values" (p 108). If that be the case though, then how is it that Islam "introduced another definition of community" which did not "preserve and strengthen . . . Kazakh cultural values" of community, but rather *changed and replaced* them through the 'introduction' of essentially new and 'other' ones?

'Come, let us reason together'. Whatever changes regarding "definition of community" which Islam *did* bring to Kazakh nationhood—and we certainly admit to changes, even still today, in the *ongoing and interconnected* flow of their religious-national history—they occurred for the most part much further back in Kazakh history than Olcott is allowing for. Likewise, although *distinctions of emphasis and expression* existed, the "definition of community" which the Tatar Muslims brought to the already predominantly Muslim Kazakhs later in their history were not "new." Those ideas had surrounded the Kazakhs from virtually all sides of Central Asia, including on their own Steppeland, for nearly a millennium. While the tides of interaction surely rise and fall across the ocean of time, the idea that throughout this long millennium "[t]he self-sufficient nomads did not have much contact with the Muslim centers of the Tatars to the northwest or the Chagatai to the south" is sorely over-emphasized. Likewise, the idea that the common Kazakh masses were only minimally influenced by the ideas of community among their own leaders throughout nearly four centuries of national history, this too is severely stretching the imagination.[74]

The fact that more (tiny) mosques, mostly Tatar built and run, appeared on the Kazakh Steppe in the 19th century does not mean that a radically new and "[. . .] other definition of community" (suddenly) created a radically new and other Kazakh community or nation. The mosque was, again, among the known definitions and forms of community which had existed on the Kazakh Steppe from long centuries back. We might even do well to remember that such things as 'nomadic mosques', i.e. portable tent-type mosques, were employed, just as 'nomadic sanctuaries' had been employed among Turkic nomadic Christians along the Silk Road. Of course, much of the argument made by those following Olcott's line of reasoning has to do with the transition from nomadic community to settled community (as well as illiteracy to literacy respectively). But this 'de-nomadization' process was never *sufficiently* accomplished, at least as far as Stalin was concerned, until Stalin conducted his 'collectivization' campaigns and forced the still highly nomadic Kazakhs to settle in 'collective farms' (i.e. 'kolhoz' and 'solhoz'), a process which saw the starvation and death of millions of cattle as well as Kazakhs in the 1930s.

As far as the Jadid ideas of community which developed among the Tatars later and their subsequent impact on the Kazakhs, we might actually agree *to some extent* with Olcott that the Tatars did *help* bring *modified and progressive* ideas of 'community' (cf. 'nationhood') to the Kazakhs which the Kazakhs *incorporated* into their *ongoing* development as a nation. But Olcott is suggesting more than this, she is essentially saying, to borrow Khalid's phrasing, that such 'definitions of community' were "something new . . . all of them were modern" (1999:84; see ch 4). We do not need to rehearse our entire response to this view all over here again. While there was definite Tatar as well as Russian influence and even assistance, it was ultimately the *Kazakh* branch of the Turkic Muslim Jadid movement which was the force pursuing autonomous (cf. also independent) Kazakh nationhood. And these uniquely Kazakh pursuits must, again, be seen as standing *primarily within and as part of* the stream of Kazakh nationhood and its own unique ethnonational aspirations going back deep into its own history, not as foreign importations of the Russians and/or their Tatar agents. This is precisely why the Kazakhs never 'changed' or 'converted' to another "definition of community" so as to be absorbed into the 'pan-Turkic nation', but instead *retained their historically-grounded idea of a distinct Kazakh nation.* They continue making the same choice today amidst the revival of pan-Turkism in the post-Soviet era.

With that in view, note here carefully that Stalin's 'de-nomadization' effort in the collectivization 'round-up' was closely tied with his purging of the Kazakh 'intelligentsia' (i.e. Alash party members and others) who had *continued* fighting for rights of independent Kazakh nationhood right down to the 1930s when they were condemned as 'nationalists' and conveniently executed. The Soviet 'creation' of the *Kazakh* SSR in 1936 was directly related to, indeed forced by, that ongoing fight for *self*-definition of Kazakh community and nationhood, a fight flowing from out of the same broad and deep historical wellsprings of

---

Kazakh nationalism as Kenesari's struggle and its connection with the former 'Kazakh State'. The Alash Party members, as Kenesari before them, originally carried on their part of this long struggle with the Tsarist Russian Empire only to *continue* negotiating its independence with and then under the Soviets.[75] The fruits of an autonomous Kazakh SSR in 1936 were primarily their achievement in broader cooperation (amidst 'infighting') with 'the Kazakh nation'. Yet these fruits never fully ripened on the vine because the Soviets refused to water the deep, historic roots of Kazakh nationalism. Nevertheless, fifty short years later, in December 1986, the same Kazakh nation took to the streets protesting the appointment of a Russian leader over their Kazakh Republic in what was a *resurgence* of those deep historical roots of Kazakh nationalism and its quest for independent statehood. In direct consequence, their long historic quest finally came *back* to full fruition in 1991 with the establishment of the modern independent nation known today as 'the Land of the Kazakhs', i.e. Kazakhstan.

We are dealing here with very important issues of historical interpretation and the concepts undergirding them of 'religious-cultural influence'. As we have demonstrated in our article "Concerning the Spiritual-Cultural (Sources and) Foundations of Religious Processes,"[76] such concepts and understandings underlie all debates over 'syncretism', 'synthesis', 'contextualization' and/or 'conversion'—that is, continuity versus discontinuity—in religious-cultural history. And the interpretation of *national* history is intimately connected with the religious-cultural history of the nation (cf. 'the way of the fathers'). This is something Olcott herself is aware of and is employing in her overall interpretation of Kazakh ethno-cultural-religious-national history.

We must raise earnest questions then regarding Olcott's classifying of 'the Kazakh elites' as 'secular' and then distinguishing them so sharply from the Kazakh Muslim 'Zar zaman' (i.e. 'Time of Trouble') scholars in her treatment of "Islam and the Kazakh Intelligentsia" (pp 107-9). For example, Olcott places her religious value judgment upon Ibirai Altinsarin (1841-1889), the great Kazakh educational reformer, saying he was "[n]ot a devout Muslim himself" (p 106). Yet he is the same Altinsarin who wrote a booklet promoting Islam (in its Jadid Muslim 'progressive', not 'secular', form) among the Kazakh people, a work for which he tried to enlist the help of the head of Russian Orthodox missions to Altai based at the Kazan Theological Academy, N. Il'minskii, to publish. If Altinsarin "was not a devout Muslim," he certainly would not have abandoned his Muslim faith and, indeed, did not abandon it in the face of ongoing invitation by Il'minskii (and his colleagues), with whom Altinsarin maintained a friendship for a number of years.[77]

———

Still more amazing though, Olcott even classifies Abai as part of the "first" group of "*secular* elites" who were educated in the new Russian educational system. Anyone who has read through Abai's 'Words' as well as his songs and poems, however, would certainly know that he identified himself clearly as a Muslim, not only "devoutly" holding onto his own Islamic faith, but promoting it among the Kazakh people as part of their traditional, *national* heritage.[78] Indeed, Abai's most celebrated disciple is Shakirim Kudaiberdi-uhli (1851-1931), whom Olcott classifies as one of the 'Muslim writers' in juxtaposition to Abai and the 'secular elites'. At the same time (as noted earlier), Olcott herself tells us that Abai "helped shape the attitude of the Kazakh intellectuals who came to maturity just before the revolution," i.e. 'the sons of Alash' behind the Alash Orda movement.

All of this means that we cannot radically separate off into two distinct groups the 'Kazakh secular elite', on the one hand, and the 'Muslim Kazakh scholars', on the other, and then only bring them together as Olcott does at some point later when allegedly "they began to work more closely," attributing this solely to "[t]he political events of 1905-1910" which "encouraged such closeness" (p 109). Certainly those events did "encourage such closeness." But it was not a 'new' closeness, rather a new *form* of closeness. The "Kazakh activists of all persuasions [who] were brought together" were brought together not only "in new political forums" in that later political context, they were brought together by their *shared* Kazakh heart for Kazakh nationhood in all its complex, yet integrated aspects. While there were surely disagreements among them as to how exactly to achieve their aims and aspirations, all of them were Kazakh, all of them were essentially Muslim and all of them shared an ongoing interest in addressing the "the political events" (not to mention the cultural, religious, social and economic events) affecting Kazakh ethno-cultural-religious-economic-political nationhood. This was both before 1905-1910 and after.[79]

While some were educated in Russian secular schools and others in distinctly Muslim ones, this does not mean the one group is "not devout" and the other is. Neither are there any solid grounds for concluding that their views on the relation of Islam to Kazakh culture "clearly showed that they were late and incomplete converts" (p 117). In the first place, their views varied on this issue and, in the second place, even if they did elevate Kazakh culture above Islam, as some of them surely did, that simple fact does not say anything about *when* they became Muslims. It does not even provide sufficient grounds for judging their 'devoutness'. Kazakhs with the same basic orientation can be found today;

some of them are surely 'devout' and almost none of them are "late and incomplete converts."

All of the Kazakh nationalists which Olcott treats, therefore, are to be properly associated (in varying ways and measures) with the Kazakh branch of the Turkic Muslim Jadidist movement (cf. Nurtazina 2002). And while this movement did, again, certainly 'borrow' *ideas relating to aspects* of modern nationhood from the Russians and other Europeans, their ultimate ideas of nationhood were not entirely 'other than' or 'new and distinct' from the Turkic nations they were already 'self-aware' of and a part of. The autonomous (or independent) nations they envisioned and struggled to achieve were *continuations* of an already established and existing nationhood *adapted* to new and changing environments. Likewise, the mere fact that some of them pursued Russian-based education in Russian schools does not warrant the conclusion that they were 'Russian created elites'. Such a view portrays them as passive agents upon whom the Russians simply imposed their will in matters of education and national ideology. Here again the intentionality of the Turkic-Kazakh Jadid scholars in actively pursuing Russian education *for their own aims and interests* cannot be overlooked.

In wrapping things up here, let us return to Olcott's original idea that Islam "provided a literate clergy who could maintain a communication network throughout the steppe." As a legitimate and important part of the ongoing debate between 'perennialists and Western modernists' (see ch. 1), it can only be pointed out that Olcott's view here reveals Western modernist underpinnings which typically associate the rise of *distinctly* modern nations with the rise of printed literature and literacy. Indeed, her whole presentation almost echoes Akiner's depiction of the Kazakhs being at some vulnerable "stage in the transition from a traditional existence (i.e. nomadic pastoralism and an orally transmitted culture) to sedentarization and literacy" in their alleged transformation "from tribe to nation-state" (i.e. their transformation from a '(primitive) ethnocultural nation' to a 'modern political nation'), during which time they were "especially vulnerable to [Russian secular education] and Soviet ethnic engineering." Of course, as noted above, Olcott actually wrote before Akiner, so we should perhaps reverse the attribution of 'echo' between the two. Regardless of order though, we should not miss the connection here between Catherine II's Islamicization strategy and the concept of the Kazakhs as an illiterate nomadic and essentially 'uncivilized', disunified tribal people. Likewise, the connection of literature and literacy with (secular) educated elites, i.e. 'intelligentsia' or 'literati', should not be missed either. The main elements of a classic Western modernist interpretation, with its distinction between 'pre-modern ethnic nations' and 'modern political nations', are all here.

In the end, the concept of 'the Kazakh nation' and its essential oneness as an ethno-cultural-political people—in spite of divisions within and among them, as with any people, throughout their history—could be, for the most part, embraced and communicated through the very strong Kazakh oral tradition combined with the speed and distance attainable through the most expert horsemanship known on the planet, namely that of the Eurasian nomads—with or without Russian education or Islam and their respective literatures to help it along. But Russian education and Islam certainly did help it along; they did not however 'create' it nor bring to it "another definition of community." Islam's definitions, as already noted, go well back into Kazakh history and were spread in both its pre-Jadid and Jadid forms through both its literature and the Kazakh oral tradition *as a natural part of the historical development of the Kazakh nation.* Indeed, the Kazakh oral tradition was sufficiently strong to both effectively spread and sustain Islamic faith among the Kazakhs centuries before Catherine had ever come along. It was certainly capable of doing the same with the Kazakh (ethno)national idea. Surely the *increased* production of literature *helped* serve national aims and ambitions, just as cell phones and computers do today. But we must call to mind in closing out this section Anthony Smith's remarks when he says: "modern nations simply extend, deepen, and streamline the ways in which members of *ethnie* associated and communicated. They do not introduce startlingly novel elements, or change the goals of human association and communication" (1986:215; see full quote in ch. 1).

The New, Modern Nation-State of Kazakhstan: Unfulfilled Promise?

Certainly Olcott provides a good deal of fair and even sympathetic treatment of the Kazakhs and their history in her now classic work on *The Kazakhs*. Olcott has done a great deal for the Kazakh people, their history and nationhood. Indeed, all of us owe much to her and a very clear, unwavering debt of gratitude is herein expressed. But whatever else may be said pro or con regarding her position on the issues historically, she remains in the end among those who share the basic Western modernist conviction that 'ethnic nation' and 'geo-political nation' should be kept distinct. This is seen most clearly in her 2002 work with its highly accusational title: *Kazakhstan: Unfulfilled Promise.* The promise she conceives is one allegedly made by Kazakhstan to become a multiethnic pluralistic nation-state, which Olcott and others of course interpret and then judge according to their own strictly Western modernist paradigm with its standard set of 'ethnic minority rights'. In chapter three on "The Challenge of Creating Kazakhstanis," she reflects this view when, as one of the "outside observers" and "advisers" to which she is referring, she says:

> Outside observers sense that for Kazakhstan to survive and prosper, its population must develop a civic-based patriotism to a common homeland rather than an ethnic-based loyalty to the land of the Kazakhs . . . This seems more difficult for the country's Kazakh-dominated leadership to understand than for its outside advisers (p. 51ff).

First, carefully note the standard Western modernist 'choice' which Olcott is offering Kazakhstan: Either "civic-based patriotism to a common homeland" and, with it, 'survival and prosperity', or "ethnic-based loyalty to the land of the Kazakhs" and, with it, poverty, social destitution and ultimately non-survival (i.e. death) as a nation. The classic Western modernist conviction is this: Ethnonationalism (i.e. ethnonational aspirations) spells death for (Western) civic-based democratic nationhood. There is little room for compromise. It is a conviction shared with the Marxist-Leninist-Stalinist paradigm of 'The Union' (cf. 'e pluribus unum' in both views).

Certainly economic and social conditions in Kazakhstan today are not what "outside observers" nor the government nor even the people of Kazakhstan themselves would like to see. If "outside observers" are not content with the social and economic situation in the nation, neither is the government or the people of the nation itself. In this, they differ little from every other nation on earth, though obviously the degree will vary between countries. Both the economic and social situation in Kazakhstan still need a good deal of improvement before they bring themselves 'up to par' (whatever exactly 'par' may be). Economically, problems with employment, working conditions, debt, poverty not to mention corruption and other matters surely exist. Socially, alcoholism and drug addition, prostitution, AIDS, issues of class, education, 'village versus city' mentalities, along of course with certain ethnic tensions and other matters are no doubt there. Scholars and common people alike recognize and discuss these issues fairly openly in appropriate times and ways. Likewise, the government has plans of action which address most all of these issues and, while certainly not to perfection, they together with the people are pressing ahead to bring those plans and aspirations to fulfillment, continually evaluating their own progress and attempting to make necessary adjustments along the way. In that process, they earnestly and openly consider input from "outside observers." The "outside observers" and even some inside ones may not entirely agree with their plans of action or be content with their efforts and we have no intention here of trying to defend and justify them in every way. *But there are no grounds for trying to pin the blame for these things on "ethnic-based loyalty to the land—or the language, culture, history, etc, for that matter—of the Kazakhs."*

We observe in this quote, then, that Olcott is placing special emphasis upon the key Western modernist term "civic-based patriotism to a common homeland." She intentionally juxtaposes this against the idea of "ethnic-based loyalty to the land of the Kazakhs," i.e. 'ethnic-based nationalism' or 'ethnonationalism'. This is the classic Western modernist dichotomy between '(civic-based) political nation' and 'ethnic nation' with its corresponding dichotomy between allegedly positive 'patriotism' and negative '(ethno)nationalism'. The latter term functions as an official term of accusation not only in Western modernist parlance, but can likewise still be heard echoing down the corridors of Kazakh history from the leftover voices of Marxist-Leninist-Stalinist propaganda. It was a condemnation of the worst possible kind which resulted in one's being classified as 'an enemy of the people'. Indeed, it was this very accusation which served as *the* grounds for Stalin to execute the 'Kazakh nationalist intelligentsia' who continued pressing for a politically independent state *for the Kazakhs* in the 1920-30s.

Perhaps the solution to the puzzle lies in her (Russian-based) view that "[t]o Kazakhs the land had no intrinsic value" (p 18). To the contrary though, as Privratsky points out, "valuation of 'land' is the one item in our list . . . that informants consistently endorsed as necessary for a Kazak to be a Kazak" (1998:119). As noted above in passing, this of course has much to do with the Kazakh ancestors, including Kazakh-Turkic Muslim saints, who are buried all throughout the Kazakh land. Such tombs go back many long centuries and give the land tremendous "intrinsic value" as *their* 'ancestral home*land*'. (Privratsky, of course, established his understanding of the Kazakhs based in their own national language and by living among them for a good number of years, something definitely lacking in all of Olcott's treatments.)

In our paper on "Issues of Kazakh Ethnonational Identity and Islamic-Religious Identity," we add to this fact a note of further and even deeper historical importance pertaining to Eurasian nomadic culture in even pre-Islamic days. Namely:

Herodotus (4:127) shows that this idea of 'sacred ancestral land' is an ancient, integral and very deep-rooted part of nomadic steppe heritage. Thus, the Scythian-Saka khan, Idanthyrsus, as far back as the 5th century BC, challenges the great Persian King Darius when the latter invades their 'sacred homeland' and chases him around wanting to subjugate Scythia as part of the Persian Empire. Idanthyrsus retorts to Darius: "If you feel you have to get to fighting soon, there are our ancestral burial grounds. Go on, find them and try to ruin them, and then you'll see whether or not we will fight."[80]

Likewise, in our "Inquiry into the Socio-Religious and Historical Relation of Ancestor, National Hero and Saint Devotion," we have pointed out the intimate relation, both socio-religiously and historically, between these various forms of 'devotion'. With special attention to 'national heroes', we note the following:

'The founding fathers' of America . . . are called forth to play their typical role of *national forefather and hero* in the moving, climactic speech of John Quincy Adams when he defends the right of freedom, based in human dignity, for a group of black African people after they were dragged in chains from their native African homeland via slave trade. A mistake in navigation by a slave ship had left them shipwrecked on American shores. The name of the ship, *Amstad*, is used as the title of the movie in which the whole scene of Quincy Adam's defense speech is dramatized.

Thus, Washington and Quincy Adams himself, along with Jefferson and some of the other great 'founding *fathers*' of America, are held forth as *admirable* (i.e. *venerable*) 'saints' of the American civil *religious* ideal . . . Indeed, Adams is shown walking past the busts of Washington, Jefferson and the others, calling upon the court to remember the 'founding *fathers*' (or 'ancestors') of America while the camera occasionally pans back on the chief representative of the black African group, who sits there understanding nothing of Adams' moving speech being offered in flowing English. Yet, unbeknownst to him until Adam reveals it at the end of the trial, he himself and his ethno-tribal-religious

126

ancestor devotion is the sourcebed and foundation of Adams' entire defense. Touche!, the head African even tells Adams by way of a translator, right after the verdict of freedom is rendered and the trial ended, that he had confidence in the outcome because he and the other black African prisoners had prayed to their ancestors for deliverance (Weller 2002:4).

The Western modernist dichotomy between "civic-based patriotism" and "ethnic-based nationalism" is erroneous. 'Patriotism' and '(ethno)nationalism' are, in fact, two sides of the same coin. The 'patrios' of 'patriotism' literally means "of one's fathers" with 'patris' being "fatherland." 'Fatherland' is none other than 'the land of the fathers' or 'land of the ancestors' or, likewise, 'ancestral homeland', all of which in the Kazakh case mean the Kazakh (and Turkic) fathers (or 'ancestors') so that 'patriotism' for the Kazakhs is indeed "ethnic-based loyalty to the land of the Kazakhs". "Civic-based patriotism" and "ethnic-based loyalty to the land of the Kazakhs" are intimately wrapped together in both our own Western terminology as well as in the Kazakh (and broader Central Asian) mind.

Western democratic convictions regarding "civic-based patriotism to a common homeland" share much in common with "ethnic-based loyalty to the land" of whoever's ancestors it may be. The main difference is that one is based in ideological kinship and descent while the other is based in organic kinship and descent. And, to recall Olcott's own recognition, "another definition of community," like that in Islam, is based in religious-spiritual kinship. This other "definition of community," by Olcott's own admission, is intimately associated with ideas of political 'nationhood'. Of course, the two go hand-in-hand rather well, for religious-spiritual kinship, like political kinship, is an ideological kinship. Western political "civic-based patriotism" is not only closely tied to "ethnic-based loyalty," it is intimately connected with 'religious-based loyalty' to the *Faith of Our Fathers*. The latter phrase is of course the title of a well-known English Christian hymn. Thus, in Western "civic-based patriotism," we find songs of similar tone such as *My Country 'Tis of Thee*, which sings of the "land where my fathers died." This theme forms a hallmark of Western democratic 'civil religion' and its "civic-based patriotism." As Robert Nisbet makes plain in his brilliant and lucid article on "Civil Religion":

> The mention of *la belle France* or of Mother Russia could send essentially religious reverberations through whole populations. . . .

In poetry, song, pageant, and sermon the divinity of the nation was celebrated, as was the glory of going to one's death for it. . . . In Europe, from France eastward to Holy Mother Russia, the continent was ablaze with newly affirmed or discovered nationalism and with the appointed destiny immanent in its historical development. In countless ways the national state appeared as the new church, recipient of functions and responsibilities historically reserved for family and religion (in Eliade, ed., *Encycl. of Religion*, 1987:V3:524-6).

It should be noted carefully here that Nisbet is *correctly* using the term "nationalism" as a synonym of "patriotism," the only difference again being that it is a "civic-based" nationalism instead of a "religious-based" nationalism with both of these being easily interchangeable with "ethnic-based" nationalism. Indeed, all three criss-cross one another's boundaries so that, adding the latter to Max Stackhouse's observation on "Politics and Religion," we must confess with him that "a broader and deeper understanding of history and civilizations reveals that politics and religion [and ethnicity] are inevitably related . . ." (in Eliade, ed., *Encycl. of Rel.*, 1987:V7:408). Perhaps then Olcott should just give up the idea of "civic-based patriotism" altogether, as many others are surely doing in the face of this inescapable conundrum. Meanwhile the Kazakhs, along with a host of other ethnonational peoples around the globe, are not ready to give up their "ethnic-based loyalty" to their historic homeland.

As demonstrated in the previous chapter of this book, however, Olcott is far from alone in her convictions. It seems we could add to the list here William Fierman, who in his article on "Language and the Defining of Identity in Kazakstan: The Mixed Blessings of Independence," concludes by saying:

Unlike the decades preceding Nazarbayev's accession to the leadership of Kazakstan, today Kazak nationalists are permitted to articulate the view that Kazakstan is above all the homeland of the Kazaks, and to press for the transformation of linguistic and other aspects of society based on this view. . . . Over the longer term, . . . Kazakstan's leadership will be obliged either to develop more creative solutions to very complex problems or to attempt to impose a particular image of Kazakstani identity with greater force. The former type of solution, though problematic, seems to offer the better chance of success" (p 7).

Fierman actually champions the Kazakh language cause, at least from a Western multiethnic pluralistic perspective. He has demonstrated his commitment to the Kazakh language cause by personally learning it. He is interviewed on Kazakhstan national television at times in Kazakh for his views on socio-political issues, including linguistic ones, relevant to the nation. In this he exceeds many. He is a highly respected and well-known scholar. Nonetheless, "the view that Kazakstan is above all the homeland of the Kazaks" and, with it, the Kazakh nationalist led effort of "press[ing] for the transformation of linguistic and other aspects of society based on this view" is clearly connected with "attempt[ing] to impose a particular image of Kazakstani identity with greater force" in Fierman's framing of the issue here. Much like Olcott, then, he subtly casts Kazakh nationalism in a negative 'light' and offers his suggestion that this is not the wise or "more creative" road to success.

As for Olcott though, like Fierman, she is definitely a respected scholar and well-mannered statesperson, but the entire chapter under discussion here (as well as her entire book) is dedicated to politely accusing the Kazakhs for failing to fulfill their alleged promise to make Kazakhstan a multiethnic pluralistic democracy *as conceived by Western, particularly American, democracy advocates*. Even her 1995 version of *The Kazakhs* reveals a vested Western political interest, namely the desire to see that "the prospects of democracy in Kazakhstan are promising" with its suggestions of a Western egalitarian view of "the Kazakhs and Russians in their common state" (1995:xi-xii). And so, eight years later (i.e. 2002), Olcott implies an accusation of 'unfulfilled promise' in her subtle, yet intentional reference to "the country's Kazakh-dominated leadership." We should recall here that these are the "descendents" of "the early Kazakh secular nationalists" of the Alash Orda movement who "had as their primary goal the preservation of a distinct Kazakh people with a consciously political purpose: they claimed that the Kazakhs were entitled to political as well as cultural concessions. They understood their 'Kazakhness' as a form of national identity . . ." (p 118). By all appearances, it would seem that Olcott is not content with the vision and efforts of either the "earl[ier] Kazakh secular nationalists" or their "descendents."

Olcott's view of the relative ease with which ethnonational identity and aspirations can be set aside and exchanged with 'civic-based democratic' ones, even her belief that it is possible, is typical of Western modernist approaches to nationhood. In her 'elitist' view of Kazakh nationalism, she seems to think that the Kazakh(stan) government could apparently convince the common Kazakh on the street to abandon his or her "ethnic-based loyalty" in favor of "civic-based patriotism." This view is somewhat bewildering after such clear recognition of the close association of Kazakh ethnic and political nationhood with all its historical depth in the era of the Kazakh khanate. Even more, it is "unthinkable" that she would even suggest such an abandonment of "ethnic-based loyalty" knowing all the painful attempts that have been made in their history to force the Kazakhs to do exactly that.

Let us ask a closely related question here: What do we think about the right of the Kazakh language to function as the 'national (or state) language' of Kazakhstan? Is it good and right for the 'modern political nation' of Kazakhstan to make the language of the 'ethnic nation' of the Kazakhs its 'national language'? Of course, if we answer 'yes', we are in essence saying that we believe it is good and right for them to expect, even require, all citizens to be able to function in the 'national language' (to a reasonable degree), otherwise its status as 'national language' has no value or meaning. If we answer 'no', then we are essentially insisting upon a continuation of the (Tsarist as well as Soviet) Russian imperial policy (or at least practice). Some have suggested a bi-lingual approach which aims at 'equality'. *But even that will never happen without special place and promotion being offered to the Kazakh language in this critical hour of its destiny.*

One thing to be highlighted regarding the language issue though is that, as with the 'terminological chaos' encountered in the more general subject of '(ethno)nationalism' (which the language issue is an integral part of), there has not been a great deal of care taken to distinguish clearly between 'heart language', 'mother tongue' and 'national language'. These terms, especially in Western usage, are often confused and conflated as interchangeable synonyms. For instance, the 'heart language', 'mother tongue' and 'national language' of many Kazakhs is Kazakh. However, for many other Kazakhs the 'heart language' is clearly Russian. This, along with the fact that most all non-Kazakhs in Kazakhstan speak Russian, leads to disputes about what 'mother tongue' is and what the 'national language' should be.

Most people seem to understand 'heart language' as the 'first language' of the speaker, i.e. the one with which he or she best and most deeply expresses the 'heart'. (And we should not miss the individualistic emphasis in this definition/perspective). On the other side of the scales, there seems to be a large measure of agreement regarding the idea that 'mother tongue' refers to the ethnonational language of an ethnic people group and that it is strongly related to and even an important part of that group's historic, ethnocultural (cf. ethnolinguistic) identity. (And here we should not miss the group-orientation of the definition/perspective). But, of course, even here disputes begin to arise. Is 'mother tongue' really an ethnonational group thing? Is it not rather 'the tongue one learns from his mother' (cf. the individualistic emphasis)? Is it really an important or even necessary ingredient in ethnonational identity? Here, then, we have a dispute about how language relates to one ethnonational group as a group as well as to the various individuals within that group. And notice not only the individualistic versus group-oriented emphases involved, but the emphases between a strictly pragmatic, 'functionalist-instrumentalist' perspective (common in Western modernist ideology) versus what we might call a combined 'functional-cultural identity view' of language (more common in organicist-perennialist views of 'nations').

Still more confusion and disagreement arises, however, over 'national language'. In the first place, are 'mother tongue' and 'national language' the same thing? Or are they something different? Of course, this question and the related dispute is connected to the dispute over whether 'ethnic group' (i.e. 'ethnos') is, can or should be a synonymous thing with 'nation'? That is, how related/similar or unrelated/dis-similar are or should 'ethnos' and 'nation' be? (See ch. 8)

If viewed according to the Western Modernist paradigm, then 'mother tongue' and 'national language' are quite distinct: the first is ethnocultural-linguistic and the second geo-political. Likewise, then, according to this same view, no ethnocultural-linguistic group should have the right to proclaim its own 'mother tongue' as the 'national language' of a geo-political nation-state, yet alone expect other ethnonational groups within the geo-political nation-state to learn and speak it. And no doubt the Russian-speaking non-Kazakh masses, as well as some of the non-Kazakh-speaking Kazakhs, who are left in a tight pinch in post-Soviet Kazakhstan, are more than happy to take up a Western modernist position on this particular issue and join the cry for 'fair and proper ideals of nationhood' based in and upon 'inter*national* human and minority rights' and especially, in this case, 'ethnic minority rights' (cf. Malik 1994:5-6).

This cry of course comes in the face of nations who, like Kazakhstan, are still trying to establish their nationhood on the no-no of Western modernist pluralist democratic socio-political ideology, that is, they are trying to establish their political nation-state, not as an 'ethnocratic state', but upon their 'ethnic nationhood'. In such a 'nation', of course, 'mother tongue' and 'national language' are synonymous. Indeed, in the Central Asian 'nations' the language of the core, historic ethno*national* group in its own historic homeland has the right to be, should be and is in fact the *national* language of the geo-political state. So in Kazakhstan, for example, everyone, Kazakh and non-Kazakh alike, who is a 'citizen' of Kazakhstan should learn and use it, *making a genuine effort* to the best of their respective ability. Here we would agree with Svat Soucek (2000:310) who notes that ". . . a demand that has been branded as 'unfair' by many Russians is that as citizens of a Central Asian republic, they acquire a decent command of its principle language; one can sympathize with people confronted by such a challenge, but not necessarily agree that the demand is unfair." Learning the 'national language' is for the sake of the unity and stability of the 'nation', not to mention for the sake of restoring what has been severely mangled and left in near ruins through past imperialism. This would be especially appropriate for the descendents of those who perpetrated and/or somehow aided the imperialism even if they are not 'personally' or 'individually' responsible. The Kazakh people still, by and large, stand amazed at the fact that most Russians make no (real) effort to learn even the most basic (i.e. 'survival' level) communication skills in Kazakh. We stand amazed with them and say there is something seriously wrong in this scenario. Regardless, (re)learning the Kazakh language would be doubly appropriate for the non-Kazakh-speaking Kazakhs, many of whom have yet to take up the task, lest they leave their own ethnonational people group divided, "a foreigner to the speakers" of their own 'mother tongue' and 'national language' in their own historic homeland.

And which side do Westerners come down on? Given that the Western modernist paradigm predominates most all Western thinking about 'nations and (ethno)nationalism' in the modern global age along with the fact that serious lack of clarity exists over definitions and usage of the terms 'heart language', 'mother tongue' and 'national language' and their proper relationship and priority, Western views and approaches seem ill-equipped to contribute sympathetically and meaningfully to the 'conundrum'. Meanwhile, our attitudes, paradigms, ideals, decisions and actions will impact the delicate situation; they are critical.

We ourselves believe Kazakh has every historic and ethnonational right to be the official 'national language' of *Kazakh*stan and, therefore, address the matter from that vantage point. But again, either way we 'slice the pie', Kazakh needs to be given priority and special treatment in the modern political nation-state of Kazakhstan. And do we really think that this can become a reality *without an "ethnic-based loyalty" to the language of the Kazakhs*? Do we really expect that the Kazakh 'ethnic nation' can detach itself in platonic fashion from its own '(ethnic) national language' and approach the whole issue on the basis of a strict "civic-based patriotism" to a common, shared language for all ethnic groups of Kazakhstan? Do we really understand what we are asking for here? Can we really expect the Kazakh 'ethnic nation' to entirely empty its own ethnonational mother tongue of all "ethnic-based loyalty" so as to view it as devoid of all *ethnonationally personal* ties and cut it loose from their ethnonational heritage to function as an entirely ethnically detached, generic 'lingua franca' for the 'civic-based patriotic land and people' of Kazakhstan?

The Kazakh language will *never* become the 'national (yet alone an equal) language' of the modern political state of Kazakhstan *without Kazakh (ethno)nationalism championing its cause and rejoicing in "ethnic-based loyalty" to see its day*. It will *never* happen and, if we think it can, we are both ethically wrong and seriously misguided in our view and understanding of the historical and socio-psychological depth of ethnonational aspirations and their close tie with political aspirations of statehood. The same could be said regarding "ethnic-based loyalty" to the *land* as well as *culture, history* and other dimensions of Kazakh ethnonational identity and being. It is all a very real part of *human identity and being* which we cannot simply 'detach' or 'de-program' from people and cast away like surplus cargo. Western approaches to and understandings of nationhood are in desperate need of coming to grips with this ethno-historic, ethno-socio-cultural, ethno-socio-linguistic, ethno-socio-psychological and ethno-socio-political fact, particularly in Kazakhstan and Central Asia.

Here let us note that it is not just "the country's Kazakh-dominated leadership" who have difficulty understanding the suggestion of these "outside observers." Such a view is again steeped in Western modernist ideas of 'elites' and their overemphasized significance in 'creating' ethnonational sentiment among 'the masses'. Based on our own discussions *in the Kazakh people's own national language* with even 'ordinary, everyday Kazakhs' regarding this precise point of debate, the suggestion of abandoning "ethnic-based loyalty to the land" as well as language, culture, history and other *integrated* aspects of Kazakh ethnonational identity seems more difficult for most of the entire Kazakh population to understand, not to mention the Uighur, Uzbek and other Central Asian national peoples living *both within and outside of Kazakhstan*. We have spoken with representatives of the 'common people' from all these other national groups and they certainly do not interpret 'multiethnic' in the same way that Olcott and the late 20th century Western modernist ideal is calling for.

One thing which must be noted again here, with all respect, is that Olcott does not *function* in the Kazakh language and is thus basing her primary research and views in the Russian and English Western domains. Neither has she lived any considerable part of her life in Kazakhstan. Those of us who do speak the language and have lived here for a considerable period of time, including most all Kazakh-speaking Kazakhs, can only agree with G. Yesim and his views expressed in an interview entitled "The Person who does not Know the Language does not Know the Mentality [of the People]."[81] Or, as one of the New Testament writers said long ago: "If then I do not grasp the meaning of what someone is saying, I am a foreigner to the speaker, and he is a foreigner to me" (1-Cor 14:11). And this is precisely the problem, one which many average, everyday Kazakh-speaking Kazakhs note. Namely, the Russians and other Euroslavic people living in Kazakhstan *do not know the Kazakh language and, thus, they remain 'foreigners' to one another.*

Indeed, apart from very rare exceptions, the Euroslavic population does not even bother to learn the simplest everyday greetings, terms for shopping, traveling, etc., i.e. 'survival Kazakh'. They cannot even buy a loaf of bread yet alone 'function' in the 'national language'. But what does it really matter? Do they not have the 'right', their 'civil liberty', to speak Russian if they so choose? Apart from diving back into historical and ethical debates, one very crucial difference is this: Until Euroslavic peoples understand the Kazakh language they will never understand the mentality and, with it, the heart of the Kazakh people and nation. They will never be able to connect personally from the heart with those living and breathing in the Kazakh language world. Meanwhile, *genuine and mutual understanding leading to genuine and mutual reconciliation is impossible without genuine and mutual understanding of one another's languages.*

The vast majority of Kazakhs know the Russian language and, with it, they understand the Russian mentality, culture, worldview, etc. They even continue, like Abai and the earlier Jadids, to promote Russian as a source of cultural enrichment for themselves not to mention as a source of communication with the Russian (and other) people, both those living in their historic homeland and those across the borders in the Russian 'fatherland'. When will the Russian and other Euroslavic peoples rise up and show the same genuine appreciation and desire to be culturally enriched as well as equipped to communicate with the Kazakh people *in the historic homeland of the Kazakhs*? When will they show their earnest respect for the Kazakh people and their worldview, grounded thoroughly in the Kazakh language, so that they can make genuine strides toward a much healthier multiethnic nation-state in today's Kazakhstan?

Strides are certainly being made among the younger generation through the elementary and secondary educational system and even in the universities. But something remains seriously mal-adjusted in the views as well as the actions being taken on these issues. It is clear not only to us but to most Kazakhs we speak with about this problem. Soucek (2000:310) is correct in saying: ". . . a demand that has been branded as 'unfair' by many Russians is that as citizens of a Central Asian republic, they acquire a decent command of its principle language; one can sympathize with people confronted by such a challenge, but not necessarily agree that the demand is unfair." All of this we say with genuine love and respect for the great Russian and other Euroslavic peoples and their languages, cultures, histories and identities as well as their rights as legitimate, integral citizens of today's Kazakh State. But the impact of Russian views of *their* rights in Kazakhstan, along with still lingering views of Russian language and cultural superiority, combined still more with *the Western modernist interpretation of the alleged Russian creation of Central Asian ethnicity and their ethnic languages*—all this continues having a rather negative impact upon the ethnonational peoples of Central Asia and their very real ethnolinguistic, cultural and political world.

In spite of all this, it perhaps should not surprise us that Olcott, in the same chapter (three) of *Unfulfilled Promises*, defends the rights of the Russian language and its cause while accusing the Kazakhs of Kazakh nationalism in regard to not only the Kazakh language, but their national anthem, national symbols and the fact they are based upon Kazakh history and culture as opposed to a more multiethnic pluralistic history and culture. She is unhappy that:

> . . . the state ideology that is being fashioned has become more explicitly pro-Kazakh. Most of the symbols of statehood are drawn from the Kazakhs' history or culture. The flag is blue, the color associated with the Turkic Khaganate that dominated the steppe before the Mongols and Kazakhs. It has a sun, an eagle, and a traditional dwelling of the Kazakh nomad, and ·is surrounded by a stylized version of a shield. The state hymn as well is designed for a Kazakh audience, describing a homeland of the Kazakh steppe and speaking of the need to preserve the mother tongue, and it is difficult to find a Russian translation of it in the country's stores and kiosks (p 59).

A fair number of other scholars publishing in the West seem to share her sentiments, as for example Taras Kuzio in his article on "History, Memory and Nation Building in the Post-Soviet Colonial Space." His language almost echoes Olcott's when he says:

The new state is both defined as a multi-ethnic society and the Kazakh homeland, although this political community is defined using only Kazakh symbols and myths. The Kazakh language is being promoted at the expense of Russian and 1998 was defined as the "year of national unity and national history" as part of the state's nurturing of the Kazakh national idea.[82]

To whatever degree Kuzio shares Olcott's sentiments, for Olcott this is all part of what she sees as Kazakhstan's "unfulfilled promise." It is a contrary development in her view, part of what she expresses her regret over when she says:

[d]espite the absence of a strong democratic tradition in Kazakhstan, the country could have developed a pluralistic or quasi-pluralistic political system . . . if its leaders had only shown the will to discipline themselves. In its first years, the country's ruling elite at least flirted with the idea of a transition to democracy . . . But these promising beginnings were abandoned over time . . . (p 2).

To the contrary, however, the "promising beginnings" which she speaks of must include the framing of the national constitution, the national anthem and the state symbols. Indeed, if we are going to judge a nation based on any 'promises' it has or has not made regarding its own national identity and intended course of development, these promises must be located first and foremost in that nation's own self-determined and self-declared identity as revealed in its founding document, its constitution, as well as its national anthem and state symbols. Here we can simply turn to the second line of the preamble to the constitution to show that today's sovereign, independent nation of Kazakhstan is a nation which "establishes [its] statehood upon the ancient-indigenous land of the Kazakhs." In doing this, Kazakhstan ensures the rightful place of the Kazakh people and their language, culture and history in their own historic homeland while at the same time "understanding ourselves [i.e. itself] to be a peace-loving civil society dedicated to the aims of liberty, equality and concord," which is the line immediately following the previous one.[83] It reaffirms this foundation and essential orientation in its national anthem when it declares the "Merciful Great Fatherland, the Steppeland of the Kazakhs" to be the "sacred cradle of concord and friendship" which "honors" and "embraces in

[its] bosom the children of all" ethnonational groups living in its midst. This is the delicate balance which it seeks to maintain in honoring and safeguarding the rights of all ethnonational groups who share in its history and heritage, with rightful, preeminent place being given to the indigenous Kazakh people and their language, culture and history in their own "ancient-indigenous land." It offers a solid, justifiable and understandable foundation for Kazakh "ethnic-based loyalty to the land of the Kazakhs" in their post-colonial context.

However, it offers no solid, justifiable or understandable foundation for alleging that ". . . the state ideology that is being fashioned has become more explicitly pro-Kazakh," since the state ideology which Olcott is criticizing here is not something "being fashioned" in a manner in which the "promising beginnings" have been "abandoned over time." It is not at all as Olcott alleges, saying:

> In the face of deteriorating economic and social conditions, the government has resorted to an age-old tactic for trying to gain support: if you cannot satisfy the material demands of a population, then try convincing them that their ideological or spiritual needs are being met instead. Kazakhstan's government officials recognize that they are no longer performing many of the tasks that the governed expect from their governors, and the elite hopes to fill this gap by arousing public support for a newly defined civic nationalism (p 59).

Here we come back to the juxtaposition of economic prosperity against (ethno)nationalism. This again is not only a Western modernist angle on things, it is one which shares the former Marxist-Communist view. Indeed, as S.R. Bowers points out in "Approaches to the Study of Soviet Ethnic Conflict," part of the Soviet thinking was that problems involving (ethno)nationalism "are largely a product of difficult economic conditions and that a stronger economy would help in the suppression of ethnic strife" and tensions. This thinking was directly connected with the "demand [for] greater efforts to form a Soviet 'community' in which people identify with an entity larger than their particular ethnic group,"[84] precisely what Olcott is seeking from the Kazakhs. Here a voice of wisdom in Walker Connor should be carefully considered. He tells us:

> A number of authorities have noted a propensity on the part of American statesmen and scholars of the post-World War II era

to assume that economic considerations represent the determining force in human affairs .... Such a prognosis again underestimates the power of ethnic feelings and ignores contrary evidence ... economic factors are likely to come in a poor second when competing with the emotionalism of ethnic nationalism (1994:46-7).

While we ourselves would not depict ethnonational *needs* and aspirations as an issue of mere 'emotionalism', one thing is certain: the placing of economic-material needs above cultural and/or "spiritual" ones is a grave fallacy of our modern (and even pre-modern) world. No one denies the importance of stable employment or the validity of requesting 'grant us this day our daily bread'. But that this should take priority over the cultural-spiritual needs of people is an overly simplistic and false dichotomy. Indeed, for those who have not recognized the quote just made, it is from "The Lord's Prayer" in the New Testament (Matt. 6:9-13), with the simple point being that economic-material needs and cultural-spiritual needs go hand in hand; they cannot be neatly cut off from or juxtaposed against one another. And it is ultimately not the government of Kazakhstan or any other government which can "satisfy" those needs; rather God is the source of both. We are not simply talking here about 'religion' and/or attending religious services, etc. Rather, just as Olcott has framed the matter, we are talking about cultural identity as a part of our spiritual needs with God as the ultimate source for satisfying those needs.

If expressing this in an academic discussion seems out of place to anyone, it only reveals how wide the unfortunate chasm between religion and scholarship has become in the Western modernist secularist worldview, which again shares on this point a great deal in common with the Marxist-Communist view. Meanwhile, the former communist government as well as people of Kazakhstan welcome this perspective and even promote it in measured proportion in public media, albeit in predominantly Islamic terms. Those who wish to understand and interact meaningfully with their perspective and approach would do well to consider the matter anew.

In a similar fashion, Olcott's juxtaposition of "social" needs over against ethnonational ones is a simple contradiction in terms. (Ethno)nationalism itself is a social issue and, indeed, a social need. The recurrence of (ethno)nationalism as a natural social phenomenon across the globe throughout the long duration of human history demonstrates this and we are simply not coming to grips with reality if we believe we can diminish or even vanquish its centrality and importance in human society through the mere "satisfying" of material needs and/or some allegedly simple swap over to 'territorial civic-based patriotism'.

Viewed in this light, ethnonationalism is not an 'elitist' conceived and driven 'ploy' for deceiving the unsuspecting masses, among whom they "arouse public support for [their] newly defined . . . nationalism," as if (ethno)national sentiments and aspirations were not already strong among those masses themselves to begin with. Indeed, in Kazakhstan as elsewhere the situation is quite the opposite. A fair number of Kazakhs with ethnonational aspirations feel the governing 'elite' are not doing enough to support their cause. That is, it is the (Kazakh) public who is seeking to arouse support from the governing 'elite' for *their* (ethno)national cause and not vice versa. Not that the governing 'elite' do not support such a cause; many of them do from their own Kazakh hearts. And precisely at this point the fact is exposed that the 'elite' are not separated off from and other than the 'public', they are a part of the public who share in public life as public servants in spite of the tensions which typically exist (in every society) between 'the government and the people'. The governing 'elite' arise from and are chosen from among the people.

In the face of the very real tensions between the Kazakh cause and the non-Kazakh (especially Russian) cause in Kazakhstan, the governing 'elite' are faced with the daunting task of balancing these often conflicting voices. We are treading on very thin ice, even bordering on arrogance, if we begin accusing them in these very complex affairs. It is hardly surprising that neither side is entirely content with the amount of support for their own cause which they receive from the governing 'elite'. All of them together must continue to negotiate a very difficult compromise in striving to strike a 'fair deal'. The continual barrage from the West (including Euroslavic sources), which naturally favors the non-Kazakh, i.e. European, prerogative is serving to increase more than decrease the tensions. No one is calling for 'carte blanche' privileges to be given to the Kazakhs, especially not in a manner which would lead to discrimination and/or oppression of other ethnonational groups. But there is surely room in Western treatment of the issues for greater recognition of Kazakh rights in relation to language, culture, history and even political governance in their own historic homeland.

Until then, the dynamic struggle between causes goes on with momentum shifting and gaining in different directions. But there is no "newly defined . . . nationalism" in Kazakhstan. The "nationalism" (i.e. national aspirations) of the modern nation of Kazakhstan, along with its "promising beginnings," are recorded in the Constitution, National Anthem and other founding documents and symbols and reveal no "resorting to an age-old tactic for trying to gain support." The "ideological [and] spiritual needs are being met," certainly not with perfection, but *in general accordance with the original 'promises' of the nation-state*.

On that note, it is perhaps ironic that Olcott's negative view of the State Symbols, National Anthem and Kazakh nationalist cause seems, in part, due to the "nagging ambivalence" over these issues in R. Stuart DeLorme's work, which Olcott uses as a part of the base for her accusations. This "nagging ambivalence" (which is a phrase borrowed from DeLorme's own assessment of the Kazakh sources) is surprising because his deep love for the Kazakh people and their ethnonational cause is evident to all who know him. He is a scholar who has lived significant portions of his life among the Kazakh people and nation. While there, he labored hard to learn, together with Russian, the national language of Kazakhstan and comprehend their corresponding inner ethnonational world. Indeed, following in the spirit of one his models, Joshua Fishman, DeLorme entitled his dissertation *Mother Tongue, Mother's Touch* as a labor of love "in praise of the beloved language" of the Kazakh people.[85] He thus built his doctoral work upon Fishman's "view of positive ethnolinguistic consciousness," noting that: "When so many western scholars warn of the dangers of nationalism, Fishman reminds us of the positive side of 'ethnolinguistic consciousness'."[86] DeLorme has made a noteworthy contribution to the affirmation, restoration and re-establishment of Kazakh as the mother tongue and national language of the Kazakh nation using an inclusive bilingual approach which offers due honor and significance to Russian.

In this light, Olcott's use of Delorme's material in an accusational context which frames the Kazakh's "need to preserve the[ir] mother tongue" as part of the "the state ideology that is being fashioned . . . resort[ing] to an age-old tactic for trying to gain support" and its alleged "abandonment" of its "promising beginnings" in favor of Kazakh nationalism seems an unfortunate misrepresentation of DeLorme's original intent. Indeed, DeLorme's conclusion to the whole matter is this:

> In its State Anthem, Emblem, and various policy statements, the current regime is constructing and promoting some *positive* metaphors to help the country become a peaceful, multiethnic, "uni-modal" nation. The government's attempts to create Kazakh metaphors for inclusion of all ethnic nationalities represent an

effort to draw from one Great Tradition *to unify a nation* out of what is now a multi-modal state of two major ethnic nationalities (and many others) with conflicting interests and sensibilities (p 108; emphasis on *positive* added).

There is no hint of accusation or warning against the dangers of Kazakh nationalism here. An overall contextual reading of DeLorme reveals that, while he is vitally aware of and deeply concerned for "the inherent tension" involved, he is predominantly positive in his view of Kazakh ethnonational consciousness and the attempts of the State as well as the people to struggle together through the very real "conflicting interests" of the "two major ethnic nationalities (and many others)" who are all rightful citizens of the modern nation-state.

Regarding these "conflicting interests," DeLorme demonstrates his vital awareness, highlighting that:

> . . . Nazarbaev is only internationalist to the extent that he must be in order to keep the political equilibrium between the huge Russian minority and the large block of Kazakh citizens with nationalist sentiments. His internationalism does not . . . keep him from publicly recognizing the role of the Kazakhs as the unequivocal leaders in implementing political, societal and economic reforms . . . . [He] insists that there is no other way, inferring, it seems, that if the regime exclusively stresses the equality of all peoples, the Kazakh nationalists will be upset and that if it only stresses the "integrating" role of the Kazakh people, the huge Russian minority will be disgruntled . . . [T]he threat of political destabilization by either nationalistic Kazakhs or nationalistic Russians is very real (1999:103-4).

Notice DeLorme's reference to "nationalistic Russians" at the very end of this quote. He equates this phrase with "the huge Russian minority" used several lines earlier. The *ethno*nationalist mentality of the Russian portion of the population, descendants of the Euroslavic colonialists who came to 'the land of the Kazakhs' precisely with and because of that ethnonationalist mentality, remains and continues to affect the dynamic of the entire situation. Only now they are taking their stance as an 'ethnic minority' being allegedly oppressed by Kazakh nationalists, appealing to the West for support in the cause of their 'ethnic minority rights', since they have now lost the privileged position in that land which they formerly enjoyed (see Malik, ed., 1994:1-15). Indeed:

> In August 1994, in a demonstration which occurred in the city of Petropavlask with the lead of active [members] of the "Lad" Slavic movement, decisions [to pursue action] with regard to the President leaving his office, local mayors being elected and Kazakhstan being joined to Russia were adopted. This movement's leaders worked to protect the rights of Russian-speaking peoples, to give political support to [those] moving and settling [in and out of Kazakhstan] and to conduct a struggle for "Russian citizenship" while residing in Kazakhstan (Weller, Babasova, Sailauov 2003:48).

This, by the way, was the major impetus for President Nazarbaev and the government of Kazakhstan to move the capital from Almaty to Astana, not the mere crazed vanity of some egotistical politician seeking glory for himself and a permanent legacy in history.

But back to DeLorme and his manner of communicating these "nagging tensions," part of the blame for Olcott's negative impressions and usage of DeLorme's material must be placed on the shoulder's of DeLorme himself. In his discussion (in chs 2-3)[87] of the drafting process of Kazakhstan's Constitution, National Anthem and State Emblem in relation to the ethnic issue and the development of the Language Law respectively, he himself says things such as:

> In summary, the most striking impression made by this explanation of the Flag is that it is *completely ethnocentric*. There is nothing which explicitly suggests the multinational composition of the country. . . . The Flag, even more than the Anthem, is *strongly ethnocentric* while expressing a welcome, symbolized by the domestic warmth of the ram's horn design and the sun that shines indiscriminately on all including those who are not native to the steppe.[88]

This represents what *could be* taken as the strongest negative statement by DeLorme in his overall discussion. We would especially note his use of the term "ethnocentric," repeated twice with the intensifiers "completely" and "strongly." "Ethnocentric" is typically used as a term of judgment and condemnation, not only in Western modernist parlance, but even in the Soviet and post-Soviet context of Central Asia. In the latter context, in both Kazakh and Russian, it is regularly used, together with ethnic-national "chauvinism," to condemn "russian-centric" and "euro-centric" ideas and attitudes. Whether DeLorme actually intended it in a condemning way in relation to the Kazakhs and their State Emblem and National Anthem is open to question, especially in light of his generally positive view of ethnonational consciousness and his overall support for the Kazakh cause. Indeed, in personal communication with DeLorme we provided him with an advanced copy of our own comments to this point on his above quote and then put this question to him, which is followed by his response:

> *Weller*: What do you intend to communicate in your choice of terminology here, particularly with respect to the phrases "completely ethnocentric" and "strongly ethnocentric"? Do you intend these phrases (and, with them, this overall statement) in a judgmental and/or condemning way, i.e. to speak against Kazakh 'ethnocentrism'? Or are you simply trying to note a 'fact', i.e. that "this explanation of the Flag" is entirely drawn from Kazakh historical sources and does not contain reference to other ethnonational groups? Similar clarification regarding the significance of the phrase "strongly ethnocentric" in relation to the Kazakh national anthem is also needed, since you refer to it with this phrase as well in comparative fashion.
>
> *DeLorme*: . . . I did not mean "ethnocentric" in a negative way. Unlike some, I see it as a neutral term. Every one is ethnocentric by default. It is part of being human. Ethnocentrism [itself] is not the culprit, *selfish* ethnocentrism is! *Unselfish* ethnocentrism, on the other hand, warmly affirms all the good of one's own *ethnos*, part of which, I would posit, would be a universal phenomenon of hospitality for those outside the *ethnos*, though the nature of that hospitality will take different forms in different times and in different places. In essence, hospitality towards the "others," the ones not in the ethnocenter, is a recognition that those other ethnocentrisms are also as valid as their own. Personally, I am profoundly impressed by the genius of the

national flag, the national symbol, and the national anthem. They are the collaborative and creative work, as I understand it, of a group of educated and sensitive artists and scholars in touch with the world at large and in touch with the genius of the great Kazakh nation. I believe that they cast a glowing vision which, like all beautiful visions, are so difficult to realize for us of the frail human race. But the surety of stumbling along the way only makes it more imperative to have such a bright vision to guide us.[89]

Unfortunately this clarification of his own heart and position was not made in the original work and his choice to use the term "ethnocentric," especially again with the added intensifiers, evoking the deep negative emotions and attitudes which such phrasing does in the Western and even (post-)Soviet world, is rather unfortunate in our view. It has obviously impacted Olcott and become fuel for her accusation regarding Kazakhstan's alleged 'unfulfilled promise', which in this case is an alleged failure to conform to Western multiethnic pluralistic democratic norms and their Western modernist underpinnings.

Likewise, in discussing the 1993 draft of the Constitution, DeLorme frames things in terms of "the inherent contradiction of the Constitutional drafts" asking: "How can all the peoples of Kazakhstan be equal if one of them, the Kazakhs, are to be the leaders?" (p 103). Certainly that is the question of the hour, but it represents a strictly Western modernist angle on the problem. That is, the question is being framed and asked from a uniquely Western socio-political perspective which sees equality for 'ethnic minorities' violated any time one ethnic group is given preeminence in cultural and/or socio-political affairs. *This is a view established on Western egalitarian multiethnic pluralistic political ideology which has been forged in the uniquely Western (including South African) Black Civil Rights, Apartheid historical context(s). In spite of its high importance and value in making comparative efforts to resolve various ethnic tensions in the international world, it is mis-applied when merely transposed and imposed upon the historical context of Central Asia* (see ch 7 below). Here again, whatever precisely his take is on the issue, it is doubtful in our view that DeLorme is attempting to argue against the unique and rightful place of the Kazakhs in modern Kazakhstan; he is more likely than not simply using the 'conventional wisdom', i.e. the predominant (Western modernist) view of his own day to help the reader feel in his gut the "nagging" tension over this issue as part of *Kazakhstan's intense struggles to establish its own fair and just form of multiethnic nationhood in its own post-colonial context within the broader international world.*

Rather than a simple polarized dichotomy framed in Western modernist terms, the choices in the post-colonial context of modern Kazakhstan seem to be essentially four:

1—A return to the spirit of the national anthem of the former Kazakh SSR which declares in bold fashion "Protectors of the nations, we express much gratitude to the great Russian people" (reflecting as this does official Soviet not to mention former Tsarist policy, including constitutional policy; the Kazakhs were forced to sing this for nearly 70 years in all kinds of school and official public settings).

2—A Constitution, National Anthem and State Symbols which grant equal place to the two main ethnonational groups in Kazakhstan, namely the Kazakhs and Russians (which would less-than-perfectly but still effectively achieve the aim and fulfillment of Russian Tsarist and Soviet policy in post-colonial Kazakhstan, including the favoring of the Russian language and thus culture, history, etc).

3—An absolutely generic, egalitarian multiethnic Constitution, National Anthem and State Symbols praising ethnic pluralism and 'the flourishing and friendship of the peoples' (which also would reflect previous Soviet rhetoric of the glorious 'Union' and would necessitate the favoring of the Russian language as the 'common language' along with its culture, history, etc, for all ethnonational groups).

4—A Constitution, National Anthem and State Symbols which allow the Kazakhs to express and develop their own unique historical relation to their own traditional homeland without excluding, discriminating against or oppressing the other ethnonational groups who have come to reside in that State, allowing all groups to restore and develop their ethnonational heritage based in a proper view of each one's circumstances within the post-colonial historical context of the nation-state of Kazakhstan.

While this book is not intended nor sanctioned to *officially* represent Kazakhstan and its government, our reading of the issue, backed up by nearly a decade of living in-country and interacting with Kazakh people in their own national language, including the reading of their newspapers, books, etc, and participation in their scholarly discussions, we can confidently say this: It is the latter (fourth) position which Kazakhstan, under the rightful leadership of the Kazakh people in mutual cooperation and counsel with all ethnonational groups residing there, has itself opted to pursue. While special place of honor is certainly given to the Kazakh (and in general Turkic Central Asian) people in the Constitution, National Anthem and State Symbols of Kazakhstan as well as in their general academic and popular discussions, the all-important question is whether there is exclusion, discrimination and/or oppression of other ethnonational peoples of Kazakhstan in those documents and symbols? In spite of the obvious inherent and ongoing tensions, according to our reading of those sources as well as our reading of DeLorme's overall treatment of them, the answer is a resounding 'no'. *To the contrary, inclusion of and concern for the rights of other ethnonational peoples is continually expressed. An explicit attitude of embrace which welcomes all nationalities to live freely in Kazakhstan and which encourages them to safeguard and develop their own ethnonational heritage is continually encountered. There is nothing worthy of accusation as a failed promise. Neither the Kazakhs, their nation nor their ethnonational aspirations deserve to be put to public, international disgrace by Western scholarship, especially that which is based on English and Russian sources, ill-informed of the inner world of the Kazakhs.*

It should observed here that, while multiple ethnonational groups live together in the genuinely multiethnic nation of Kazakhstan today, most all of these are from ethnonational people groups who have an ethnonational homeland of their own where their own language and culture prevail. This includes the vast majority of the population, particularly the dearly loved and highly respected Russian people, who make up nearly 35% of the population in the first decade of 2000 together with the Kazakhs at approximately 55%. This leaves 10-15% of the population, with the major ethnonational people groups represented by this sector having again their own homelands where their own national languages and cultures prevail. This includes the Ukrainians, Germans, Uzbeks, Kirgiz, Uighurs, Tatars, Turks, Azerbaizhanis and others.[90]

Here we offer an extended quote from President N. Nazarbaev:

> It is right for all the peoples of Kazakhstan to have ownership over the full restoration of their cultures but it is, without dispute, mandatory to give priority to the Kazakh culture, that is, the culture of the people who gave their historical name to the state,

because it cannot be sufficiently developed in a true sense in any other place other than Kazakhstan. The true spiritual maturity of the Kazakh people, who have been victimized by colonial policy for centuries, and the flourishing of their culture will adequately benefit the socio-cultural situation. The cultures of all the people of Kazakhstan will be developed as envisioned, pleasantly joining together and helping each other. According to the general stipulations of the U.N. Commission on Human Rights regarding non-discrimination, a point of view is both just and necessary which attempts for the sake of its culture to correct the real discriminations allowed in the past against the indigenous people of the nation who have been subjugated for a long period.[91]

Contrary to Olcott's contention that Nazarbaev and the government are departing from their original democratic foundations, this policy statement by Nazarbaev was published in 1993 as part of the "promising beginnings" of Kazakhstan's modern democratic nationhood. It acknowledges the right to develop an "ethnic-based loyalty to the land of the Kazakhs" as *part of* the vision of multiethnic democracy in post-colonial Kazakhstan. Indeed, the vision itself, like the Constitution, National Anthem, etc, is established *in part* upon "ethnic-based loyalty to the land of the Kazakhs."

As DeLorme himself points out (p 105-7), the U.N. document which Nazarbaev is referring to here, "The Rights of Indigenous Peoples," states in its opening paragraph that:

Indigenous or aboriginal peoples are so-called because they were living on their lands before settlers came from elsewhere; they are the descendants . . . of those who inhabited a country or a geographical region at the time when people of different cultures or ethnic origins arrived, the new arrivals later becoming dominant through conquest, occupation, settlement or other means.[92]

The "ethnic-based loyalty" for which Olcott accuses the Kazakhs is a part of both Kazakhstan's own founding documents and the U.N. declaration on "The Rights of Indigenous Peoples." In this light, Manash Kozibaev, a well-known and respected 'white-beard' and Kazakh scholar of history, is right to say "the Kazakh term for citizen (lit. 'azamat') is wider than the official term.

Its roots lie in the national history, the national language and mentality (lit. 'dil'); its wellsprings are in the world spiritual, humanistic contributions" (2001: 241; *Civilization and Ethnicity*).

In genuine concern for ethnonational groups without their own homelands, Kazakhstan even goes so far as to declare in official policy that "there are a few representatives of ethnonational groups who do not have their own (ethno)national statehood (lit. 'uzindik etnikalik memlekettigi zhok'), and the responsibility of this nation [of Kazakhstan] with respect to protecting their original cultures continues being increased."[93]

All ethnonational groups residing in Kazakhstan today are warmly welcomed and embraced as genuine citizens of the nation. They are, on the whole, being treated rather fairly. No one wishes them to depart. Certainly Kazakhstan has become their home. They are even encouraged to preserve and develop their own ethnonational heritages as citizens of Kazakhstan. But if they cannot find it in their hearts to recognize and contribute to the cause of Kazakh language and culture within the Kazakh homeland as genuine citizens of the nation founded upon it, no one is denying them the right to return to their own original 'fatherlands' where their own national language and culture *already* prevails. This would be especially true in the Russian case. Those who choose to stay, however—as again they are entirely free and welcome to do—should not be undermining Kazakh ethnonational rights within the historic Kazakh homeland with accusations that their 'human rights' and/or 'ethnic minority rights' are being violated, a heart-tugging cry which most Westerners and/or their own respective ethnonational 'homelands' are all too quick to take up on their behalf (cf. Abduvakhitov in Malik, ed., 1994:75).

Instead, as Nazarbaev states in his "Defining the Way for the People of Kazakhstan" ("Kazakhstan halkina zholdau") in the new millennium: "We must expend all our energy and aspiring strength to further develop one of the primary factors in unifying all Kazakhstanis—our nation's state language, the mother tongue of the Kazakhs."[94] This concern for the mother tongue and national language of the indigenous ethnonational group of the state would extend, in principle, to its national culture, history, etc—again without exclusion, discrimination and/or oppression of other ethnonational peoples within that state context. Here again we have grounds for the development of 'ethnic-based loyalty to the language, culture and history of the Kazakhs', not as the sole base of loyalty, but as a rightful *part and component of* loyalty to the modern nation-state of Kazakhstan. This, of course, is especially important for the Kazakh sector of the population.

As T. Gabitov notes immediately after highlighting the dichotomized views of 'civic' versus 'ethnic' nationhood (see ch 3), "[d]evelopment of the pan-Kazakhstani national idea is one of the issues discussed in the book by N. Nazarbayev, *In the Flow of History*" as well as some of his other writings.[95] Indeed, it is not only discussed, it is pursued *in fair balance* within the complex of ethnic relations viewed properly in historical perspective. As Gabitov (2001:314-5) elsewhere observes then: ". . . no matter how valid negative evaluations of the Soviet Union are, one thing has to be acknowledged: The friendship of peoples was not a false slogan, but it truly became an intentional virtue of common people," including Kazakhs. It is not a virtue which was cultivated strictly under the Soviets, though. It is based in the strong hospitality custom of traditional Kazakh nomadic society, a custom reinforced by the hospitality tradition of Islam. Note then that the development of a 'pan-Kazakhstani' identity is synonymous with efforts to develop the 'Eurasian' identity. But it requires, as Gabitov points out, the understanding that "a Eurasian cultural type must unite with the Kazakh traditional culture. Otherwise, the Eurasian Kazakh culture will be dominated by marginal features" (ibid). And this requires special concessions for the Kazakh people in their own historic homeland with respect to language and culture rights and even the balance of political power since all these deeply affect the destiny of the entire nation.

In trying to understand Kazakhstan's earnest efforts to achieve this delicate balance, this might be the best place to pause for a reading of Kazakhstan's National anthem:

1. We are a heroic people created in honor
who have been burning with zeal
on the road to freedom.
From the anvil of fate, from hell itself
We have come safely through,
we have come safely through.

*Soar high, eagle of freedom,
Call (us) to nationhood in (our) living!
The strength of greatness is in the people;
The strength of the people is in unity.

2. Honoring their mothers, valuing their wisdom
We have embraced in (our) bosom the children of all.

149

The sacred cradle of concord and friendship
Is our merciful, Great Homeland, the Kazakh steppe!

3. We have come through so much, (now) obliged to the past,
The days ahead are (filled with) wonder,
the future great (and vast).
Our traditions of honor-integrity,
mother tongue, wisdom,
heroism and nationhood
are entrusted in safe-keeping to the next generation.[96]

(On January 06, 2006 Kazakhstan adopted a new national anthem! Visit www.ara-cahcrc.com/ca-nationhood.pdf for appended discussion.)

But to return to the problem of language choices in DeLorme, he notes regarding the 1993 draft of the Constitution that:

> There is one phrase in the second modifying clause of the preamble, however, that seems to contradict the prevalent theme of inclusiveness, that is, "Kazakh statehood" instead of "Kazakhstan statehood." The former phrase implies statehood as defined by the Kazakh people. The phrase is interpreted by Kazakh nationalists as statehood (primarily) of the Kazakhs. Note the wording of the first basic principle of the Constitution immediately after the preamble: "The Republic of Kazakhstan, as a form of statehood self-determined by the Kazakh *ult*, "ethnic nationality,' ensures the equal rights of all its citizens." How can ethnically non-Kazakh citizens of the Republic of Kazakhstan be ensured equal rights, if they have already been excluded from one of the most basic rights of democracy, that is, determination of the fundamental nature of their own state? Evidently, the Kazakhs are first among equals: they lead in the process of statehood formation without entirely excluding the contribution of others. [But] the Kazakhs do not arrogate all state power . . . (pp 88-89).

Here again, DeLorme continues to use terminology such as "contradict(ion)" to express "the inherent *tension*" of the hour. Indeed, "tension" is a much better choice and he employs it elsewhere. "Contradiction," on the other hand, is a term which leaves much room for misunderstanding, especially in light of the Western modernist context in which it is being used and particularly when juxtaposed against the idea of "inclusiveness," interpreted again from a Western socio-political angle. In that context, his attempt to clarify that this is only an appearance, i.e. that it (only) "seems" to be the case, should not be missed, but it may not carry the force it should due to the manner in which it is framed and the context in which it is being read.

Also on the positive side, DeLorme offers balance to his assessment by noting that the Kazakhs "lead in the process of statehood formation *without entirely excluding the contribution of others . . . the Kazakhs do not arrogate all state power . . .*" Here, then, we have a clarification of the fact that the phrase "Kazakh statehood," even in this 1993 draft, according to Kazakh intentions, is in no way intended to be "exclusive," i.e. unaccepting and unembracing of other ethnonational groups.

In this light, it must be pointed out that these comments are only *part* of DeLorme's broader discussion of the drafting *process* in relation to the 1993 *draft* version. We understand DeLorme, therefore, to be offering honest critique of the *process*, but not *at this stage of his discussion* to be pronouncing any final judgment upon its conclusions. DeLorme is simply revealing in honest fashion the frail humanity which besets not only the Kazakhs, but all ethnonational groups as they attempt to grapple with, yet alone express accurately in official (and non-official) sources, these very complex issues. Indeed, he soon after clarifies that:

> In the place of the phrase "Kazakh statehood" in the 1993 Constitution, the 1995 draft version substitutes the phrase "statehood on the *aezhelgi*, 'ancient,' Kazakh land," which the final version . . . changes to "statehood on the *bajyrgy*, 'indigenous and ancient,' Kazakh land." The implication seems to be that the right and privilege of active involvement in the formation of statehood is not confined to the ethnic Kazakhs only, but should nevertheless be profoundly influenced by the fact that this land has historically belonged to the Kazakhs (p 90).

As suggested above, this resolution of the alleged 'contradiction' is, in our opinion, entirely fair and just in view of the post-colonial historical context. The fact that *the Kazakhs and Kazakhstanis together*, under the leadership of President Nazarbaev and the Kazakhstan government, worked through these very complex matters and made significant advance toward clarifying and perfecting a proper balance is only to their praise. Far from blame and accusation for an alleged devolving away from a healthy balance of multiethnic nationhood, they achieved significant strides toward it, all as part of their original "promising beginnings," the very foundations of their nationhood.

But DeLorme uses other language elsewhere which misrepresents the issue, i.e. which creates negative impressions. Namely, he alleges that: "The preambles of both the draft and the final versions of the 1995 Constitution address the inherent tension between equality of human rights and the Kazakh prerogative" (p 89). Once again, "the inherent tension" is real enough and remains to this day, not only in the Constitution, National Anthem and other official documents, but in non-official books, articles, discussions, etc. The problem with DeLorme's language here, however, is that it pits "the Kazakh prerogative" against "equality of human rights," as if "the Kazakh prerogative" is not itself an issue of the "equality of human rights," especially again in such a post-colonial context where, for nearly 200 years, the Kazakhs and their ethnonational aspirations, including their national language, were suppressed and even at times condemned. The wording should, in more fair terms, be: 'the inherent tension between the Kazakh prerogative and the prerogative of the non-Kazakh (particularly Russian) citizens of Kazakhstan, which are both issues of the equality of human rights in the post-colonial context of modern Kazakhstan'. After sending an advanced copy of this critique to Delorme, he himself noted in personal correspondence (03 Dec 2005) that he "particularly appreciate[d]" this clarification of the issue.

Indeed, as shown above in his overall conclusion, DeLorme seems to be nearer rather than farther from this suggested revision. He comes closer to a fairer portrayal of the issue when he speaks at a later juncture about ". . . the . . . nagging ambivalence which haunts the State symbols and the other government level documents examined so far. Specifically, what *is* the priority in state policy: the rights of all citizens to develop their cultures or the rights of the indigenous peoples to do the same?" (pp 96-97). He thus makes the issue on both sides of the scales equally an issue of human "rights." Here again though, he oversimplifies the matter by framing it in terms of a mere dichotomy. "The rights of the indigenous peoples" are actually included within "the rights of all citizens." The question is how the balance of rights for all citizens *in relation to the question of indigenous versus non-indigenous* is worked out. Here again, DeLorme specifically quoted this clarification as one which he "particularly appreciated" within our overall critique of his work. This was part of his sentiments expressed regarding the overall critique, of which he said in conclusion: "You have further clarified my own thinking on this issue. Bravo!"[97]

Be that as it may, DeLorme could have chosen better terms than "the nagging ambivalence which haunts." This "nagging ambivalence" ultimately "haunts" his own original treatment of the issue. It is something which Olcott seems to have interpreted quite negatively from her Western modernist viewpoint, ultimately using DeLorme's work to warn against the dangers of nationalism even though DeLorme himself never intended such a warning, especially not to such a degree as to warrant any idea of an 'unfulfilled promise' on the part of the Kazakhs and Kazakhstan. Indeed, as noted above, the foundation and center of DeLorme's entire approach and treatment is "in praise of the beloved mother tongue," based in the conviction that, "[w]hen so many western scholars warn of the dangers of nationalism, Fishman reminds us of the positive side of 'ethnolinguistic consciousness'." This would transcend language to include 'ethnonational consciousness'.

In this light, Olcott's warning against Kazakh nationalism in relation to "the need to preserve the mother tongue" as reflected in the wording of the national anthem and her immediate, direct connection of this with the allegation that "it is difficult to find a Russian translation of [the national anthem] in the country's stores and kiosks" are contrary to DeLorme's intent. Indeed, DeLorme only notes in passing that: "Interestingly, I could not find a single Russian version of the Anthem in bookstores in Almaty City . . ." (p 67). Olcott thus intensifies DeLorme's merely "interesting" and matter-of-fact observation into arsenal proof to warn against the Kazakh nationalist cause. Not only this, however, Olcott likewise takes DeLorme's locating and limiting of this merely 'interesting' and ephemeral circumstance to "bookstores in Almaty city" and inflates it to extreme proportions which cover the entire "country's stores and kiosks." Thus the city of Almaty in DeLorme becomes the entire country in Olcott where the bookstores are interpreted to include the whole multitude of kiosks throughout the land. Still more, Olcott is basing her 2002 case against Kazakh (linguistic) nationalism on a rather outdated and merely 'interesting' passing observation by a pro-Kazakh language scholar which was made back in 1994 or 95, which is when DeLorme was living in Kazakhstan and doing his field research.[98]

But even if Olcott has visited certain bookstores and kiosks herself, we can only wonder how many she has visited. Has she traveled the entire country visiting all the nation's bookstores and kiosks? We have not only visited, but lived in this country between 1995-1999 and 2002-2006. We make it our habit to visit all the major bookstores as well as kiosks *in Almaty city* (including the various outlets of the large chains Yevrika and Ekonomiks) on a regular basis. Without exaggeration, contrary to Olcott's claims, we have as of yet (in the period from 2002-2006) been unable to locate a single Kazakh-only copy of the 'National Anthem', without the Russian given in parallel. This is not to say that a few Kazakh-only copies do not exist somewhere. But let the point be well taken, for it is a very true and accurate one.

Why does Olcott not instead champion the Kazakh language cause by noting the *fact* that many bookstores in Almaty (and *presumably* throughout the nation) continue to carry predominantly Russian language materials with only the slightest stock of Kazakh language resources (e.g. those on the lower east corner of Auezov-Timiryazov, Auezov between Kurmangazi and Shevchenko and Abai between Mate Zolka and Pravda, to name just a few). This would include numerous kiosks selling newspapers and magazines, etc, (as for example the kiosk midway between Zharokov and Aimanov on Zhandosov). We have even asked the owners of such kiosks why they do not carry Kazakh language materials in a kiosk in *Kazakh*stan. The standard answer is 'Why, what need is there?', i.e. 'Russian is the primary language of this nation and is sufficient for (most) everyone'. Some do not even have one newspaper or magazine in Kazakh (as was formerly the case on Zhandosov between Aimanov and Zharokov; perhaps our prompting helped?! They now carry two Kazakh language newspapers!). But let us add to that the problem of menus, signs and a host of other documents, school texts, etc, to say again: If any language is still looked down upon, discriminated against and in need of special attention in 'the Land of the Kazakhs', it remains after 200 years by all means Kazakh.[99] Here again, the contribution of DeLorme and others is only positive, praiseworthy and necessary.

Toward Greater Appreciation for 'Ethnic-based Loyalty' in 'the Land of the Kazakhs'

The issues at stake here involve not only "ethnic-based loyalty to the land of the Kazakhs," but ethnic-based loyalty to their language, culture, history, etc. These all come wrapped together in 'the unified ethnonational complex' which Olcott and a host of other Western modernist and post-Soviet Euroslavic scholars are attempting to confront and even undermine, particularly now in Kazakhstan (and broader Central Asia), as they press their agenda for multiethnic pluralistic nationhood in the modern global world along the lines of Western socio-political ideals, norms and values. The issues are crucial for, as in the

Alash Orda movement of the 1920-30s, still "at stake [are] the development and advancement of [the] Kazakh nation" (Olcott [1987] 1995:210).

But when considering 'the development and advancement of [the] Kazakh nation' (as well as other Central Asian nations), surely we must realize, as G. Yesim and a host of other Kazakhs themselves do, that "[t]here is no perfect democratic society or nation in the world," a truth which prompts Yesim and all of us to ask "which nation can be the example of genuine democracy?" (2003:5, *The Price of Freedom*). While no one nation deserves to be singled out as *the* one true "example of genuine democracy," Westerners are still quick to suggest France, England, the United States and other Euro-American nations, giving little if any serious thought to the East. In this, they fail to realize, as President Bush has come to do in his second 'Inaugural Address' (20 Jan 2005), that "when the soul of a nation finally speaks, the institutions that arise may reflect customs and traditions very different from our own." This, we insist, would include customs and traditions which concern the proper relation of 'ethnic nation' and 'political nation'.[100] If we can truly say in that light, as President Bush did in continuing his thoughts, that "[o]ur goal . . . is to help others find their own voice, attain their own freedom, and make their own way," then perhaps we will be drawing nearer to the right path toward helping "evolve . . . *alternative approaches and methods* to handle . . . nations and peoples who seek fulfillment of ethnic aspirations."[101]

Indeed, through Kazakh scholars like T. Gabitov in his treatment of "The National Idea of the Kazakhs as a Problem of Cultural Study," "the soul of a nation finally speaks" and says:

> . . . a 'rootedness' in his own culture, existence on this 'land', among this very 'people', place, . . . This is the root and foundation of a national mentality and character . . . Within the last century the Kazakhs have been in three completely different types of civilization (colonial nomadic community, totalitarianism and transitional society in the [modern] Republic of Kazakhstan). The new independent Kazakhstan is still less than two decades old, *but it does not require an entirely new national idea.*[102]

Democratic nationhood has a long history of "approaches and methods" which have "handled" and can continue to "handle" such "nations and peoples who seek fulfillment of ethnic aspirations" (cf. the three steps outlined above). The question is: can hardcore Western modernists insisting on the separation of 'ethnic nation' and 'political nation' in 'the modern age of nations' find a way to achieve *genuine* "greater appreciation of the inner 'antiquity' of many modern nations" (A. Smith 1986:backcover)? And can they then work this into current ideals and models of nationhood, including ideals and models suitable for today's democratic nation of Kazakhstan (as well as other nations around the globe)? And *can they do this with a view to the historic rights of the Kazakh 'ethnic nation' within the bounds of their historic 'political nationhood' without excluding, oppressing and/or discriminating against all other ethnonational groups who have come to reside in and are now rightful citizens of modern Kazakhstan in the process?* It is a tall order and the attempts of Kazakhstan to fill it are bound to, and obviously do, disappoint a great many in the Western world. But the State, including both its Kazakh and non-Kazakh citizens alike, are working and struggling together to resolve the critical tensions they face in their post-Russian imperialist context. They are doing a surely less-than-perfect, but nonetheless still highly commendable job on the still long road ahead. They, as well as the 'inner antiquity' of their Kazakh-based identity and history, deserve more respect, support and affirmation from the Western world than they currently seem to be 'enjoying'.

—Chapter Six—

TOWARDS UNDERSTANDING THE DYNAMICS OF INTERNATIONALISM, PAN-NATIONALISM AND ETHNONATIONALISM IN KAZAKHSTAN AND CENTRAL ASIA

Appreciating the Complexity of National Rebuilding in the Post-Soviet Era

While we affirm the rights of ethnonational groups to pursue both ethnosocial and ethnopolitical aspirations *in principle*, a realistic view of the powerful and unpredictable nature of (ethno)nationalism should certainly be borne in mind. With respect to the state, 'illusions of grandeur' should not be entertained, for all states, like all people, 'fall short of the glory of God' (Rom. 3:23) as well as the longings and dreams of man (cf. 'utopia'). All governments are accountable to God, their people and one another for their actions and remain ever in need of humility in confessing their failures, seeking forgiveness and achieving genuine reconciliation, including restoration for any damages done (in as much as reasonably possible). The 'international world', a world of nations interrelating with one another, provides the context for interhuman, interethnic and international relations and is, in theory if not always in reality, a good and healthy thing.

It has been claimed by some that the Kazakh State, at both the national and local levels, has sometimes used its (ethno)nationalist agenda to exploit and mistreat people, both its own citizens and expatriates. Being acquainted with certain unpleasantries ourselves, we are unable to deny certain of these claims. Certainly neither the government nor its policies would offer support for such abuses. Likewise, defensive attitudes and actions, while not excusable, are at least understandable in light of their predicament, a predicament which includes not only their post-colonial dilemma, but the literal bombardment of socio-political accusations being leveled against them now, which are rather quick to come, in the international arena which they have only recently entered. We have known hospitality and commendable treatment far more than not, especially when we demonstrate our respect and appreciation for the "inner antiquity," i.e. the Kazakh foundations, of their modern nation-state. There are no grounds for seeing the State nor its people, particularly the Kazakh sector, as failing alleged promises nor for viewing their (ethno)nationalism as evil in and of itself.

All who deal with this land, especially those living and working there, should display genuine respect and appreciation for the incredibly difficult task they face. They are trying to rebuild a nation after 200-300 years of foreign imperialist oppression which used Kazakhstan as a politically strategic sending base for literally millions of Euroslavic colonialist settlers as well as a dumping grounds in the later Soviet era for multiple 'seditionist' ethnic groups and 'intelligentsia'. This included not only the confiscation and redistribution of thousands of square miles of land from the Kazakhs to the Euroslavic settlers, but outright persecution and annihilation of several million of their own people, a situation which left them, by the middle of the 20th century, a serious minority in comparison with the Euroslavic Russian-speaking majority in their own land. If we can somehow find it in our hearts to see it through their eyes, all of these 'foreign' peoples brought their 'foreign' religions, cultures, ideals and values with them into 'the Kazakh Steppe'. While all citizens of Kazakhstan today deserve whatever is ultimately deemed to be fair and just treatment as well as proper citizens' rights in all civil affairs, this remains the historical reality which has shaped the present conditions and dynamics of this nation. It affects all religious, cultural, social and political discussions and debates, including all debates over the proper relation between 'ethnic nation' and 'geo-political nation' and the related debates over language, culture and history in the ancestral Kazakh homeland. It has certainly shaped, as has been seen, the writing of today's national anthem of Kazakhstan (see ch 5).

Against this complicated and painful background, this national rebuilding is also taking place in the face of a new, international world which now brings multiple new 'foreign' powers and influences into their historic homeland, each with their own new religions, cultures, ideals and values. They all want the Kazakh people and nation to 'listen to us' because, of course, they all feel that 'we know best'. But the Kazakhs have heard the concerns and felt the pressures of these kinds of 'big brothers' before in the 'great games' played out between Russia, Britain, China and other foreign powers surrounding them from all sides. After such a long history of exploitation still rather fresh in their minds and hearts, trust in the allegedly 'pure and philanthropic motives' of such foreign powers does not, will not and cannot be expected to come easy, if it ever should. The age of globalization in the post-Cold War era, though not entirely 'Western', still has much to do with the extension and imposition of Western economic and political power in the world. There are certainly good, humanitarian motives and actions involved, but it is a very mixed bag, with the balance of the scales unfortunately seeming to tip more toward the side of exploitative self-interest instead of the other. For example, in the book *Central Asia: Its Strategic Importance and Future Prospects*, in his chapter on "Central Asia and American National Interests," Graham Fuller, notes that:

> "Two . . . positive U.S. national interests [in Central Asia] are: 5. Supporting the growth of human rights, democracy, free market economics and a cleaner global environment. 6. Enabling the United States to play a role in the economic development of the region, especially its raw materials" (1994:130).

It is no mistake that "human rights, democracy, [and] free market economics . . ." are all mentioned in the same breath here. As we have seen, "human rights" and "democracy" are largely bent on establishing a 'multiethnic, multireligious pluralistic civic democratic nation-state' which demands the separation of 'ethnic nation' from 'political nation' and thus ultimately undermines Kazakh ethnonational rights, including language and culture rights, in their own historic homeland. Likewise, the "free market economies" so closely tied to this agenda have in view "enabling the United States to play a role in the economic development of the region, especially its raw materials." To borrow from the 'dependency world-system theory' of Wallerstein and others, this simply strikes too close to the heart of capitalist exploitation of peripheral nations in the global economy in the name of one's own national economic benefit and interests to go unnoticed. It is certainly similar to past (Tsarist and Soviet) Russian exploitation of the same "raw materials" for the benefit of the Russian state and its empire. This concern is only reinforced when we hear, for instance, that in regard to the U.S. goal of promoting "a cleaner global environment," President Bush announced on Saturday, March 31, 2001 that the United States would not sign the Kyoto agreement aimed at international environmental protection against global warming "because it is not in the economic interests of the United States."[103]

The task for Kazakhstan of rebuilding its nation in the aftermath of Russian colonialism, which ushered it suddenly face-to-face with the international-global world, is by no means an easy one, especially when that international-global world now thrusts them inescapably into the post-911 'War on Terror' with all its consequences for religious freedom and national security. Whatever its failures—which most certainly exist in a world of imperfect peoples and nations—Kazakhstan, especially as an entire nation, does not deserve to be publicly disgraced before the entire international community by accusations of 'unfulfilled promises', especially when those accusations are grounded in Western modernist demands for conformity to its own vision of multiethnic, multireligious pluralistic nation-states, and even more so when they come from scholars who have not lived for extended periods of their lives in that nation and/or likewise who cannot function sufficiently in the national language and, therefore, who cannot properly comprehend the inner ethnonational world of the people and nation they are leveling such serious accusations against.

The Delicate Balance of (Ethno)National and International in Comparative Perspective

It is a curious fact that, while a number of Western voices seem to accuse the government of Kazakhstan for promoting and following a predominantly ethnonationalist agenda, other Western voices insist that the State 'elite' are more internationalist in their outlook and perspective. They believe the government officials of Kazakhstan represent 'Russian-educated, Russian-speaking Kazakhs' who heavily favor the international in their outlook and do not concern themselves with nor participate in the (ethno)nationalism of 'traditional village Kazakhs'. But perhaps this is because they, like those who accuse them otherwise, want to see Kazakhstan become more 'international' and not because it actually is, at least the way they would like it to be. This kind of 'international(ist)' perspective has been common of Westerners' inability to properly understand and interpret, not to mention *appreciate*, both Turkey and Japan as nations which are highly 'international', yet which are built upon 'ethnic cores' and remain strongly *(ethno)nationalist* in response to the international world they find themselves in. Consider here the comments of John Whitney Hall (1970:243-44) in his classic study of *Japan: From Prehistory to Modern Times*. He notes how in the mid-19th century . . .

160

... Japan found itself on the threshold of what was to prove the most traumatic chapter in its entire history, when within a brief century nearly every aspect of its life—its government, economy, social structure, and style of living—were all to be radically altered under Western influence. Japan's confrontation with the West, like the earlier encounter with Chinese civilization [in the 7th century], was to force a major turning point in its history. But the common assumption that Japan was simply overwhelmed by foreign influence holds no more for the nineteenth century than it did for the seventh. ... [Even] In twentieth-century Japan a long established cultural tradition and deep-running internal currents of change commingled with influences from the West to produce a modern society which nonetheless has retained an identity of its own.

There is an important and clear distinction to be made between 'class' and 'ethnicity' (see Connor 1994:156 quoted on pp 78-79). Neither the Turkish, Japanese nor Kazakh State need partake whatsoever of the 'rural' mindset and condition, which is an issue of 'class', to embrace a sophisticated, educated and socio-political ethnonational orientation. And they can do this without being 'artificial inventers' of (ethno)national identity as well as without losing a proper balance on the international. With that balance in mind, both 'rural nationalism' and 'State nationalism' for all three 'nations' are grounded in the same basic ethnonational identity of 'Turk', 'Japanese', and 'Kazakh' respectively so that, in general, rural community and state mutually support and encourage each other. After numerous generations of openness and interaction with the international world, neither Turkey nor Japan have abandoned their essential ethnonational orientation, including their 'traditional religions', in favor of 'foreign' options being offered to them. The Kazakhs will doubtfully prove any different—and we again have no real blame or accusation to level against them for it.

The 'eye for the international' is, *perhaps*, because we have been partly 'blinded' at the ideological level from out of our Western worldview and its values. And this *could* very well be related to a lack of understanding of the various paradigms of nations and (ethno)nationalism and their *significant ramifications*. The importance of this concerns vital issues of ideals and ethics as they affect the glasses through which we view not only the "Central Asian conundrum," but other situations involving ethnonational identity issues throughout the *international* world.

And, indeed, it is a 'conundrum', a "multicultural riddle." Even more, it is a downright 'clash of civilizations' (i.e. paradigms) at the level of ethical standards and values in the attempt to address and resolve this 'riddle'. The assumption that 'internationalism' in the international nation-state system of world politics, with its new vision of late 20th century multiethnic, multireligious pluralistic democracy, offers the 'best' (i.e. 'most ethical') option for handling the "multicultural riddle" is simply ill-informed and Western-Euro-centric.

In many ways, developments in the balance of national-international emphases within Japanese history during the Meiji Era (1867-1912) seem to be repeating themselves in Kazakhstan in the post-Soviet era:

> The Japanese search for national identity in the face of Western [cf. international] influence had thus gone through three distinct phases—from eager all-out advocacy of Westernization, to assimilation and modification, to a return to certain aspects of Japanese tradition. The resultant amalgam of thought typified the 'enlightened conservatism' of the late Meiji intellectual.

This, of course, is not surprising nor is it anything unique to solely Japanese or Kazakh history. It has occurred in broad and similar fashion in many times and contexts of human history. Thus, these brief and passing comparisons of developments in ethnonational consciousness between the Japanese in the Meiji era of their history and the Kazakhs of modern Kazakhstan are only intended in broad and general manner. They should certainly not be used as grounds for warnings or forebodings that the trends of Kazakh nationalism are on some kind of predetermined course which will only wind up in similar tragedy as the Japanese when the latter group ultimately, decades later, wound up joining forces with German and Italian ethnocentrism and plunged itself into World War II. No doubt Japanese, German, Italian other ethnonational histories should be compared with instructive and even sobering lessons drawn therefrom. But we have no intention here of joining in with the "many western scholars [who] warn of the dangers of nationalism" (DeLorme 04 Dec 2001), often using such tragic and extreme experiences as fuel for their Western modernist fires.

All in all, the situation in Kazakhstan today seems much like that in modern Turkey, Japan and a good many other nations. The government participates in the international nation-state system in order to enjoy the rights *which it should have* to the same basic benefits as all other 'nations' of the world. But this does not mean that it favors or should favor 'internationalism' over and above its concern for its very real (ethno)national dimensions and aspirations. Indeed, it retains a strong (ethno)national focus in the overall balance between the two.

In view of the close connection between 'separation of religion and state' and 'separation of ethnicity and state' in Western democracy, we can bring the closely related issue of religion into the mix at this point. The State not only in Kazakhstan, but again in Turkey, is careful, for example, not to associate with Islam 'officially' mainly because it knows this will create tensions in its international relations by violating all 'sacred ideals' of late 20th century Western democracy which are grounded in 'the separation of Religion and State'. It takes a similar approach to 'the ethnic problem' because of the pressure which Western democratic nations apply to 'the separation of Ethnicity and State'. Thus, whenever (it senses that) it is under the scrutiny of the "international" community with respect to its religious relations with Islam (or, in the case of Kazakhstan, any major 'secondary' religions like Russian Orthodoxy), or that it is being monitored with respect to its policy of treating 'fairly' all ethnic groups within its borders, it will be very cautious regarding any 'official' identification with its core group or religion. In this way, it avoids the accusations (which are quick to come) that it is being 'non-democratic' by virtue of its religio-political and/or ethnopolitical policies (with these two being strongly tied together, of course.)

Regardless, in the case of Turkey for example, since it is founded upon the ethnonational identity of the Turks (i.e. Turkish ethnosocial, ethnocultural, ethnolinguistic, ethnoreligious, and ethnopolitical identity), it remains established upon its core ethnonational group, the Turks, and offers what might be considered special support for Islam as the traditional 'ethnonational religion' of its core ethnonational group. It thus remains (ethno)nationally centered at its core, with Islam functioning as an 'officially unofficial' and 'unofficially official' religion of the nation.

Of course, it looks upon Islam more socio-culturally than religiously, that is, primarily as a 'social movement' with religious foundations. It views this movement as one which helps provide socio-political stability for the core ethnonational group (i.e. the Turks) and, therefore, the entire nation-state, as indeed it does. *If the Turkish government does not lend a 'healthy' measure of favor and support to both the core ethnic group and their traditional religion, the foundations of the entire 'nation' will become unstable and, with those foundations, the political authority of the government. For one and the same ethnonational group comprises the core of the nation, both politically and religiously as well as culturally and linguistically.* While Turkey may be emphasizing the international aspects of its identity in its ongoing efforts to join the European Union, this essential balance of relations between ethnicity, religion and politics will not change in any drastic measure. It has survived since the founding of the secular state by Ataturk in 1923 and even before in the Ottoman era and there are no signs of significant change on the horizon.[104]

The dynamics described here are at work not only in Turkey, but in various 'nations' across the Middle East, Central Asia, Japan and Korea, and elsewhere across the world. The precise balance of these factors and their exact outcomes are all unpredictable because they depend upon the freewill choice and actions of spontaneous human beings. No direct cause-effect relationship can be established which would enable us to predict their directions via some type of socio-psychological determinism. The various nations respond differently with regard to how they balance their international and national identities in the global age. They are certainly affected, however, by particular, identifiable factors and perimeters, including a concern for continuity with their historic identity acting from a group-oriented paradigm. This is why we must strive to understand those factors to the best of our ability. These nations are sensitive to the international world and are, for the most part, striving to work out a fair and just balance between their own ethnonational and international dimensions.

One thing may be said, though: With respect to the Turkic peoples of Central Asia, the history of the region, especially throughout the 19-20th centuries in the Turkic Muslim Jadidist movement, demonstrates that all of them have their ethno-historic *national* welfare at the center of their visions and interests (see ch 4), something for which we certainly do not blame or accuse them. Those entertaining ideas that the post-Soviet era will prove different, in favor of (a Western interpretation of) the 'international'—especially those basing their hopes in a view that ethnonational identity and its presence and force in their history are merely artificial and imagined social constructs—are setting themselves up for a good deal of disappointment not to mention a potential 'clash of civilizations' if they continue to approach and confront the issues from that angle.

Varieties and Interrelational Dynamics of Ethnoreligious and Ethnolinguistic Nationalism in the 'Pan-Turkic World'

To shift from a socio-political to more of a linguistic angle—though the two cannot be neatly compartmentalized and cut off from one another—it is not only the Russian-educated elites who are believed to be more international than national in their outlook. Because Russian still functions (by default) as the 'inter-ethnic' (cf. 'international') language of communication for the various ethnonational peoples of Central Asia, the general population of Russian-speaking Central Asians are believed to be 'internationally' and not (so much) '(ethno)national(istical)ly' oriented. It is believed by more than a few Westerners that the Russian-speaking Central Asians constitute a generally 'nationalism-free zone', or at least that (ethno)nationalism is but a minor, relatively unimportant issue among them. Some have even suggested that discussion of '(ethno)nationalism' by both expatriates and nationals in relation to the Russian-speaking Central Asian native peoples is empty, fruitless and vain. These sentiments have been expressed in the context of (sometimes heated) debate over the rightful place of national languages versus the Russian language in Central Asia. The problem is particularly acute among the Kazakhs, but also affects the Kyrgyz, Uighur and other Central Asian ethnonational groups.

In discussing the matter of (ethno)nationalism in relation to Russian-speaking Central Asians specifically, let us first note that we are using 'Central Asia(n)' in its broadest though 'Russian-language restricted' sense here. Likewise, we should note the problem of exactly who to 'categorize' as a 'Russian-speaker' versus a 'Kazakh speaker' or a 'Tatar speaker', etc. We must all be painfully aware that there are not two simple, distinct and separate 'black and white' categories. The ability of various native peoples to speak their national language versus Russian is best visualized as a scale representing a large continuum between those who speak their national language fluently but struggle hard in Russian to those who speak Russian fluently but do not even know how to say 'hello, how are you' in "their" national language. People fall at various points all over the scale in the continuum between these two extremes.

Regardless, it certainly remains possible to speak of "Russian-speaking Central Asians" or perhaps "Russian-speaking Turks" in the broader Jadidist sense of 'Turks or Muslims of Russia'. But we can be sure that a good many of these Russian-speaking Central Asians are some of the strongest '(ethno)nationalists' we may ever meet, whether it be a pan-Turkic-Muslim *form of* (ethno)nationalism or a more limited ethno-cultural-political (e.g. Kazakh, Uzbek) *form of* '(ethno)nationalism.

Directly related to this, we must bear in mind that (ethno)nationalism across Central Asia has various forms and dimensions, and they are all dynamically overlapping and inter-related. If we are not careful, therefore, we will wind up, as so commonly happens, confusing and conflating the broader, general *category* of (ethno)nationalism in Central Asia (in all its various forms and dimensions) with one particular and common *aspect* of those (ethno)nationalisms, namely Kazakh (and other) 'pro-national language' positions. Though pro-national language positions and (the various forms and levels of) '(ethno)nationalism' do go hand-in-hand, *the two are not the same thing*.

We should also call to mind here again that, along with other things, particularly things like land and culture, both 'national language' and 'Muslim identity' are closely related, *yet distinct*, elements in the (ethno)nationalism(s) of Central Asia. Some emphasize 'national language', some 'Muslim identity', and still others both, together with culture and land emphases. Often, then, 'Muslim identity' very easily can and does replace 'national language' as a rally cry of (ethno)nationalism for a great number of the Russian-speaking (and even 'mother tongue' speaking) Central Asians. As most of us are aware, the far greater majority of *Central Asians who value their Muslim identity as Central Asians* do so *precisely because* they view their Muslim identity as inseparably linked, and quite often synonymous, with their *Central Asian* 'national' identity. This is true whether this association be at the more limited and ethnopolitical level or the broader (pan-) cultural-ethnic (i.e. 'meta-*national*') level, or both. No matter how we slice the pie, (ethno)nationalism at the more restricted 'Kazakh', 'Uzbek', and other (ethno-cultural-) political levels and (ethno)nationalism at the 'pan-Turkic' level(s) are both still *forms of* (ethno)nationalism. They are inter-related and inseparable, as study of the late 19th-early 20th century Turkic Muslim modernist movement known as Jadidism and its resurgence in the post-Soviet 'pan-Turkic' movement will bear out (see again ch 4). And Muslim identity as well as Central Asian cultural-ethnic identit(y/ies) are a part of both of these (ethno)nationalist forms. We would, again, even have to throw 'Tengrism' into the mix here in order to treat all the dynamics occurring (see near beginning of appendix).

The various forms and levels of (ethno)nationalism across Central Asia work in mutual dynamic *tension*, at times with and at times against one another, keeping Central Asia (generally) united on the whole but divided at the ethnopolitical level. This is true regardless of which language is involved, whether it be one of the 'national languages' like Kazakh or the 'meta-national' language of Russian. Ultimately (ethno)nationalism is not to be associated strictly with the various national languages and the speakers of those languages in Central Asia. Muslim identity for the millions of Russian-speaking Central Asians is intimately connected with and thoroughly grounded in a pan-Turkic *(meta)national* identity, which itself assumes and thrives on a definite kind of broader Turkic (ethno)nationalism. The same basic Muslim identity is also involved in the more restricted ethnopolitical nationalisms of that same Turkic world of Central Asia. And the Russian language, just like the various national languages, participates in all the various forms and levels of Central Asian Turkic nationalism(s), crossing back and forth between the elusive boundaries of each. We simply cannot discuss Muslims or Turks or Central Asians and their identit(y/ies), regardless of their language, without discussing (ethno)nationalism.

Language is language is language, whether Russian or Kazakh or Uzbek. Though Russian transcends the cultural-political boundaries of the other more restricted Central Asian Turkic national languages, it still has its own cultural-political bounds with its own unique history in relation to those Turkic Muslim peoples. If the Russian language is associated with Turkic peoples and/or Central Asian Muslims (or any other particular religious group), then Russian simply replaces the pan-Turkic language which Gaspirali and others (even today) promoted among the (Turkic) 'Muslims of Russia' in order to unite them in their pan-Turkic cause. Here it should be readily visible that Russian is *not* the language of Turkic peoples and/or Muslims in northwest China, the Middle East or North Africa. This gives it clear '(meta)national' (i.e. 'nationalistic') dimensions and character. As soon as a specific ethnonational and/or religious group (e.g. Turkic and/or Muslim) is singled out and delimited by a specific language domain (e.g. Russian or a pan-Turkic language) within a (broad but) specific geographical as well as historical context, we have the indisputable and primary ingredients of '(ethno)nationalism'.

Ultimately then, whether we in our own view see '(ethno)nationalism' for better or worse, if any position ignores or excludes it from its discussions when '(ethno)nationalism' is inescapably a (core) part of the reality of the broader Central Asian Turkic world, regardless of language or religious domain, then such a position is certainly eclipsing very important aspects of Central Asian Turkic identity. Likewise, any position which sees it as little other than a negative, destructive force producing only social unrest, tensions, strife and conflict as well as economic poverty and demise—such a position is sadly ill-informed, mis-representing Kazakh and Central Asian (ethno)nationalism and, thus, only itself contributing to the ethnic tensions, strife and conflict for which it accuses the (ethno)nationalists.

—Chapter Seven—

ISSUES OF COMPARATIVE HISTORY: THE USA, SOUTH AFRICA AND KAZAKHSTAN

Borders, Treaties and Other Matters of Debate in Modern Kazakh Nationhood

In 'answering the Western assault' on Kazakh and Central Asian nationhood, we must go to the roots of the problem. These roots lie in the unique history and experience of the West, particularly its 20th century experience of World War II, the Black Civil Rights Movement and Apartheid. These ethnonational events of the 20th century have largely determined the fundamental ideals, values and convictions of the West in responding to the whole problem of the relation of ethnicity and state.

Here, then, we must say a few words about 'borders' and other matters of historical continuity versus discontinuity in Kazakh nationhood in comparison with other nations, the United States and South Africa in particular. Note that what we say is from the heart with genuine love for our own nation (i.e. the USA), including all its dearly loved and respected ethnonational peoples, lest our love for any other nation—Japanese, Kazakh or otherwise—prove merely reactionary and full of contradiction. How can someone love another nation and not their own? And precisely here we would do well to bear in mind the words of Jesus which apply to all of us, ourselves first, when he said in rather straightforward tone:

> Judge not, that you be not judged. For with what judgment you judge, you will be judged; and with the measure you use, it will be measured back to you. And why do you look at the speck in your brother's eye, but do not consider the plank in

your own eye? Or how can you say to your brother, 'Let me remove the speck from your eye'; and look, a plank is in your own eye? Hypocrite! First remove the plank from your own eye, and then you will see clearly to remove the speck out of your brother's eye" (Matt 7:1-5).

With that in view then, let us quote a more modern source here concerning the issue at hand. Svat Soucek (2000:225), *A History of Inner Asia*, informs us that:

> A frequent statement in the voluminous Sovietological and post-Sovietological literature produced in the West is that the borders created through national delimitation are "artificial," and minority pockets in many parts of Central Asia are mentioned as proof of that; moreover incidents like the bloody fighting between the Uzbek minority and Kyrgyz nationalists that occurred during June 1990 in the Osh region of Kyrgyzstan are adduced as portents of catastrophic upheavals in the future. The answer is that perfectly monoethnic and monolingual populations in a territory they consider their homeland and dominate politically are a rare occurrence in any part of the world, and that every national state must devise a compromise on how to deal with one or more minorities.

Ultimately then, the arguments, like those pursued by Akiner (see ch 5) and others, that the borders of today's Kazakhstan were "staked out" and drawn up by the Soviets and do not match the original borders of the Kazakh khanate or other periods of Kazakh history—these arguments are sorely over-emphasized. The attempt is, again, to disconnect the historical Kazakh State with the modern one so that today's state will not be a 'Kazakh', but a 'Kazakhstani' state. Here again, the issue of 'ethnic nation' versus 'political nation' stands front and center in the controversy.

Some even wish to argue that the Kazakhs, as nomads, had no idea of 'borders'. But this fails to understand nomadism, viewing it as an aimless and entirely unattached way of life instead of as it truly is, namely a very territorially-based lifeway which has *designated* land it calls its own and uses in systematic fashion throughout the turn of seasons. As Olcott herself notes with respect to the Kazakhs, "each tribe . . . migrated within an established geographic zone"

([1987] 1995:17). As graphically depicted in the 2005 Hollywood movie *The Nomads*, which concerns the 18th century Kazakh defense of their homeland against the Zhungarian attacks, it is this land which nomads seek to defend from intruders as their own rightful homeland. The movie concerns the all-important historical battle in Turkistan where the Kazakhs managed to protect their land from the Zhungarian invaders. Indeed, the Kazakh version ends the movie with a message encouraging the Kazakh people to value the restoration of their independence in modern Kazakhstan, thus seeing a very intimate connection between their ancient homeland and today's political nation-state. And so, this attachment to homeland remains even if at times "[t]he Kazakhs . . . were unable to protect their lands," as with the Russian takeover (Olcott [1987] 1995:26).

The idea that nomads had no borders also fails to understand that natural geographical boundaries, such as rivers, mountains and other phenomena have served throughout the entire span of human history, right down to our own day, to mark legitimate and clear 'borders' between 'states', 'nations' and 'nation-states' as well as kingdoms and empires. And so, as Anuar Omarov puts it in his brief article on Kazakh nationhood entitled "There Before, and Still There in Days to Come":

> The Kazakhs did not descend down from out of heaven. Neither did they emerge from out of the earth. For centuries they trotted about in the daytime without releasing the reigns of their horses and went about cold at night, bequeathing as an inheritance to their offspring the boundless and spacious Great Steppe.[105]

To cite certain evidences, then, showing that the Kazakh borders pre-existing the Soviet and even Tsarist Russian expansion into their homeland generally and *sufficiently* correspond to the modern nation-state of Kazakhstan, we can first note, as various Kazakh historians themselves do, that previous Kazakh borders actually included portions of modern southern Russia, i.e. some of the Siberian regions just north of modern Kazakhstan (e.g. Yesilkul and Karasuik) as well as the region of Astrahan in the West. Certainly large numbers of Kazakhs still live there today. Kazakhs even contend over the southern borders. Thus, Omarov declares: "If China asks, we simply gave [it] in trimmings; if Russia asks, in carvings. My heavens, can 500,000 square kilometers even be put into words?" (see previous ref).

Our concern here, however, is not with defining exact borders and then entering into the dispute over them. We would actually agree on this count that, while there may indeed be certain historical grounds for dispute, it is wiser to leave the borders inherited by the Soviets in tact, accepting them as *part* of the historical development *of borders* for the Kazakh nation. Our emphasis on "part" and "borders" here is to help emphasize again that we are not suggesting in any way that Kazakh nationhood as a whole was 'created' by Soviet ethno-engineering. The Soviets, like the Tsarists before, did impact the historical development of Kazakh nationhood. But that nationhood was pre-existing and their impact upon it was significantly and *sufficiently* determined by Kazakh views of and demands for their own nationhood. Indeed, Omarov himself draws from one of his Kazakh kinsmen who was involved in helping define the current borders in negotiation with the Soviets as part of the Kazakh branch of the Turkic Muslim Jadidist movement. From Kazakhstan's national archives, Omarov (2005:2) quotes:

> Alimhan Yermekov, who says: "On May 18, 1920 I took in my hand my Mandate No. 2043 which had been issued by a[n official] 'Decision of the (Bolshevik party organization) Kirvoenrevkom' and set off on a work trip to Moscow in order to give a report regarding the conditions and borders of the Kirgiz (Kazakh) steppe. During the four months [I was] in Moscow I interacted regularly with the members of the Kirvoenrevkom, receiving from them the necessary instructions regarding the establishment of an autonomous republic and the defining of its borders. I participated in a meeting which was conducted under the chairmanship of V. Lenin after [he had] come to Moscow, giving a report on the situation of Kazakhstan."

Omarov then adds immediately that: "In this historically decisive meeting the ruler of the day himself [Lenin] supported the demonstrated and consistent proposals of Alimhan Yermekov and, in accordance with the decision [reached] in April 1921, it is known that the provinces (lit. 'oblistar') of Semei and Akmola and the Caspian coast were joined to the extent of [what made up] Kazakhstan. That is, there were borders!"

Our primary concern here, then, is with the fact, as evidenced by this above historical proof itself, that the Kazakh borders pre-existing the Soviet and even Tsarist Russian expansion into their homeland generally and *sufficiently* correspond to the modern nation-state of Kazakhstan. Olcott herself recognizes this when she notes that "by the last quarter of the seventeenth century [the Kazakhs] controlled most of present-day Kazakhstan" (1995:10). However far back we take it though, this is important to understand because it means that the modern nation-state of Kazakhstan should be viewed properly as part of the longer and deeper history of the Kazakh State, a subject we will again return to in broader and deeper detail in the next chapter. Here (as we shall soon clarify in relation to other nations) we can and should acknowledge that changing borders certainly mark 'discontinuity' between past and present *forms of* the nation *within and as part of that nation's history*. But this in itself is entirely natural and in no way nullifies the existence of a nation and the overall continuity of its history as a single, genuine and integral nation.

With that in view we can turn to still further and deeper historical evidences to demonstrate the overall continuity of today's nation-state of Kazakhstan, particularly here its boundaries, with the previous Kazakh State. For example, the territory of modern Kazakhstan, with special emphasis on its northern parts, is shown by Kereihan Amanzholov in his treatment of the *History of the Turkic Peoples* to have properly belonged to and been inhabited by the Kazakhs during the 1800s. He relates the following:

> Before us lie several geographical maps. The first map was made in the year 1816. It is named 'Map of sections connected with the lands of the Kirgiz-Kaisaks [i.e. Kirgiz-Kazakhs], Karakalpaks, Turkmen and Bukharans.' The second map is called 'Head platoon of the border between the Kirgiz (Kazakhs) of Siberia and Orenburg.' [Its] . . . production in the year 1841 is specified in writing. The third is a map made in the year 1864 depicting the border between the Kazakhs of Siberia and Orenburg. These maps foster no doubt that the western, northern and eastern regions are the land of the Kazakhs. They brand the borders of the Russian land and the Kazakh land, making it like the brand imprinted upon a young colt. The limits of Kazakhstan are not a steppeland which laid unowned, unnamed and without evidence; its mountains and valleys, rivers and lakes were recorded with Kazakh names, its boundaries are recognized as those of a nation whose borders have been clearly delineated. . . . These kinds of historical evidences which were drawn up by the hands of Russia's own representatives in the Russian language, and preserved in the cultural-civilizational archives demonstrate that

the land of the Kazakhs of the Little zhuz and Middle zhuz was not the possession of the Russian empire.[106]

Amanzholov focuses his attention on the northern region because he is giving special attention to the claim by certain of Kazakhstan's Russian citizens in the north that the northern territory belonged properly to the Russian Empire. This is in connection with the 'Lad' Slavic movement and other groups who were calling for Kazakhstan's northern territories *where they lived* to be 'returned' to Russia after the breakup of the Soviet Union. But the first map of 1814 which Amanzholov references covers the regions to the south as well, i.e. "Karakalpaks, Turkmen and Bukharans." Along with the map, it should also be noted that in the south, the Sir Darya River has functioned as a natural border between 'Mawarannahr' (i.e. 'Transoxania') to the south, which is essentially modern Uzbekistan, and the 'Kipchak-Kazakh Steppe' to its north since well before 1814, even back into the BC era.

Respecting Amanzholov's contentions regarding the northern regions though, we should consider the reference made by Robert P. Geraci in his article on "Going Abroad or Going to Russia?" In the opening paragraphs he notes as part of his depiction of the era that:

> Until the recent construction of a bridge, the [Irtysh] river had been an obstacle between the Russian village and the steppe, where most of the Kazakhs lived as nomads, and was thus known colloquially as 'the border' or 'barrier' (*granitsa*). In Russian, to go 'beyond the border'—*za granitsu*—is, idiomatically, to leave one's country, to go abroad. So to cross the river was, in local parlance, to move not only between two places, but also between two different nations or peoples.[107]

Judging by the dates Geraci is treating, special note should be taken of the fact that *it was the Russians* who held the idea that even still in the latter part of the 1800s a clear border existed "not only between two places, but also between two different nations or peoples," namely the Kazakh nation and the Russian nation. This evidence cited by Geraci certainly supports the contention of Amanzholov that "[t]hese kinds of historical evidences which were drawn up by the hands of Russia's own representatives in the Russian language, and preserved in the cultural-civilizational archives demonstrate that the land of the Kazakhs . . . was not the possession of the Russian empire." Omarov looks back to both the Tsarist and Soviet eras and declares in similar fashion:

> . . . in yesterday's Soviet era the rulers who had fixed their staring eyes upon the Kazakh's land were not few [in number]. If, as those certain ones go about saying, it was ownerless and unclaimed, by this time no land, not even so much as a horse's saddle flap, would have remained with us. They would have left none. If we take it from one angle historically, and if we draw from another angle officially, it was only because they had no other choice but to acknowledge all of our rights that they were not able to do so.

Here we must realize that we are actually dealing with two distinct yet interrelated issues: 1—the question of whether the current borders of the nation-state of Kazakhstan are (radically) different from the previous land(s) inhabited *and possessed* by the Kazakhs and, 2—the question of whether the Kazakhs ever turned over rightful sovereign control of their land to the Russians, making it effectively part of 'Russia' and thereby forfeiting *historic* rights to 'the land of the Kazakhs'. The answer on both counts is 'no'.

If we bring our attentions back to focus on the first question, the map in Soucek (2000:176) depicting "Central Asia in approximately 1825" is also of importance here. Soucek's map shows the Kazakhs 'fixed' on the territory essentially corresponding to today's Kazakh nation.

All of this to say that, while the modern borders drawn by the Soviets do not *precisely* match those of the pre-Soviet Kazakh 'nation', there should be little dispute over the fact that since the 1600s the Kazakh people have possessed and inhabited the territory which, generally speaking, corresponds with the nation of Kazakhstan today. The modern nation-state of Kazakhstan is properly seen as *the* historical continuation of the more than 500 year history of the Kazakh nation.

But if we really wish to follow the reasoning regarding borders in the Kazakh case, then we should apply the same basic reasoning to the USA, to name just one example. In that case, the latest boundaries "staked out" (cf. Akiner above) by the nation would certainly not match its original ones of 1776. Or did the early Americans even have *the same identical concept* of precise borders which we speak of in relation to "today's" America? Of course, we should confess at least some continuity since rivers and other natural geographical markers continue to serve as boundaries between various political units, i.e. states, within the nation, such as the Ohio River between Ohio and Kentucky. They even serve as *national borders* between the USA and other nations, such as the Great Lakes and their rivers flowing between Canada and the USA and the Rio Grande River marking the divide with Mexico. Of course, on that note, Mexico still disputes the borders between the USA and itself!

But we should even go so far here as to ask whether the proper date for the beginning of U.S. history is 1776 or not? If "modern" democratic nationhood requires a constitution, the U.S. constitution was not drafted and adopted until 1787. Here we should note the comment by the host of BBC's *Dateline* (Aug 28, 2005) regarding how the USA took their 'good old time' in drawing up their own constitution in stark contrast to how they now pressure Iraq to have theirs completed as quickly as possible *in order to firmly establish and legitimize their full, independent nationhood*. We should also note here the 'proud fact' which some Americans seem rather fond of in emphasizing how the U.S. constitution has never undergone any serious revisions in comparison to those of other nations, including Kazakhstan (cf. the 1993 draft versus 1995 final version). Indeed, after taking 11 long years to write it we should only hope that no serious revisions were or are needed, though we can only wonder how many were made in the course of those 11 years—a span of time equal to or even greater than the span in which Kazakhstan has made initial revisions to its own constitution. Of course, not only the constitution; neither did the USA elect its first president until 1789. Perhaps then the grand 200th anniversary of America in 1976 was celebrated prematurely? Perhaps it should have been 1987 or 1989?

Or is nationhood to be counted as commencing with a 'declaration of independence' according to 'the right to self-determination of nationhood', i.e. "we the people" in "government by the people, for the people"? If so, is this a 'human right' which is only valid for and granted to civic multiethnic 'nations' and not 'ethnic nations'? And if this be so, then why should the nationhood of the U.S. be recognized as commencing with its 'Declaration of Independence' in 1776 when the Caucasian (i.e. 'white') European descendents who framed that 'Declaration' did not include the African-*American* and native *American* Indians, but only the Euro-American (i.e. 'white') 'ethnic nation' who stood at its core? When the Kazakhs recognized themselves as Kazakhs, i.e. an 'ethnic nation', from the mid-15th (or 16th) century onward and established their 'khanate' on the core of this 'ethnic nationhood', does this not count? And remember here that the Kazakhs did this on their own historic homeland and that of their ancestors, not on someone else's which they had sailed to and taken over through colonialist-imperialist force.

On that note, if we wish to stress divisions between the various tribal or ethnic groups *within* a nation, we could certainly stress the division between Caucasian Euro-American and African-Americans (i.e. 'whites' and 'blacks') as well as Caucasian Euro-American and native American Indians in the USA until at least the 1970s (and beyond) as much as we could stress the division between the Kazakh tribes in their alleged 'pre-modern', i.e. 'pre-national' history. Perhaps then U.S. nationhood and history proper should not be counted with the 'Declaration of Independence' in 1776, the drafting and adoption of its first Constitution in 1787, the election of its first president in 1789 or even the 'Emancipation Proclamation' finally signed almost a century later by Abraham Lincoln in 1863. Maybe it should be counted from 1868 when the United States government finally ratified the 14th Amendment of the Bill of Rights granting citizenship to the African-American ethnic group in its midst? But even then the question of *full, fair and just* citizenship, including the right to vote in 'free elections' according to true democratic *nationhood*, would still be hanging uneasily over us, at least for another 100 long years until President Lyndon B. Johnson signed the 'Voting Rights Act' in 1965, finally granting *full powers of* citizenship to the African-American community some two centuries late in that *nation's* history.

If we were to turn our attentions to the treatment of native American Indians by the Caucasian Euro-American (i.e. 'white') government of the U.S., then we could begin by mentioning the various tragedies in 'pre-national' history when, for example, the Indians in Virginia were "crushed" in wars spanning from 1622-44 and the Pequot 'nation' of New England was "massacred" after war broke out between them and the Caucasian Euro-American (i.e. 'white') settlers in 1636. All of this and much more was part of what John Quincy Adams referred to as the "extermination" of the native Indians by the Caucasian (i.e. 'white') Americans, something he warned would surely bring the judgment of God upon the nation. Within U.S. 'democratic' history proper, though, attention should at least be drawn to the "Indian Removal Act" of 1830. It was "signed by President Jackson" and "authorized the transfer of southeastern tribes to land west of the Mississippi [River]. Indian resistance was met by illegal force; Jackson even ignored a Supreme Court order upholding the land rights of the Cherokees."[108] Likewise, "[i]n 1855, the defeated Nez Perse tribes were given land in the northwestern states, but when gold was found in the area they were again forced to move. . . the California gold rush also led to the overrunning of Indian lands and to the death of thousands of Indians [from] 1848-58" (in Rosenbaum, ed. in chief, [1982] 1993:613-4). Indians of the western lands were engaged via war and their lands forcibly taken from them throughout much of the mid to late 1800s. This would include the Navaho and their defeat by Kit Carson in 1863, the Apache, whose last war chief Geronimo surrendered in 1886 and the Sioux, Apache and Cheyenne who "were subdued [between] 1870-90 by a combination of military force and the depletion of buffalo herds" (ibid). In 1871, in the middle of these conflicts, the U.S. government had "ceased to recognize Indian tribes as independent nations" (ibid).

It does not end in the 1800s however, for according to the personal testimony of certain Caucasian (i.e. 'white') Americans still living today, Indians continued to be hunted and shot for sport in California and presumably elsewhere in the western U.S. in the early 1900s.[109] Whatever other incidents there might be to recount throughout the 20th century though, these long-standing historic problems have still not been resolved even at the dawn of 21st century modern democratic America. As Tom Gorman of the *Los Angeles Times* reported in the July 22, 2002 edition of that newspaper: "The Danns and other traditional Shoshone Indians—as well as a host of historians, attorneys and international human rights commissions—note that the tribe never ceded its territory to the U.S. government nor lost it to Western conquest" (p. A8).[110] An incredible legal battle over the proper boundaries of U.S. nationhood and government jurisdiction involving much of Nevada, southern California and other large tracts of land in the pacific west—namely 24 million acres—still rages in our own day.[111]

And so we come back around full circle to the question of political types and structures of government, constitutions and their 'democratic' laws and the continuity-discontinuity of all these *within* the history of one 'nation' as well as in comparative perspective between various 'nations' and their respective histories. That is, we come back around full circle to the question of 'pre-modern' *versus* 'modern nations' and just where we draw the line between the two? Indeed, perhaps we should judge U.S. nationhood and its rather checkered history based on the Kazakh model instead of vice versa?

One thing is sure though: If (especially a Caucasian Euro-American) proponent of true and just multiethnic and pluralistic democracy wishes to write a book about the 'unfulfilled promise' of any nation, they should surely make their first book one about the more than 200 years of "America:

Unfulfilled Promise," which continues being unfulfilled right down to our own day, before they venture off to write one about the 11 years of Kazakhstan's alleged failures.[112] Here we would do well to reflect on the words of Martin Luther King, Jr., one of the greatest Americans and, indeed, world heroes of the 20th century. They are taken from his address on February 25, 1967 in Los Angeles, California concerning "The Casualties of the War in Vietnam." He reproves us, saying:

> . . . We often arrogantly feel that we have some divine, messianic [or secular humanistic] mission to police the whole world. We are arrogant in not allowing young nations to go through the same growing pains, turbulence and revolution that characterized our history . . . We are arrogant in professing to be concerned about the freedom of foreign nations while not setting our own house in order. . . . We must undergo a vigorous re-ordering of our national priorities.[113]

Likewise then, if any (especially Caucasian) American (or even other) scholars wish to criticize someone's national anthem and symbols, then they should start with America's and its exclusive representation of the Caucasian Euro-American (i.e. 'white') history standing at the heart of its flag and reflecting its origins, i.e. the 13 alternate red and white stripes representing the 13 white founded and led colonies of the Caucasian Euro-American (i.e. 'white') settlers. Where is representation of the 'nation' of African-*Americans* or the various 'nations' of *American* Indians? Red, white and blue are likewise colors chosen by the Caucasian Euro-American (i.e. 'white') people because of the special significance they carry in their own culture for their own history. The whole thing "originated as a result of a resolution adopted by the Marine Committee of the Second Continental Congress at Philadelphia on June 14, 1777" in which no African-American or Indian voices participated.[114]

If borders themselves, though, be the primary issue, then those originally established for the USA in 1776 were radically altered in 1803 with the Louisiana Purchase, then again with the purchase of Florida from Spain in 1819, the annexation of Texas in 1845 and the Gadsen Purchase of 1853 bringing in much of New Mexico and Arizona. After this the nation was split into two during the Civil War (1861-65). Should its unbroken, 'perennial' history end here and be made to begin again? Do we have the start of an essentially new, previously unconceived nation here? But back to borders, without even rehearsing all the various states and their dates of individual incorporation we can at least note the purchase of Alaska from Russia in 1867 and the annexation of Hawaii in 1898; these added still more new territory, but the territories were not made an official part of the nation, i.e. declared 'states', until 1959.[115] The speculation regarding Puerto Rico becoming the '51st' state might also be mentioned. Beyond that, we might note that the USA, in relation to its presidential elections of 2000 and 2004, is again being described in the late 20th-early 21st century as 'a nation (being) divided' into "two nations."

Again, none of this is shared in any 'anti-American' spirit. To the contrary, we love our nation and thank God for it, including the rights, freedoms and privileges we enjoy with it. For all its blemishes and failures, we have no regret for being born and raised in the USA and we have no intention of 'blaspheming' it or 'desecrating' its national anthem or symbols. The United States of America has done much good in the world of nations, including its own, in attempting to provide relief and restoration for pains and damages experienced in the ongoing course of human history. It deserves full credit for this. But when it comes to criticizing and even judging other nations for their ideas, policies and/or practices, we will have to begin at home and take a good look at ourselves in our own land with our own 'checkered' history. A similar 'checkered' history could be rehearsed for many a nation in world history, including for example Kazakhstan's respected neighbors, Russia and China, as well as France (cf. Connor 1994) and others.

In the end, the argument about borders having been drawn by the Soviets and/or not precisely corresponding with earlier or original boundaries as well as the attempts to emphasize disunity of 'tribes' or other points of discontinuity—these do little if anything to undermine the genuine 'inner antiquity' and rightful historical and ethnonational roots and foundations of today's Kazakh nation, i.e. Kazakhstan.

We should remind ourselves here, by the way, that while Lenin, Stalin and company surely engaged in intentional drawing of borders to cut across ethnic boundaries in a 'divide and rule' strategy, they nonetheless founded those nation-states on *real historic* ethnonational cores—namely Kazakh, Uzbek, Kirgiz, Turkmen and Tajik—which had already been determined by those peoples' own 'self-aware' conceptions of themselves far more than any Tsarist ethnography or Soviet 'ethno-engineering'. As Svat Soucek (*A History of Inner Asia*) notes: "the scientists, in this instance Russian linguists, anthropologists, and politicians, had done fairly competent work," so much so that they "correctly identified principal nationalities" (2000:225, 238).

Important Distinctions of Ethnonational Issues in U.S., South African[116] and Central Asian History

We stand then in much greater need of deeper and more accurate comparison-contrast of the unique histories and ideals arising out of the ethnocentric catastrophes of World War II, the Black Civil Rights Movement in the USA and Apartheid in South Africa with ethnonational issues of other historic circumstances. Only then will we understand just how the histories of the respective peoples and nations compares and contrasts in order to know just what ideals from the WWII, Black Civil Rights and Apartheid cases should or should not be applied to the ethnonational issues of those other historic circumstances.

With respect to Kazakhstan and Central Asia, a more careful look reveals that while the whole problem of Europeans coming to the 'new world' and overrunning the native Indian and African peoples has certain shared phenomena with the (Tsarist and later Soviet) Russian colonization of Central Asia, these situations differ significantly in the fact that America and Africa were both entirely separate and very distant land masses from the colonizers original European homelands whereas Russia and Central Asia are one connected land mass into which the Russians simply 'extended' their territorial boundaries. The colonizers from Western Europe (as opposed to the Slavic Russians of Eastern Europe) left behind their homelands to find new ones, namely those of other peoples while the Russians 'merely' sought to extend the borders of their own nation.

If we wish to compare the respective situations from this angle, then in the case of the Caucasian (i.e. 'white') Europeans we can see similarity in the way that, *after* they established themselves in their 'new' homeland, they then (like the Russians in Central Asia) proceeded to overrun the native American Indian or African tribes, 'simply extending their territorial boundaries' into Indian and African domains. But even then it will need to be acknowledged that the only 'just' solution the United States government could work out, for example, with the *native* Americans was to return to them their own 'nations', albeit in the form of 'reservations'. Thus, Paul Stuart can write a book as late as 1989 entitled *Nations Within a Nation*.[117] We are essentially speaking here about American Indians of today who live (not as 'ethnocratic', but) as distinct ethno-political (semi-)autonomous 'nations' within the geo-political boundaries of the USA. And this has much to do with land, language and culture rights among other things.

Likewise, in the South African predicament the whole idea of establishing 'homelands' for the various black ethnonational peoples (between the 1950s

180

and 1970s) was an ethnopolitical solution similar in principle at least to the one in the USA in connection to the native Americans, only on a larger scale and organized not technically within, but alongside the Afrikaner state. The main problem with that solution for the black peoples of South Africa was not so much that they received ethnopolitical nationhood; *no one protested against or rejected the proposal on those grounds.* The protest and ultimate rejection of the attempted solution is more to be found in the description offered by *Encyclopedia Britannica* in their article on 'History of South Africa'. They explain how the government . . .

> . . . began to consolidate the scattered reserves into 8 (eventually 10) distinct territories, designating each of them as the "homeland" of a specific African ethnic community. *It also manipulated homeland politics so that compliant chiefs controlled the administrations of most of those territories.* Claiming to match the decolonization process that was taking place in tropical Africa, the government devolved powers onto those administrations and eventually encouraged them to become "independent." Between 1976 and 1981 four accepted independence: Transkei, Bophuthatswana, Venda, and Ciskei. *However, like the other homelands, they were economic backwaters, dependent on subsidies from Pretoria, and not a single foreign government recognized them. Conditions in the homelands rapidly deteriorated* . . .[118]

Or, as another source describes it: "In practice, the homelands [were] poverty-stricken, generally poor in soil and in natural resources, depending to a large extent on South African aid and revenues generated by commuter workers, those who work[ed] in white areas but reside[d] in homelands."[119]

Again, the ethnopolitical solution itself was not abandoned because it was viewed as inherently evil. Neither should the "conditions in the homelands [which] rapidly deteriorated" into "economic backwaters" be blamed on the idea of an ethno-based nation, as if 'ethnic-based nationhood' automatically means poverty, disease and despair. Such arguments, as we have already seen, are surely heard in our day. Olcott herself attempts to juxtapose 'prosperity' in Kazakhstan, for example, with 'Kazakh ethnic nationalism', as if the two were diametrically opposed to one another. With respect to South Africa, the white Afrikaner government, when designating the 'homelands', intentionally drew up the borders to exclude mineral resources and other sources of natural wealth.

Likewise, they intentionally kept the quality of education low among the black nations to keep them from potentially prospering and becoming powerful. Thus, the ethnopolitical solution simply did not work *primarily* due to other factors, namely those of ongoing manipulation, oppression and the poverty and dependency created by the Afrikaner government.

Eventually then the problem of Apartheid became intimately intermingled with the crisis of segregation raised in the Black Civil Rights Movement in the USA. Thus, many of the voices which have been raised against Apartheid echo the same basic civic democratic ideals which emerged in the American context, i.e. 'a multiethnic state' via the demand for complete separation of ethnicity and state with the assumption that this will provide absolute justice and equality for all ethnonational groups involved. While this solution seems to be meeting with basic success in the South African case and is even accepted by the black majority (approx. 85%), and while all Afrikaner and British descendents living in South Africa are embraced as genuine, full-fledged and equal citizens of the new nation-state, it cannot be overlooked that the government is essentially a 'black government'. Indeed, this is the phrase used, not officially of course, but by the average people in the streets when making simple matter-of-fact reference to the government. But it carries no inherent negative connotations; rather, it is viewed as essentially good and right in light of South Africa's history. While one might say this is simply the result of democratic process in free and fair elections and/or point out that the 'black government' does not represent one distinct ethnonational people group, it remains a very important fact of ethnopolitical significance. This is especially true for the black peoples of the nation who are by no means ready to see a white majority in government again any time soon because they want to ensure proper control of their own ethnonational heritage and its destiny.

Note here by the way that 'ethnic minority rights', a phrase and concept popularized in the uniquely American context, does not really apply to South Africa, since the black peoples were by far the majority. This fact, along with other similar situations, urges caution in simplistic association of 'dominant ethnic group' with 'oppressor' and 'ethnic minority group' with 'oppressed'. It also urges caution against simplistic transference and application of 'ethnic minority rights' ideals from one historic context to another.

Regardless, we can find some common ground when comparing South Africa with Central Asia. But important differences remain, particularly in the fact that the various ethnonational peoples of Central Asia do have their own distinct homelands as opposed to them all being joined together in one pan-

Turkic Central Asian 'multiethnic' state. Likewise, while they may have been the last to secede from the Union—due mainly to concerns over China and the Middle East—they did not choose to remain in or create a single multiethnic nation-state which included within its embrace their colonizing oppressor, i.e. they did not combine Kazakhstan or any other Central Asian states with Russia to create one 'new' multiethnic one. Certainly many Russians and other Euroslavic peoples live now as citizens in the various Central Asian nation-states, but this too is an important difference with the South African situation, where the colonizers and their national domains were all incorporated into one nation-state with the various black ethnonational groups. All of this is critical to understand in attempting to apply or not apply 'civil rights' ideals from post-Apartheid South Africa to post-Soviet Central Asia.

If we return to the comparison between the USA and Central Asia, the differences are even greater. Indeed, when attempting to apply lessons and/or socio-political ideals from the 'situational ethics' which arose out of the Black Civil Rights Movement, we must recognize that the history of Caucasian (i.e. 'white') Euro-Americans (cf. 'WASPs') dragging black Africans from their homeland and taking them to and then subjugating them as slaves in what essentially became their (i.e. "the white man's") 'new' homeland and forcing segregation upon them (i.e. mixing prohibited)—may God, the African-American peoples and the world forgive us!—is almost entirely opposite to a history of Caucasian (i.e. 'white') (Slavic European) colonists invading the native Central Asian people's homeland(s) and then forcing desegregation (i.e. mixing imposed) upon them *in their own land*. The issue of 'dragging' the black African peoples into their homeland aside, the contrast between segregation (i.e. forced separation) versus 'desegregation' (i.e. forced mixing) would actually hold true between South Africa and Central Asia as well. And here we should listen from the heart to the cry of a Kazakh ethnonationalist writer reflecting upon "The Ethnography of [Russian] Colonization." He summarizes the matter in this way:

> The greatest wrong-doing in the history of the sons of men is the socialist system's sending off of over 200 national peoples into *a pulverizing mix of obliteration* through totalitarian rule. In consequence of this, almost 100 tribes and national peoples went off to complete destruction. That is, nearly 100 *national cultures which had been preserved throughout centuries have perished forever, and the cultural-spiritual essence of the surrounding land has been*

made formless and void. Never before has mankind known the likes of this kind of deep sorrow. In the place of this destruction and engraved sorrow, they themselves, trampling down the national cultures which had been preserved throughout thousands of years, ended up a group of 300 million [strong] who reached to a healthy state of being.[120]

This is not to say that Russians did not generally 'keep their distance' from, what in their view were, the 'cultureless, uncivilized' Central Asians. Different residential areas developed among other things. Much of this was due to the Central Asians' own desires and efforts to retain their own homogeneity however. The Russian aim was to establish a strong Russian presence *in their midst*, mixing with them and thereby influencing them linguistically, culturally, religiously, socially and politically, turning them into 'citizens' of the Russian empire, not official slaves who were intentionally sectioned off from them in all aspects of life and only permitted to be present when serving their masters.

With that in view, we should note that later in the same section Seidimbek refers to this "pulverizing mix of obliteration" as "ideological whoredom." Note well that the Kazakh nationalist cry says their nationhood has been violated by foreign powers and this has resulted in severe breakdown of their historic peoplehood and homeland. This concerns, of course, the issue of 'Russification' as well as forced ethnic mixing and relates to matters of ethnic rights of homeland, language, culture, and even religion.

Still, Westerners seem to look at the Kazakh nationalist movement of today—especially these aspects of it—from eyes of 'White supremacy' racism as it occurred in the context of the immigrant nation of the USA. Within less than two decades the Kazakhs have gone from being the object of sympathy as an oppressed 'minority' group to being viewed as a 'dominant' oppressor of other 'ethnic minorities' in the traditional Kazakh homeland.[121]

We cannot of course allow mere license to be given to their sinful abuse of these issues as if all of their attitudes and responses are somehow sanctified. Still, one of the hardest ethical issues to face is that the Kazakh cry concerns, amongst other things, a violation of their ethnonational unity as an ethnic people group, i.e. they have been *forcibly* internationalized and heterogeneized and this has caused the breakdown of their ethnonational identity as well as that of many other Turkic Steppe peoples. This was the result of Russian Tsarist imperial policy which sent millions of Euro-Slavic peoples to Kazakhstan to colonize it in the 18th and especially 19th centuries, a policy aimed at strengthening Russian control on the Kazakh Steppe, which included the aim of promoting the 'civilizing' influence of Russian language and culture among the ethnonational peoples over and above their own 'uncivilized' ones. To repeat something from earlier, the dearly loved Russian (and even other Euroslavic) people have not yet, after some 200 years, moved beyond this same basic attitude of cultural superiority. While exceptions can be found, by and large they refuse to this day to demonstrate their respect and genuine appreciation for the Kazakh people and their language; that is, they do not count the Kazakh language worthy of any effort to learn or use. Regardless, after the Tsarists, in the Soviet era, Kazakhstan was one of the primary lands specifically and intentionally used by Stalin and other Soviet leaders as a 'dumping ground' for 'seditionist' (i.e. 'nationalist') ethnic groups and political offenders. It was the same era, i.e. that of Stalin in the 1930s, in which more than two million Kazakhs either starved to death or were intentionally executed for being 'nationalist' betrayers of the 'Soviet brotherhood' and its aims and ideals.

History certainly does not favor the idea that the Kazakhs descended on other ethnonational peoples' homelands and took them over or, similarly, dragged all the various ethnonational peoples into their land and then began oppressing and imperializing them. Thus, Hafeez Malik, as editor of the book *Central Asia: Its Strategic Importance and Future Prospects*, offers a different perspective on the matter, explaining how:

> Russian immigration started to change the demographic picture of Turkistan. "Net Russian immigration was 206,000 in the decade from 1896 to 1905 and 834,000 in the period from 1906 to 1916; some 300,000 to 500,000 settlers [had already] arrived by 1896." By the end of World War II, this trend resulted in the Kazakhs becoming a minority of 36 percent in their own state, while Russians, Ukrainians, Volga Germans, and other European nationalities constituted the majority of the population. After 1992, Russia turned the Russian settlers' question into that of human rights issues and the acme of international law and morality. The western powers are now being wooed to support the Russian contention ([1994] 1996:5-6).

One must be careful how he or she is interpreting 'ethnocentrism' and 'racism' in its historic context. Ethnocentrism and racism can certainly wind up in separatism, i.e. segregation and Apartheid, but it can just as easily result in the opposite extreme of forced assimilationist efforts aiming hard at 'social integration' via intentional mixing of the 'ethne' together. Through such 'mixing', dominant groups can often influence and ultimately change, 'subdue' and control the language, culture, political power, etc, of ethnic 'minority' groups, as was the aim in Russian colonization with its program of 'Russification' (and 'Christianization').

So we ask: Do the Kazakhs (and other ethnonational groups in human history) have a right to their ethnonational cry? If we take the definition seriously that "an ethnic social group" is a group "with . . . enough unity to be regarded as a corporate whole" (cf. Kaiser 1978:103), then actions and efforts which threaten or infringe upon that "unity" and 'corporate wholeness' must be deemed detrimental to the well-being of the ethnonational group itself. Can we then violate (even by accusation) the freedom of the ethnonational group to its corporate ethnonational identity and unity? Even worse, is it right to locate sin in outward social or political structures instead of the heart? Granted it is wrong to promote 'pure race' ideas out of a superiority complex which typically involves despise or hatred for other ethnonational groups and which may even lead to dangerous ideas such as 'purification', i.e. 'ethnic cleansing'. But the Kazakhs and others have been forced to accept these almost irreversible violations of their peoplehood and nation. Is this any better? They are in deep pain and frustration, even a state of confusion, over this "pulverizing mix of obliteration." Does anyone feel the depths of their pain and sympathize with them? Can people from a multi-ethnic immigrant homeland such as the USA or other multi-ethnic democratic states even begin to relate to or sympathize with this kind of situation?

It is not primarily a problem of 'mixed or impure blood' or even of casual 'mixing' in the course of life. The Kazakhs have a genuine love and respect for other nationalities living in their midst. Much of that love and respect is grounded in their strong tradition of hospitality flowing forth from their nomadic heritage and reinforced by their Islamic one. Rather, it concerns the deep damage done to the ethnonational people group's kinship solidarity and unity *as a people and nation* which in turn is closely tied to and grounded in issues of national language, culture, social values and norms, political authority and even national history. It is a steep uphill, indeed 'up mountain', battle which they must fight daily, struggling 'against' the deeply entrenched dominance of Russian language, culture, worldview and even political authority, etc. Many from the West and Russia want them to simply 'forgive and forget' and accept the conditions which have been come to pass. But this is too simplistic, it is too much of a 'historical fatalism'. Either that, or they engage in historiographical attempts to undermine any indigenous ethnonational rights to language, culture, political rule, etc, by depicting the language, culture, political rule, etc, of the particular ethnonational group in question to have no genuine or rightful historical connection with the particular nation-state in question. But all such approaches seem too conveniently in line with the Western and Russian agendas of promoting egalitarian ideals of 'multiethnic nationhood' as well as protecting the 'ethnic minority rights' of the remaining Russian and other citizens in the various Central Asian nations today. And again, these two agendas work hand-in-hand.

Towards Applying Ethical Standards in Comparative Historical Perspective

Once again, the 'ethnic nation' and the 'geo-political nation' are much more intimately bound together in the minds of Central Asians, as well as a great many other Asian and African peoples, than the late 20th century Western modernist mind would ever care to imagine. We have no grounds for accusing them nor for coercing them to conform to our own Western ideals, convictions and values. 'Genuine democracy' certainly offers no grounds for accusation nor does it make any attempts to conform them to late 20th century Western ideals. Rather it upholds the right of the people to self-determination of nationhood. Nationhood, in the case of the Kazakhs and other Central Asian peoples, was determined not by the Russians or other Euroslavic groups who colonized their lands, but by the titular ethnonational groups of Central Asia well back in their respective national histories *in accordance with that democratic right of self-determination*. Those histories, and with them those nationhoods, cannot be cut-off from the history of the modern Central Asian nations.

While circumstances have changed in the course of history, the mere fact that they have emerged as 'multiethnic nations' does not mean that the nature of this 'multiethnicity' is the same as in the Western cases. Thus, Western standards, ideals and models of 'multiethnic nationhood' cannot be superimposed upon them. It is their own unique histories which must be consulted in order to resolve any questions of 'ethnic rights', whether 'minority' or majority, native or non-native, etc. The same stands true for issues of (ethno)national reconciliation and questions of restoration, restitution, etc, which are intimately wrapped up together with them. We cannot simply follow a philosophical-ethical approach to nationhood which takes one set of standards, ideals and values regarding ethnicity and state as determined in one or even several limited historical contexts and then try to impose them upon all nations without any view to the history of the particular nations in question. *Drawing from the experience of other situations can surely be helpful, but it could actually wind up violating the ethnonational rights of peoples if applied uncritically to situations and circumstances in different historical contexts.* In determining proper 'rights' for various ethnonational groups within the context of various nation-states, the particular histories of those particular nation-states must be the primary sourcebed from which all seeds of thought regarding ethnonational rights in those nation-states should sprout, form and take their shape.

This makes one's understanding and interpretation of a particular nation's history of deep importance. It likewise means that (ethno)national reconciliation and, with it, interethnic peace and harmony, can only be achieved through resolving the issues in historical perspective. Thus, for example, the European Union (EU) demands of Turkey in 2005, as one in a list of requirements, that Turkey change their view of the 1915 Armenian catastrophe before they are accepted into the EU. Of course, it will not end with merely changing their view; that is only the first step. Turkey realizes that if it did change its view, issues of *reconciliation* and (reasonable amounts of) *restoration-restitution*, etc, would immediately arise. We take no position on the issue in question. We only use it as an example of the fact that in our world today, views of history and *right* action resulting from them are acknowledged as valid, integral issues in the struggle to determine right interethnic and international relationships both inner-nationally and internationally.

If an ethnonational group's land—including political control of that land and the issues of language, culture, etc, that inseparably go together with it—have been violated historically, then wrongs must be righted. This includes special concessions for the ethnonational group within their own historic homeland with respect to national language, culture, history and even political authority. The Kazakhs and other Central Asian peoples today have rights to such special concessions in their own historic homelands, i.e. in the 'new' Central Asian nations. While we do not support all of their agendas, attitudes or actions or offer any idea of 'carte blanche' privilege to them, we are obliged to support these basic ethnonational *human rights* in the international world of our day—with a proper view to their history.

—Chapter Eight—

THE "SINGLE ETHNIC UNITY" OF THE KAZAKH PEOPLE AND THEIR NATION IN HISTORICAL PERSPECTIVE

Our purpose in this chapter is not to provide a detailed account of Kazakh history. Rather, it is to offer an historical overview of Kazakh ethnonational aspirations throughout their history in order to reveal the undying embers of that flame, including its political dimensions, in spite of the ebb and flow of tide amidst varying socio-political contexts. We have already offered significant discussion of key issues in chapters five through seven. While repetition of certain points is inevitable, the unique aim of this chapter is to provide a unified and interconnected overview in flowing fashion without becoming sidetracked by or buried in finer points of debate.

If we consider the case of Kazakh ethnonational identity and its corresponding (ethno)national aspirations (i.e. [ethno]nationalism), we can first note several important books by Kazakh scholars treating this issue which have emerged in the post-Soviet era. For example, Tursin H. Gabitov and Aktolkin T. Kulsarieva, with contributions from Nagima Baitenova and Zhusip Mutalipov (2006), *Kazakh Religion, Culture, Society and State in Historical Perspective*; Dosmuhammed Kishibekov (1999), *Kazakh Mentality: Yesterday, Today and Tomorrow*; Zh. Moldabekov (2003), *Kazakh-ology*; Kabdesh Zhumadilov (2000), *My Vast Nation, My Kazakh . . .* ; Mukhan Mamanzhanov (1999), *I Labored for My Nation*; Rahmankul Berdibai (2000), *If We Say We Will Be a Nation . . .* ; Murtaza Bulutai (2001), *Our Muslim Kazak Nation* and Manash Kozibaev (2001), *Civilization and Ethnicity*.[122] There have also been a number of conferences treating the matter. For instance, a series of (so far) three conferences has been organized through the Faculty of Philosophy and

Political Science at Kazakh National University, one in 2003 with its publication of articles entitled *Kazakhstan Civilization in the Context of Globalization and Finding Ways for Cultural Identification*, another conference in 2004 with its publication on *The Problem of Forming a Civilizational Mindset [within Kazakhstan]*, and a third one in 2005 with its publication on *The Civilization of Kazakhstan: Problems of Socialization and Accommodation of People*.[123] "Temirkazik's" scholar's roundtable discussions have also provided significant opportunity for dialogue on these matters. In particular, the December 2004 gathering on the topic of "The Kazakh Ethnos and (Its Proper Relation With the) State" should be noted here along with its December 2005 discussion on "The Spirit of December" in honor and memory of the December 1986 uprising in Republic Square in Almaty. It publishes annually the main presentations given in those gatherings.

Turkic Nationalism in
the Streams of Pre-Kazakh History

Regarding the historical development of Kazakh ethnonational identity and its manifest aspirations in ethnonationalism, discussions of the streams of pre-Kazakh history contributing to their later ethnogenesis would take us all the way back to the more distant past of their nomadic ancestors of the Eurasian Steppe, the Scythian-Saka and Huns. While much debate, at least among Western scholars, surrounds the actual ancestral connections of the Kazakhs with those early peoples, the cultural and territorial ties are clearly very strong. Closer though still distant associations can also be touched upon in relation to the 'Kok' (i.e. 'Blue') Turkic khaganate of the 6th-8th centuries AD. This is because, as R.S. DeLorme points out in relation to the blue flag of the modern Kazakh nation:

> *Koek*, 'light blue,' is a color of historical significance to the Kazakhs: their ancestors, the Turks of the Turk Kaghanate (Sinor, 1990:285-316), founded in the seventh century A.D., were known as *koek*, 'blue,' Turks, meaning "heavenly Turks" or "divine Turks." Shajmerdenov writes: "under this precious flag which is the color of the sky, they breached the walls of their merciless enemies and defended every last inch of their vast homeland. A distinguished, distinct civilization known as 'nomadic culture' was established. And the original place, the homeland of this Turkic people was our Kazakh nation. According to the conclusions of scholars, the

Kazakhs are the people who have most assimilated and kept the characteristics of the [Blue] Turks".["124]

Here we might pause to note that some would cast this connection off as a purely 'imagined' one based on a mere political agenda which reinterprets the past arbitrarily. Of course, all historical study is 'arbitrary'; no historian can cover every detail of the past. They must *selectively* choose, according to some selecting and organizing principle(s), what to include and what not to include and how to arrange the included events and facts. They must then interpret the significance of those arranged facts. The connections of today's Kazakh people and nation with the ancient Turk khaganate are certainly distant, but they are more than merely 'imagined' or 'invented traditions'. How much more is a question we will leave unanswered as one of the finer points of debate with which we do not wish to become distracted at this juncture.

Beyond the ancient Turk khaganate, the Qarakhan Turkic khaganate (960-1211 AD) centered in modern N Kirgiz, SE Kazakh and NE Uzbek territory would also provide some background for understanding later Kazakh ethnogenesis and the development of their identity historically. This would be the era of Zhusip Balasaguni, who wrote his famous *Kutadgu Bilik* or *Wisdom of Royal Glory* in ancient Turkic, not Arabic or Persian, in 1069 AD.[125] It would also be the era of Mahmud Kashgari, who wrote his famous *Diwan lughat al-Turk* or *Dictionary of Turkic Languages* in 1076. And last but not least, it would be the same age in which Firdowsi wrote his famous *Shahnama* or *Book of Kings* (998-1036), which "was a kind of Iranian nationalistic memoir. . . . Firdowsi galvanized Iranian nationalistic sentiments by invoking pre-Islamic Persian heroic imagery."[126] Thus, if we note the emphasis on Turkic, not Arabic or Persian, in the two famous Turkic Muslim scholars of this era, we might detect signs of Turkic (ethno)nationalism at work in dynamic interaction with Arabic and Persian culture and language in the ancient Turko-Persian Muslim world of Central Asia. Indeed, As Robert Canfield ([1991] 2002:9) points out in *Turko-Persia in Historical Perspective*: "The Qarakhanids . . . cherished their Turkic ways."

Thus, Svat Soucek (2000:90) in his work on *A History of Inner Asia*, notes that, along with his knowledge of Firdowsi,

> Kashgari also knew the rich philological literature devoted to the Arabic language produced by Arabs and non-Arabs alike, including Farabi's *Diwan al-adab fi bayan lughat al-Arab*, 'Literary

dictionary explaining the language of the Arabs'. In contrast there was little or nothing on Turkic, and we can thus visualize how the sophisticated and perhaps somewhat homesick Qarakhanid scholar-aristocrat decided to compose his priceless work. The introduction is revealing: '. . . God Most High had caused the Sun of Fortune to rise in the Zodiac of the Turks, and set their Kingdom among the spheres of Heaven; that he called them 'Turk', and gave them rule; making them Kings of the Age, . . .'

Soucek also records Kashgari as saying: "the Lord Himself bestowed the name *Turk*, for [it is] a statement traced back to the Noble Prophet . . . , who said: 'The Lord says: I have a host whom I have called Turks and whom I have set in the East . . . '."[127] He thus founds Turkic nationalism on a saying attributed to an Arab, namely Muhammed, grounded in Islamic hadith tradition! Indeed, it was even the God of Islam who "had caused the Sun of Fortune to rise in the Zodiac of the Turks." In this way, Kashgari's work, as T. Gabitov (2001:247) notes, "not only contains information about the cultural life of the Karakhanid State, it also includes a wonderful description of ancient myths and legends of Turkic culture, particularities of traditions and customs, deification of Heavenly Tengri, the Sun and natural phenomena by the Turks." Gabitov (2001:246) notes in similar fashion that "[t]he roots of the creative work of Zhusip Balasaguni are to be found . . . first of all, in the cultural legacy of Turkic peoples. *Kutadgu Bilik* [i.e. *Wisdom of Royal Glory*] is not copying Arabic and Persian literature, as some claim."

All this would provide an important 'snapshot' of early Turkic nationalism in comparison with Turkic ethnonational movements of later generations, especially Turkic nationalism in the Muslim Jadidist movement with its distinctively Kazakh branch. This early Turkic nationalism continues affecting these later movements right down to our own day. It is part of the reason the Soviets sought to cut them off from this history, minimizing and grafting it into the history of 'the great Russian people'.

The Strength of Kazakh
Ethnonational Identity Over 500 Years

As we press ahead, then, we might also note the relation of the Kazakh people with the Turkic Kipchaks who inhabited the Eurasian Steppe as an important historical source for understanding Kazakh ethnonational identity. But if we come to the Kazakhs themselves, we have already noted (in ch 5) how the Kazakh scholar A. Abdakimuhli (1997:54-5) offers a list of at least seven historical evidences tracing the earliest possible occurrences of the term 'Kazakh' back to the 10-11th century, long before Tsarist colonial ethnographers ever appeared on pages of history or their alleged 'imagining' of Central Asian nationhood were ever re-imagined in the minds of Western modernist scholars. These include the following as quotes directly translated from Abdakimuhli's work:

- In looking at certain historical evidences, the name of a field of the Kuban River was known as "Kazakhia" in the 10th century.
- The 10th century Arab writer Matsuda, in his own publications, speaks of a nation and people called "Kashek," [and/or] "Kazhek."
- The historian Ibn al-Uardi in the 10th century writes about "Kazakhs."
- Ferdoisy (in the 11th century) in his own well-known publication of "Rustem dastan" gives [us] information about "the Kazakhs and Kazakh khans."
- "The Annals of Nikon" mention that in the time of the first invasion of the Mongols in the year 1223, they came passing through the land of "the Kasakhs" like [it was the open] sky from out of the Karkaz Mountain sides.
- In the year 1282, the '*Bestau sherkesteri*' show that they called themselves "Kazakh."

Beyond this, most scholars, including most Kazakhs, look to the middle of the 15th century for the actual beginnings of a tangible, traceable history of the Kazakh people and nation, *with ethnic formation largely preceding and undergirding state formation.* Taking it from this point forward, we would be in essential agreement with Privratsky (2001:8), in *Muslim Turkistan: Kazak Religion and Collective Memory*, when he says:

> The strength of Kazak ethnic identity over a period of 500 years is suggested by Kazak attacks on Uzbek cities in the 16th century, resistance to Jungar incursions on the Kazak steppe in the 17th and 18th, uprisings against Khoqandian and Russian rule in the 19th, anti-conscription riots against the Tsar in 1916, the Alash Orda government of 1917-20, and a series of revolts against Stalin's collectivization program. Rebels from Sozaq attacked the Turkistan telegraph station as late as 1930. When Stalin was gone and national identities were again allowed limited expression in the 1950s and '60s, an aggressive public resurgence

of Kazak culture occurred, including the national reclamation of the Yasawi Shrine in Turkistan.[128]

We can show this "strength of Kazak ethnic identity over a period of 500 years," including its ties with Kazakh nationhood, in greater detail with the following historical overview. It can be covered under three major periods, namely the pre-Russian independent, the Russian imperialist and post-Russian independent eras. The trek begins in the first period with a quick glance back at the clear break which the Kazakhs and Uzbeks made between one another around 1466.[129] *The search for the origins of Kazakh ethnopolitical nationhood is centered in this era.* In this we agree with the Kazakh scholar B. Kumekov who opens his article on "Problems of Kazak Statehood" with the declaration that: "The history of Kazak statehood proper is connected with the Kazak khanate formed in the 15th century."[130] In close harmony with this, we would also agree with the Kazakh scholar O. Ismagulov in his treatment of "The Ethnogenesis of the Kazak People" who says: "Historically the Kazakhs represent by themselves a single ethnic unity . . . with original cultural features and with its own language on the territory of contemporary Kazakhstan. . . . from out of the ashes of the Mongol Empire the Kazak tribal unions went to a new, higher quality level of ethnic self-consciousness. The clear evidence of this is the formation of the Kazak khanate . . . "[131] With respect to that "single ethnic unity" and its ethno-socio-political aspirations "on the territory of contemporary Kazakhstan," we should not fail to mention the national unification efforts which achieved a nomadic Kazakh State under the khans Kerei (1458-73) and Zhanibek (1473-80) and then developed and maintained basic (though fluctuant) unity under Burunduk Khan (1480-1511), Kasim Khan (1511-1523) and Haq Nazar (1538-1580). This spanned more than a century in the foundational 'golden age' of the Kazakh khanate, i.e. the Kazakh State.

After this, the Kazakhs experienced a period of inner struggle marked by certain measures of disagreement and disunity between their three main tribes. But we would not conclude with Orhan Soylemez (1995:243) that "[p]ower struggles in the region among the various nomadic groups prevented the Kazaks from emerging as a Kazak state or a nation until the annihilation of the Oirats by the Manchus in 1757." He is following here Chantal Lemecier-Quelquejay and his article on "The Kazaks and the Kirgiz" in the volume on *Central Asia* edited by Gavin Hambly. We have already treated the Western modernist paradigm of Kazakh and Central Asian nationhood, including Hambly's view of the Tsarist and Soviet 'creation' of Kazakh (ethno)national identity, in the previous chapter. This position, again, corresponds to the alleged 'age of nations' (ca. 1750-1914) and, with it, the rise of nationalism within the Western modernist framework (cf. ch 3). Times of disunity, sometimes even long ones, mark the histories of many 'nations'. They do not preclude genuine nationhood from having "emerged" in the period(s) prior to such disunity nor from it being genuinely sustained throughout those periods. Whatever disunity there was in the Kazakh case—and we must certainly acknowledge some—the fact that it was ever set in tension with desires and strivings for national unity only serves to prove the point. The Kazakhs laid the genuine foundations of their nationhood (i.e. ethnic-based statehood) in the 15th and 16th centuries. These served as the pillar and guide of that nationhood in all ensuing eras.

'O, My Nation!'

With that in view, mention must be made of the forces significantly shaping Kazakh (ethno)national identity and giving rise to Kazakh heroes in the era of conflict with the Zhungarians or 'Oyrats' (ca. 1690-1758). It was a period of extreme hardship and tragedy when the Kazakhs felt themselves on the very edge of destruction. Indeed, it is known in Kazakh as 'aktaban shubirindi' or 'barefoot wandering' since many were left homeless and starving with no shoes on their feet. It is also described by the phrase 'alkakul sulama' or 'circle of dead bodies around the lake', depicting the many who died even as they dragged themselves near the lake shores in search of water and other nourishment during this era. These terms are applied specifically to the years 1723-28, but also function to describe the entire era. "There is not a Kazakh who does not know the song of mourning 'O, My Nation!' which emerged in these difficult years."[132] Indeed, it is the first song of many hundreds whose lyrics are given in the 2002 publication entitled *Kazakh Songs*, which is part of the 'Precious Heritage Series'. The Kazakh title is 'Yelim-ai!' It is a 'folk song' or 'song of the people' which is etched in the national memory. It goes like this:

> They come, moving down from Karatau (Black Mountain),
> Every time they move, a young horse*,
> [having lost in war the child
> who should be riding it], comes along empty.
> O my nation, O my nation!
>
> It is clear that being cut off
> from the people and nation is an evil [thing],

The youth come along glossy-eyed
and tear-filled in [their] black eyes.
O my nation, O my nation!

This time is what kind of time;
it's a long [hard] time,
O be again once more the time as long before.
O my nation, O my nation!

Sons from their fathers,
daughters from [mothers] in-laws are cut off,
I shall make flow the tears of [my] eyes and form a lake.
O my nation, O my nation!

This time is what kind of time;
it's a time [of life] cut short,
a time when the bird of happiness has flown far away.
O my nation, O my nation!

Dirt and dust storm down from the blue heavens,
more wicked than the winter in January
[with] its cold days.
O my nation, O my nation![133]

The use of the term "nation" (Kzk. "yel") as the central refrain throughout this song should be well noted.[134] "This time is what kind of time?" It is an important time in the *ongoing* formation of Kazakh ethno*national* identity, a formation which included deep reflection on their 'nationhood' amidst struggles to regain inner national unity while defending 'the land of the Kazakhs' from outside foreign invasion in the late 17th and early 18th centuries.

Kenesari and 'the National Liberation Struggles of the Kazakh People Against Russian Colonialism'

And with that we come to the second period, that of Kazakh (ethno)national development and (ethno)nationalist movements occurring under and in reaction to both Tsarist (1731-1917) and Soviet (1920-1991) Russian domination. We have already encountered (in ch 5) that it is here we enter the most controversial realm of Kazakh history, especially with respect to the question of relations between the pre-Russian Kazakh State, its development under and during both phases of the Russian period (i.e. Tsarist and Soviet) and its identity and standing in the post-Russian era. To expand on an earlier quote from Vucinich (in Olcott 1987:xvi), he notes:

> The most important questions in this connection are interpretations of historical significance of the Kazakh submission to Russian rule and the significance of the Kazakh anti-Russian movements . . . . The essence of the problem is whether the Kazakh entry into Russia was a Russian 'conquest' or a 'lesser evil'—that is, a release from feudal oppression, hence a 'lesser evil'.

"The Kazakh entry into Russia" refers to the 'agreements' made between the Kazakhs and Russians between 1731-42 by each of the three Kazakh leaders. These were arranged in connection with the Kazakh request for Russian 'protection' against the Zhungars, the essence of which from the Kazakh vantage point was assistance in defending their homeland against the Zhungarian attacks. It was not an invitation for the Russians to come take over their land; that was precisely the thing they were seeking assistance against. One's view on this matter corresponds directly to one's view on "the significance of the Kazakh anti-Russian movements." Note also that the 'conquest' versus 'lesser evil' interpretations in connection to Tsarist Russian domination are especially concerned with later Soviet views on this whole problem, hence the Marxist idea of 'release from *feudal* oppression'. While they did go back and forth depending on the occasion, the Soviets for the most part took the 'conquest' view in the earlier part of their reign when they were still trying to wean the national peoples away from Tsarist control and win their allegiance to the Soviet vision. *They did this because it resonated in the hearts of most of the 'conquered' peoples, i.e. it was essentially the view of the conquered peoples.* But after those conquered peoples realized that they had been re-conquered by the Soviets and so began aiming their former anti-Russian Tsarist hostilities at the Russian Soviets, the Soviets realized that stressing such interpretations only added fuel to (ethno)nationalist fires which had already been burning from long decades and even centuries before. And so they stressed the more positive choice of a 'lesser evil'. Beyond this, we have already covered the main problems relating to 'borders' and rightful possession of land and the significance of those questions in relation to the development of Kazakh nationhood under the Soviets (in the last chapter).

With those matters properly in view, we can move on to look at the ethnonational resistance movements themselves. Again, they should in no way be taken to imply that Kazakh (ethno)national identity was first 'conceived' (cf. 'genesis' or 'ethnogenesis') in mere reaction to or as a product of Russian colonialism. They should rather be viewed as efforts to revive, strengthen and defend an already existing identity which had over 200 years of socio-political self-governance 'under its belt', even if it *includes* times of *measured* disunity between the three main tribes.[135] This identity, likewise, embraces an even deeper historical heritage of religion, culture and language going back hundreds upon hundreds of years.

As E. Valikhanov covers, then, in his article on "National Liberation Struggles of the Kazak People Against Russian Colonialism," these struggles include the early efforts at resistance in the NW regions in 1783-97 under Batir Srim Datov, the mutually supportive struggles of 1820-35 under Zholaman Tlenshiev and 1824-36 under Sarzhan Kasimuhli as well as the joint efforts of Isatai Taimanov and Mahambet Utemisov in the western regions of Kazakhstan from 1836-1840.[136]

But the aspirations of all of these movements, and the many smaller ones across the then colonized *nation*, were ultimately though only temporarily fulfilled in the decade long struggle from 1837-47 under Kenesari Kasimuhli (1802-1847). He was the grandson of the great Kazakh khan Abilai (1711-81) and he succeeded in *re*uniting the three Kazakh 'tribes' in the stand against Russian rule. He was "elected khan of the whole Kazakh people in 1841" and is thus counted the last khan of the Kazakh khanate before a Russian provincial governing system was instituted on the Kazakh Steppe.[137] This event restored a national unity whose desire remained alive, if not in outward political circumstances, certainly in many Kazakh hearts since the original 'golden age' of the khanate between 1488-1580.

Olcott quotes Kenesari, who certainly bemoans his people's condition, saying: "We the children of the Kazakhs, what would we be if we had unity? Until now we have been split, because we have no unity?" (1993:65). But there are plenty of national leaders who have bemoaned there own people's lack of unity without making them forfeit the genuine status of nationhood. Indeed, an overly literal interpretation of this obviously poetic genre would be unreasonable. The sentiments of Kenesari's expressions here are very near to those we shall encounter later in the poem-songs of the Alash Orda writers. Besides, as just noted, he ultimately succeeded in *re*-uniting the three Kazakh tribes and was made khan over all of them.

As Vucinich (in Olcott 1993:xvi) notes, Kenesari "was at first viewed as a leader of a 'progressive' native endeavor to win liberation from Tsarist oppression, but later the same movement was rejected and assessed as a reactionary undertaking." As just pointed out above, both interpretations were Soviet, one in the early Soviet period when they sought to distinguish themselves from the Tsarists and emphasized promises of helping the Kazakhs achieve their national independence, the other in the later Soviet period when they realized that such interpretations only served to fan still burning embers of desire for liberation from Russian rule, *Tsarist or Soviet*, back to flame. Here again, the original Soviet interpretation of the event actually 'rode on the back of' the Kazakh view.

It still remains a Kazakh view today as, for example, Zh. Kasimbaev demonstrates in his 2002 article on "The Ethnonational Independence Movement of the Kazakh People Led by Kenesari Kasimuhli." He makes clear that Kenesari, when conducting his campaign, "set before himself the [clear] intention of *restoring the territorial solidarity and independence . . . of the Kazakh nation*. Before commencing any armed revolt he sent letters on numerous occasions to the rulers of the Russian empire setting forth the required demands."[138] Olcott confirms this, saying: "In his [1838] letter he argued that the rule of the Kazakhs should be returned to the Kazakhs themselves and the institution of the khan restored."[139]

Although in the end unsuccessful, Kenesari led the most important, and by far, the largest 19th century Kazakh national independence movement. In the words of one post-Soviet Kazakh account: "The ethnonational independence uprising lead by Kenesari Kasimuhli—which was a struggle on behalf of his own people's independence and freedom, with its impact upon the political situations of Russia and neighboring states as well as Kazakhstan's inner life, distinguished by its extended duration and great reach, and likewise its persevering determination—is found to be a most noteworthy event of great significance within the history of the Kazakh nation."[140]

'Awake, Kazakh':
The Kazakh Jadidist National Movement

Taking its start even earlier and running parallel to this would be the other great Kazakh national resistance movement, one which took the route of education and cultural-political activism as opposed to armed confrontation. This was the Kazakh branch of the Turkist-Jadidist reform movement (1820-

1920) treated so masterfully in Sabit Shildebai (2002), *Turkic Nationalism and the Ethnonational Independence Movement in Kazakhstan.*[141] It was during this movement that such great national scholars as the father of modern Kazakh language-based education Ibirai Altinsarin (1841-1889) and the great Kazakh poet-prophet Abai Kunanbai-uhli (1845-1904) emerged. Altinsarin promoted Russian studies as part of a Kazakh curriculum and was among the first to recommend a change to the Cyrillic from the Arabic script for the Kazakh language.[142] In this, he shared much in common with Abai, who went so far as to advocate that:

> One should study Russian; wisdom and cattle [raising] and scholarship—the Russians have them all. In order to avoid their harm[ful ways, yet] partake of their profits, one must know their language, studies and scholarship. For that they [themselves] knew the world's languages, this is how it was [achieved]. If you study their language, your inner-eyes will be enlightened. The person who knows the language and skills of someone [else] will with that enter into equal standing with them; he will not have to plead [for help] and be debased [with] exceeding shame. [Such] knowledge, it is even beneficial for religion. . . . Russian learning and culture are the keys to the world; for the one who knows this the world will be brought down to him with much less expense.[143]

But the idea that Altinsarin or Abai (and even Shokan Ualihanov, 1830-65) were agents of the Russians, mere propaganda tools whose 'national hero' status was created and used by especially the Soviets to promote their agenda of 'the superior Soviet person' (which was essentially a continuation of the old Tsarist agenda of 'russification') does not hold. Abai and company were Jadidists, not Russian cultural-political agents, even though the Russians used them to accomplish their own aims. Abai critiqued his people in true Turkic-Jadid heart and style, admiring and emulating Russian cultural-political achievement but applying it to and safeguarding their own national Kazakh-Turkic heart and heritage. He thus proclaims in his thirty-eighth 'Word':

> The mullahs of this (present) time are enemies to the name of (Muslim) scholarship. . . . The learning of scholarship these days is in the tradition of the old medreses (or Muslim religious schools),

they have no profit for the present time. . . . Choosing to remain uninformed of this world's scientific knowledge is great [and] harmful (darkened) ignorance, it is reproved in the Qur'an.[144]

As N. Nurtazina (2002:175, *Kazak Culture and Islam*) notes regarding the Jadidist admiration and borrowing of Russian and European culture: "Even though it sounds like a paradox, it turned out necessary to learn and embrace many things from another culture in order to save Islam and [our] ethnonational identity." It is a clear Jadid perspective and approach which, in spite of its critique of 'old' traditional Islam, may even be heir to a deeper Islamic tradition of critique going back to the glory of Islamic scholarship which flourished in Central Asia in the middle ages.[145]

Regardless, Abai is rightly honored today as a Kazakh national hero, indeed one who stands out as 'a Kazakh of Kazakhs', representing historic Kazakh identity in the modern era. In this regard, it is to be noted that he yearned for his people and nation to be wise and righteous. He addresses good government established on the precedent of historic Kazakh statehood enshrined in "all the laws passed down from our forefathers," saying:

> What we mean by this [aforementioned] authority is not something which any [randomly] elected person is capable of among our Kazakh people. For [the proper execution of] this [authority], it is essential to know Kasim khan's 'Straight Path', Yesim khan's 'Ancient Pathway' and Az Tauke khan's 'Seven Decrees' which came in the daily council on top of Mount Ash. But since the times have changed, he would have to be a person who could discern which of these ancient ideas may have become outdated, no longer standing in harmony with this new era, and in their place [offer] sound judgments put forth [with] full measured authority; such people are rare [however], if there are even any [around].[146]

Kasim khan ruled from 1511-1523, Yesim khan from 1598-1628 and Tauke khan from 1680-1718. Together they mark over 200 years of 'national law' (cf. 'constitution') in Kazakh political tradition. The national laws which they drew up for their people—just like Al-Farabi's (870-950) works on *Road Map to Happiness, Policies of Citizenship* and *Outlook of the Residents of the Merciful City* as well as Zhusip Balasaguni's (11th century) *Wisdom of Royal Glory*—were all still useful for the Kazakh nation in Abai's day. The Kazakhs hold this same view today.[147]

But, as evidenced in Abai's quote, neither Abai nor the Kazakhs entertain 'archaic' ideas about such things, as if they were seeking to go 'backwards in time' and/or restore and preserve an ancient, inflexible 'monolithic' cultural-national identity. Long before Bob Dylan, they like many others understood that "the times they were a changing" so that any "ancient ideas [which] may have become outdated, no longer standing in harmony with this new era" must have new ones offered "in their place." That is, they must be 'modified' in accordance with the times.[148] Here again, Abai's genuine Jadidist (lit. 'new method') roots are revealed. These 'new method' roots remain alive today. They are real roots which go beyond mere 'ethnosymbolic' reinterpretation and its seeming Leninist-Stalinist type idea of 'ancient in form, modern in content' to actually draw on the ancient content itself, though carefully adapting it to the modern age. It thus retains an actual grounding, not a mere appearance of one, in its own real history.

Sharing these same Jadidist roots with Abai was the 'Alash Orda' with its 'Alash party' for political "democratic" independence and sovereignty (1905-1920). This movement gave rise to such national heroes as Alihan Bukeihanuhli (1866-1937), Akmet Baitursinuhli (1873-1938), Sultanmahmut Toraigirov (1893-1920), Magzhan Zhumabaev (1893-1938), Zhusipbek Aimauituhli (1889-1931), Mirzhakip Dulatuhli (1885-1935), Muhammedzhan Seralin, and Shakirim Kudaiberdi-uhli (1858-1931). It is probably Mirzhakip Dulatuhli's stirring poem-song of 1909, 'Awake, Kazakh!', which can rightfully be called the 'national anthem' of this era. In the spirit of Kenesari Kasimuhli, though with a different 'call to arms', Dulatuhli made a passionate call for 'national awakening' when he pleaded:

> Open your eyes, awake, Kazakh, lift [your] head,
> Without passing the time* in darkness in futility.
> While [our] land is gone, [our] religion impoverished,
> [and our] condition desolate,
> My Kazakh, lying down now is not becoming [to you].
>
> Wretched Kazakh straying off in darkness,
> without the moon rising,
> or even his sun appearing, or the day dawning.
> How is it possible for a man
> who sees an unextinguished fire [still] burning
> to rise without sinking down into [his] soul?![149]

This was the spirit that resonated throughout the age. As soon as it was written, Dulatuhli's poem-song "passed from hand-to-hand, mouth-to-mouth, [and] in little time it took the reputation and glory of the poet to distant peoples in very far away [places]" (Ismagulov, ed, 2002:10). He contributed many poems and articles to the journals and newspapers which functioned as the mouthpieces of the Kazakh Jadidist movement, such as *Aikap* (1911-15), *Kazakh* (1913-18) and others. The impact of his heart and work remained strong, inspiring for example a poem in *Aikap* journal in 1914 entitled 'Arise, Kazakh'. It apparently was written by its well known publisher and editor, one of Dulatuhli's close companions, Muhammedzhan Seralin. It reads:

> Arise now, Kazakh, from slumber,
> It's not the time to sleep, this hour*.
> [A life] built on strumming
> the dombra [guitar], [and] amusement
> That time is gone, never to come [again].
>
> Be not lazy, my Kazakh,
> Laziness is no profit to manhood.
> You may one day descend to hell,
> If you become ignorant [and] unresourceful.
>
> Don't go about left to regret,
> sons of six alash Kazakhs.
> Gather into crowds [your] city, your land,
> It's been cut off, the exile* of the nation.
>
> Thinking past times shall come again,
> Don't shed the tears of your eyes in vain.
> Thinking the bullet you fired will fire again,
> Don't exhaust [your] eyes, don't wait in vain.[150]

This independence movement would actually carry us all the way into the 1930s and Stalin's sweeping executions of the 'intelligentsia' for their involvement with "nationalist" causes (which explains the short lifespans of the Kazakh national heroes listed above). It should be noted in connection with this particular Kazakh nationalist movement—i.e. the "Kazakh political party" (or 'Alash party') and its efforts to seek "an independent state" within a "democratic republic"—that the governing body which the Kazakh 'elites' proposed made clear concession for the rights of non-Kazakhs then living in 'the land of the Kazakhs', including the provision that up to two-fifths (2/5) of the governing body itself could consist of non-Kazakh members.[151] Today's government in Kazakhstan, likewise, allows for fair participation by non-Kazakh peoples who share together in rightful citizenship with the indigenous Kazakh people. It even allows for participation by international advisors and others, though it retains its own rights to full national sovereignty and independence.

Whatever exact points and measures of continuity-discontinuity there may be, the Alash Party's efforts to rebuild Kazakh statehood in the early 20th century are properly seen as tied to the earlier efforts of Kenesari Kasimuhli, with both of these looking back to the previous generations of the Kazakh State all the way to its founding in the mid-15th century. Kenesari and the Alash Party both shared the basic view of Abai which looked back to a centuries long tradition of Kazakh national law and government to establish Kazakh government in their own day based, not on an inflexible archaic view, but a conservative reformist approach. The government of Kazakhstan today continues this tradition, looking back to Abai as well as the founding fathers of the Alash independence movement and their writings, and even beyond them to Kenesari and the previous generations of the Kazakh State, finding in them inspiration as well as guidance for rebuilding the Kazakh nation in the wake of Russian imperial collapse. Whatever Steven Sabol had in mind, then, in naming his 1999 doctoral dissertation *Awake, Kazak! Russian Colonization of Central Asia and the Genesis of Kazak National Conscious*, we can be sure that the genesis of Kazakh national conscious goes well back beyond the Alash efforts to *re-*establish an autonomous (or independent) "Kazakh government" and 'nation'.

The December 1986 Demonstrations:
'For Every People Their Own Prince'

In moving ahead, we will leap beyond the '1916 Uprising' and the later uprisings against Stalin's collectivization campaigns—all of which mark continuing Kazakh desires and efforts to resist and ultimately break free from Russian rule—and come to the end of 'the Russian period'. This would bring us to the 1986 December nationalist uprising in Almaty which was sparked by the former Kazakh SSR ruler, D. Konaev, being replaced with a Russian leader named Golbin. The uprising resulted in the clash of Soviet (including of course Kazakh) police with some 1000-2000 Kazakhs proclaiming in Republic Square outside the Presidential Palace 'For every people their own prince'. This latter declaration indicates that the uprising should not be taken as any kind of indicator of simple 'anti-Russian' attitudes on the part of everyday Kazakhs. It is not a problem of Russians and Kazakhs living together in Kazakhstan (cf. DeLorme 1999:92). It is simply a fact of ethnonational history that ethnonational groups do not wish to have 'foreigners' ruling over them. It is a sentiment going long back into the history of peoples and nations, reflected even in the Law of Moses, which declared:

> When you come to the land which the LORD your God is giving you, and possess it and dwell in it, and say, 'I will set a king over me like all the nations that are around me,' you shall surely set a king over you whom the LORD your God chooses; one from among your [own] kin you shall set as king over you; you may not set a foreigner over you, who is not your kin (Deut 17:14-15).

There has been a great deal of debate, however, over whether the uprising should properly be labeled 'nationalist' or not. Indeed, after reviewing the matter it was officially labeled 'nationalist' by the Soviet government in 1987, but that declaration was later publicly withdrawn and the whole thing written off to untamed youth under the influence of alcohol and drugs. Of course, being labeled 'nationalist' under Soviet policy was to be 'black listed', it was one of the most heinous crimes of betrayal against the Union which one could commit, so even the Kazakhs protested against labeling it 'nationalist', at least according to Soviet standards of the time. Those standards still have deep influence upon interpretations today, even among the Kazakh people.[152]

But after independence a fresh look at Kazakh history, especially by the Kazakhs themselves, was and remains in order. Many now look with pride on the event as a clear expression of their ethnonational aspirations for freedom, that is, they look upon it as proper 'love of one's ethnonational people' ('ultzhandilik') or even more straightforwardly as 'ethnonationalism' ('ultshildik', lit. 'passion for one's ethnonational people'). G. Yesim (2003:16) looks back on the event in this way in his work entitled *The Price of Freedom*:

> ... the 1986 December event comes to my mind. After the December event, an official decision of the Soviet Central Committee was released; in it the clarification of [the event as] "Kazakh (ethno)nationalism" was made. We all disputed over their

saying "the Kazakhs are (ethno)nationalists." Actually, in [that] decision our enemies properly clarified who we are for us. What is wrong about (ethno)nationalism? Being (ethno)nationalist is wrong for those at the center [of control, i.e. Moscow]. For us it is right. The word '(ethno)nationalist' [lit. 'passionate for one's nation/ethnos'] is the word 'peoplist' [lit. 'passionate for one's people']; if we had not been (ethno)nationalist, then we would not have longed for [national] sovereignty, we would not have attained it. The action of the youth was right. The foremost idea of being an independent state is being (ethno)nationalist. We came to define (ethno)nationalist as internationalism's counterpart, that is, with the mistaken Leninist [based] understanding. When the [heart of the] matter comes to light, the 1986 movement was a manifestation of (ethno)nationalism.

Yesim elsewhere devotes an entire article to the December 1986 event entitled "If Kazakhs are not (ethno)nationalists, then who?"[153] We express our essential agreement.

We should perhaps note here that our reason for placing the 'ethno' part of '(ethno)nationalism' in parentheses is because in the Kazakh mind 'ethnic nation' and 'geo-political nation' are *not* dichotomized. It seems the best way to get the full sense of both dimensions across to the Western mind, i.e. the combined ethnic and political dimensions of their 'nationalism'.[154] We should also not fail to recognize something very important here: namely, this position of the Kazakh 'elites' (and many 'common, everyday' Kazakhs) does *not* build off of Soviet ideas of nationality policy, i.e. it is not founded upon the ideals about nationality which the Soviets 'inculcated' in the national peoples and their 'elites', an idea which the standard 'Soviet fiat' view (covered in previous chapters) bases itself upon. This view of the Kazakhs rejects outright the Soviet view and rises up to break free of its chains, to recapture a passion which resided in their hearts before the Soviets (or Tsarists) came along and suppressed such aspirations. They simply found new freedom for unhindered expression with the collapse of the Union.

It may be said that the December 1986 (ethno)national uprising was a key turning point on the path to establishing the modern Kazakh nation-state. It cleared the way for the appointment of a Kazakh, Nursultan Nazarbaev, as head of the nation in 1989. The course of the nation's development soon led to the Kazakh 'Language Law of 1989', the declaration of sovereignty in October 1990 and the declaration of independence in December of 1991.

Ethnic-based Loyalty in
Modern Independent Kazakhstan
(and Central Asia)

This would lead us into the third period of Kazakh (ethno)national development and (ethno)nationalist movements in historical perspective, namely the era of independence (1991-present). As declared in the second line of the preamble to the constitution, today's sovereign, independent nation of Kazakhstan is a nation which "establishes [its] statehood upon the ancient-indigenous land of the Kazakhs." In doing this, Kazakhstan ensures the rightful place of the Kazakh people and their language, culture and history in their own historic homeland while at the same time "understanding ourselves [i.e. itself] to be a peace-loving civil society dedicated to the aims of liberty, equality and concord".[155] It reaffirms this foundation and essential orientation in its national anthem when it declares the "Merciful Great Fatherland, the steppeland of the Kazakhs" to be the "sacred cradle of concord and friendship" which "honors" and "embraces in [its] bosom the children of all" ethnonational groups living in its midst. This is the foundation for understanding the self-determined nature of modern Kazakhstan and any promises it has or has not made regarding its nationhood.

In this period, as in all previous periods, at least two major *dimensions* of the "single ethnic unity" of the one Kazakh people and its ethnic-based loyalty to 'the Land of the Kazakhs' may be discerned: social (i.e. popular) *and* political. And these 'social and political' dimensions make the compound term 'socio-political' very meaningful. While it has taken on new dimensions and emphases in new contexts, 'ethnic-based loyalty to the Land of the Kazakhs', which formed early on in their history and underlay the ancient Kazakh State, has not fundamentally changed for the Kazakhs today. They still view both people and land as ancestral, with authority being determined largely by right of descent and inheritance *at the (ethno)national level*. Thus, the 'state' (i.e. the aspect of political rule of the land) becomes intimately linked with ethnonational identity so that there is indeed a 'Kazakh-predominated leadership' in the nation today. But they do not form an 'elite' who 'manipulates' the views and attitudes of the common Kazakh in the streets. Both ethnosocial and ethnopolitical

nationalism become intertwined and complimentary—indeed inseparable—
though the two remain distinct at the same time in their particular emphases
and (some of their) goals. Official as well as non-official, academic, political,
and 'common' peoples share in both the ethnosocial and ethnopolitical forms
of Kazakh nationalism (though participation in the political is more restricted,
of course, yet not limited to politicians and scholars). In both of these *dimensions*
there are three or four major emphases: language, culture (including traditions
and customs as well as social structure), religion and land. And these would all
in turn include historical aspects making '(ethno)national history' a
foundational issue in all other dimensions of their '(ethno)national identity'.

Concluding Thoughts

The dimensions of Kazakh (as well as other Central Asian peoples')
ethnonational *human identity* involve issues of ethnonational *human rights*
which form an integral part of the international human rights agenda in the
modern global age. All such rights must be pursued and resolved in accordance
with the (ethno)national as well as international and interethnic history of the
states and peoples involved. The impact of colonialism and the questions of
cultural, linguistic, religious, social and political restitution and restoration
must be taken into account as part of the historically-grounded resolution.

This book aims at *Rethinking Kazakh and Central Asian Nationhood.* It
defends the rights of national language, culture and history as well as primary
political control for the indigenous ethnonational groups in their historic
homelands in Kazakhstan and Central Asia. While our treatment of the issues
makes no claims to being exhaustive, it addresses key points of debate over
Kazakh and Central Asian ethnonational identity within the broader context
of academic debate over the proper nature and relation of ethnic nationhood
and political nationhood in the modern global age. We expose a rather 'low'
view of Kazakh and Central Asian nationhood among (Euro-American and
Euro-Slavic) Western modernist scholars, one which recurs like a chorus
throughout their works and results in negative and oppositional attitudes toward
the rights of the Kazakh and other Central Asian *nations* in their post-colonial
context. Important contributions to (ethno)national development were certainly
made in the former colonial context in both its Tsarist and Soviet Russian
forms. Nonetheless, far from 'creating' ethnonational identities in Central Asia
via 'ethno-engineering', the colonial powers and presence significantly oppressed,
broke down and worked against the ethnonational identity and rights of the
indigenous peoples and their nations. The post-colonial context has now ushered
those peoples and their nations into 'the international world' and has brought
them face to face with a 'Western modernist assault' which is proving its

determination to continue the same calculated stance against their ethnonational identity and rights with its deep-seeded convictions of "civic-based patriotism" inherently opposed and calculated to work against any type of "ethnic-based loyalty" in relation to political statehood. This Western modernist view is little else than a modified Marxist approach to ethnicity and national identity applied to Western ideas and ideals of democratic nationhood in the post-World War II, post-Civil Rights, post-Apartheid era of the late 20th, early 21st century.

This work has been especially concerned with the Kazakh 'ethnic nation' and its history in relation to today's 'political nation' of Kazakhstan. It provides an overall reliable framework grounded in essential continuity and unity for interpreting its history and identity. Varying degrees of emphasis and difference of view (i.e. 'diversity' as well as 'disunity'), along with transitions and transformations of cultural-religious, social as well as political structure, *within* the *one* Kazakh nation and its history are recognized. But these are not viewed as grounds for breaking apart *the one nation's continuous (i.e. 'perennial') historical development, of which the modern nation-state of Kazakhstan is an integral part.* While recognizing dynamic interaction with and influence from other sources, Kazakh ethnonational history and identity is seen as predominantly *self*-determined, not as a mere mental 'imagination' or 'invented tradition', but one grounded in a historical, linguistic, cultural, religious, social, economic and political reality which is a genuine, integral and natural part of human history and identity within the created world. This overall framework supplies the proper basis for understanding and interpreting the further details of that history and nationhood and emerging with a deeper understanding, respect and appreciation for it.

This work thus provides the proper basis upon which to approach the questions of rights in relation to language, culture, history, religion and politics in modern independent Kazakhstan, one which values and honors all ethnonational groups living there today as rightful citizens and sharers in that history and nationhood, yet which gives proper place to the Kazakh people along with their national language, culture and history in their own historic homeland.

—Appendix—

CLARIFYING PARADIGMS OF ETHNONATIONAL IDENTITY

We have no intention in this work of suggesting an overly rigid, inflexible idea of ethnonational groups and their corresponding ethnic cultures, as for instance in the case of Oswald Spengler and his 'closed-system' theory of culture in his classic work on *The Decline of the West*. We likewise share due concern for "the reifying tendencies of primordialism" and recognize that there have been and *potentially* still can be "politically dangerous ideas of organic nationalism" (A. Smith 2001:77). We should take special care to avoid sociobiological versions of ethnicity. Notwithstanding the ethical questions involved then, we acknowledge plainly that ethnonational 'people groups' die out and new ones form from a mixing of pre-existing ones as well as that 'cultures' and 'civilizations' have overlap (i.e. 'shared culture') and sometimes 'hazy borders'. Likewise, problems of kinship, language, religion and land associations exist, sometimes rather deeply. However, these problems are not sufficient cause for giving up on or, worse yet, denying the reality of 'nations' and their nationhood, especially in light of what has been said concerning their organic foundations and nature in human history. This is a historical reality which is affirmed by the Jewish-Christian-Muslim tradition. While not sharing his 'ethnosymbolist view, A. Smith's (1986:209ff) observation is significant here: "*Ethnie* and nations are not fixed and immutable entities . . . ; but neither are they completely malleable and fluid processes and attitudes, at the mercy of every outside force. . . . [W]e can treat *ethne* as both mutable and durable at the same time, and ethnicity as both fluctuating and recurrent in history." In *The Nation in History* he likewise affirms "the durability and the transformation of ethnicity in history and the continuing power and persistence of nations and nationalism at the start of the third millennium" (2001:77).

Here would also be the place to note the intimate relation between the socio-political and the ethical-moral paradigms of ethnicity, nations and nationalism (set forth in ch 2). In line with our earlier comments regarding the need to look beyond humanity for help in understanding and responding to these issues, we believe that it is only an organicist-creationist paradigm which can provide the true and proper foundation for not only valuing, but actively, intentionally and whole-heartedly seeking to nurture, preserve and protect (ethno)national identity within human society in balance with our individual and international-global identities. It thus leads properly to 'the Paradigm of Positive Activism: (Ethno)Nationalistic Internationalism'. Perennialism can at best lead to a fair valuing, i.e. a half- or three-quarters-hearted concern for (ethno)national identity, but it leaves us without the firm foundation for an uncompromising active pursuit of (ethno)national well-being in balance with concern for individual and international-global identities. Thus, perennialism logically results in either 'the Paradigm of Perfect Neutrality: Preferred Internationalism/Globalism' or 'the Paradigm of Positive Passivism: Popular Internationalism'.

Here, too, we should not fail to recognize the common ground upon which the perennialist and (Western) modernist paradigms of nations and nationalism both stand. They both ground ethnicity, nations and nationalism in the circumstantial processes of history itself. The only real difference is that perennialists argue for the perennial presence (i.e. 'long duration') of nations and nationalism in history. They do not limit nations and nationalism to 'modern' (i.e. post-18th or 19th century) history, with its corresponding idea that nations and nationalism are uniquely related to the historical processes which led to a transition in society from (European) feudalism to industrialization and modernization (i.e. modernity). The latter is the hallmark of the modernist position, a hallmark which it shares with the Marxist view of ethnicity, nations and nationalism, indeed a hallmark which Western modernism seems to have taken over from Marx with the only distinction being that their application of it is to the 'union' of all ethnic groups within civic democratic nation-states (cf. 'e pluribus unum') instead of a socialist-communist 'union' (i.e. the former Soviet Union). Nonetheless, *because perennialists and modernists both ground ethnicity, nations and nationalism in history itself, they are both willing, indeed logically obliged, to embrace the idea that historical circumstances may lead to the dissolution and ultimate disappearance of 'nations' just as much as they have led to their appearance and sustenance in history.*

Along with the difference in view concerning the depth and duration of nations in history, the other key differences between these two views would be these. First, perennialists have a harder time believing that the dissolution and disappearance of nations will really take place by mere virtue of their perennial presence throughout the long duration of human history, at least up to the present. Second, modernists lay far more stress upon the psychological dimension of '(ethno)national consciousness', indeed to the point that many of them insist that (ethno)national identity is little more than a psychologically (i.e. mentally) constructed or fabricated identity based in nothing but myths, falsehoods and human imagination. Such a view hardly offers any positive support for valuing and preserving (ethno)national identity in human society. And this is why it logically leads to 'the Paradigm of Negative Intolerance: Modernist Civic Nationalism/Globalism' or, at best, to 'the Paradigm of Negative Tolerance: Modified Civic Nationalism/Globalism'.

Endnotes

Foreword, Reviews & Preface

[1]   These reviews are based on and also appear in the Kazakh edition (2005, *Kazak pen ortaazialiktarding ulttigi men eldigin korgau*), though some of them have been edited down in size for inclusion in the English. The portions edited out involve mainly parts simply summarizing the book's content. Slight modifications and clarifications occur in a few minor places with respect to exact wording and order. All translation and editing has been done in consultation and full agreement with the original authors.

[2]   Lit. "places me in a streambed of hope" ("umit arnasina salip otirgan").

[3]   The reviewer is not basing this latter idea of Central Asia descending into ethnic wars on our work, he is clearly drawing from other readings he himself has done on this issue.

[4]   The quote is from Porkhomovsky (in Naumkin, ed., 1994:21). It is taken from the main text of the book.

[5]   For those concerned for literalism, we are quite aware that this rendering is 'loose'. Also, note that most all of the translations from Kazakh into English are our own, except perhaps DeLorme's. We do not include transliterations for longer texts; the original sources are cited and can be accessed by those interested, just as in any other research quest. The transliterations which we do provide in this work, mainly of shorter texts or book and article titles, follow the 'Weller Arbitrary System' and not any standardized system. Our reasons for this are simple: no single world standard has yet been developed. Anyone who knows Kazakh well enough to read and understand it should be able figure out the actual words lying behind the transliterations in 98% of the cases and will also know how they should be pronounced and who or what they are referring to historically, etc. If they do not and are really in need of knowing a term here or there or clarifying a source, they can drop us an email or do their own homework. Those who do not know the language will not need to concern themselves with the whole problem

---

anyway. And beginning or intermediate students should not expect this kind of book to help them struggle through their own problems of limited grammatical knowledge; other works are designed for that, including our own 450 pp book entitled *Using Kazakh Grammar* [*Kazakh tilining grammatikasin mengeru*]. Unfortunately, variants of Kazakh and Central Asian terms in English are numerous across the scholarly world; we will try not to increase them and will likewise strive for consistency of transliteration *within* this work; but no attempt has been made herein to coordinate with other systems because again they themselves are not coordinated with one another. Indeed, some are not even coordinated with themselves! One problem arising from this is that our choice of transliteration may at times be different from the choice of sources we quote from. We have chosen to leave all transliterations within quotes as originally given. This conflict is impossible to avoid because we quote from various scholars. E.g. in our treatment of 'Kasim khan' (our rendering) we quote from two scholars who each use different renderings, in the one case, 'Qasim Khan' and the other 'Kasym-khan'. This whole problem of English transliterations and translations of Kazakh, including the added confusion of having them come via Russian, is currently being addressed in the doctoral research of Nursaule Rsalieva of Kozha Akmet Yasawi University in Turkistan, Kazakhstan. As for a final note of personal opinion on the subject, we do not personally care for the attempt to assign one (or two) Latin letter(s) to one Kazakh letter and force its usage on every occasion; phonemic contexts, especially from the pronunciation angle, sometimes call for variation because readers will naturally interpret the phonemic clusters according to their own deeply entrenched native language environment. Either that, or they must be expected to learn new phonemic values for letters, i.e. essentially learn a new alphabet, re-assigning new and different phonemic values to letters they are already very familiar with, something which is simply too cumbersome and confusing in our opinion, at least until a single world standard for transliterating Kazakh at both the phonemic as well as terminological level can be agreed upon. One special case we will mention is that of 'Kazakh' itself. The government went from originally using 'Kazakh', later to 'Kazak' and then back to 'Kazakh' in its official transliteration. Both forms are encountered in various works. Our system is to use 'Kazakh' unless it occurs in an English quote or book title. In those cases we have left it as given in the original English sources.

6   Anuar Omarov, assistant chief ed., *Ak Zhol Kazakhstan* (newspaper), No. 30 (152) 02 Sep 2005, p 2. By permission of the author and newspaper we have translated this brief article into English and posted it on the web ('www.ara-cahcrc.com/CAHCRC/nation-kzk-borders.pdf').

7   I am using the term 'Black' here simply because it is the term historically associated
with the movement. In general, American citizens of African heritage today are
more properly referred to as 'African-American' and we entirely respect and value
this identity as well as their heritage. We would be grateful if understanding were
granted to our use of the term 'Black' in relation to discussing the Civil Rights
Movement as well as other issues of African-American history in the course of
our treatment.

8   With Martin Luther King, Jr. as one of my primary heroes and models,
permit it to be clarified here that, while his contributions to Altaic / Central
Asian scholarship certainly deserve and receive our attention and even
admiration in the broader study of Kazakh ethnonational history and identity,
it is not my purpose or goal to follow in the tradition of N.I. Il'minskii in his
approach to and efforts among the Altaic / Central peoples (see esp. Geraci,
"Going Abroad or Going to Russia? Orthodox Missionaries in the Kazakh
Steppe, 1881-1917," in Geraci and Khodarkovsky, eds., 2001, *Of Religion and
Empire*). Indeed, I sympathize greatly with the critique of Il'minskii and his
work by Muslim Kazakh scholars. I likewise have genuine concerns and even
criticisms, some rather deep ones at times, regarding (especially Western)
Christian missionary efforts in Central Asia, particularly those who display
little or no regard for ethnonational issues or, if they do, either insist on a
Western multiethnic understanding of things and/or follow more along the lines
of the exploitational model of Il'minskii and company, seeing history, culture,
language and other ethnonational identity issues primarily as 'tools' for conversion
to a heavily Westernized faith (cf. also the Leninist-Stalinist approach to
nationhood covered in ch 4). Nonetheless, I do not and cannot as a Christian
myself simply condemn Christian missions wholesale, not even in Central Asia.
I rather admire a good number of missionaries, particularly those who have
made and continue to make vital contributions to worthy cultural, social,
economic and even political causes in our world. Likewise, in spite of the
recent revisions to Kazakhstan's religious laws in July 2005 calling for more
restricted and tighter control on Christian and all religious activity in their
country (which I understand and generally support), the Kazakhstan government
does not ultimately forbid or condemn Christian or other religious missionary
activities either. But, even given the legal freedom to pursue such a path, as a
Western foreign scholar of general Christian persuasion who is attempting to
make genuine contributions to Kazakh and Central Asian nationhood in joint
cooperation and dialogue with national (as well as Western and other) scholars
of Muslim, Tengrist, secular and other persuasions, I choose not to engage in

proselytizing activities (i.e. 'missions' in the more narrow sense of the term). Propogation of and conversion to various faiths is ultimately something the nationals themselves will have to debate and carry out. As for myself, I see myself as much closer to the model of perhaps Jean-Paul Roux, the Catholic Turkologist, or Isman Kongir Mandoki, the Hungarian Christian scholar who participated as a Turkologist in, among other academic pursuits, the production of the *Kazakh Sovet Encyclopediasi* in the early 1970s. If I understand correctly, he is even buried in Almaty in the same cemetery as D.A. Konaev. He is honored each year across the nation on television, in schools, etc, on the occasion of his birthday. The Kazakh scholar Sultanmahmut Toraigirov (1893-1920) would also be a model who, as one professing 'the way of Jesus', participated in the social-national renewal movement together with 'the sons of Alash' at the turn of the 19th-20th century and is rightfully honored among the Kazakhs for his contribution to their cause. In the end, while not a 'missionary', in proper honor of God within my work and human society, I make no attempt to hide my faith from anyone. To the contrary, the fact of it has been known from the beginning of my presence in Kazakhstan where I am accepted properly as a scholar of history, religion and culture on those terms by the Kazakh national scholars—Muslim, Tengrist, secular and otherwise—with and under whom I work, study and write. In this, they demonstrate their genuine commitment to mutual respect and dialogue in the world of nations and its world religions and perhaps even exceed the West in this regard in their commitment to democratic principles (cf. e.g. 'The Congress on World and Traditional Religions' held in Astana in September 2003 under the direction of President Nazarbaev himself).

Chapter One

⁹   1994:29, 73. "Chapter Two: American Scholarship in the Post-World War II Era," which is a re-print of the article, "Nation-Building or Nation-Destroying?," *World Politics* 24, April 1972:319-55.

¹⁰   Mary Kate Simmons, ed., 1995, *Unrepresented Nations and Peoples Organization*, The Hague/London/Boston: Klumer Law International.

¹¹   Smith actually uses the terms 'modernist' and 'primordialist' in his earlier work (1986) *The Ethnic Origins of Nations* and 'modernist' and 'perennialist' in the later work (1999) on *Nationalism and Modernism*. First note that we use the term 'organicist' instead of 'primordialist' because of the latter term's rather negative connotations. Relatedly, our choice to use 'organicist' instead of 'perennialist', as will be clarified in more detail later in the main discussion, is because not all 'perennialists' are 'organicists', even though all 'organicists' are 'perennialists'. We

have chosen to use the term 'organicist' in order to properly include the 'organicist' features, which include the perennialist ones, while at the same time being careful to avoid falsely attributing them to perennialists. Both the organicist and perennialist paradigms clash with the modernist paradigm, so the basic issue at stake does not change. It seems that Smith shifted his own focus away from 'organicism' to 'perennialism' because 'organicism' on the whole has been largely abandoned in especially the last several decades. The reasons for these choices, shifts and clashes will become more evident as we move through the course of our study.

12 It is perhaps worth mentioning here that the position of one professor under whom we studied was (and perhaps remains) a rather 'hardcore' and classical western modernist. The professor demonstrated himself to be almost inflexible in his insistence that the 'nations' of today are unique and novel 'creations' which have no real likeness to 'nations' of antiquity. This of course is one of the standard dogmas of the western modernist view. And he had no desire to consider or even acknowledge the actual existence let alone possibility of any alternative positions. We are not exaggerating either. Indeed, he silenced us with no recourse or appeal when attempting to make a comparison of modern and ancient nations during discussions in class on one occasion. And he was so upset with our position and found it so disagreeable to his taste that he refused to finish reading our term paper, noting its unworthiness of being read with several exclamation marks somewhere beyond the half-way point. Of course, as it turns out, our position does indeed present serious challenges to the push for 'multiethnicity' and its corresponding ideal of 'multiculturalism', which happened to be the new direction which he (and at least a few others at the institution) were wishing to move people in. And in moving them in that direction, it was not coincidental that they suggested on repeated occasions that 'the time to move beyond a focus on ethnicity was upon us with the dawning of the global age'. Perhaps we should mention as well the 17-page heated email debate we found ourselves unexpectedly engaged in with another Western (post-)modernist scholar over these same basic issues. Likewise, there was the three-hour debate with yet another professor of political science from Britain teaching at a university in Central Asia while hosting a seminar on 'ethnicity, nations and nationalism' in his city in the spring of 2002. All of these 'clashes of paradigms' and the debates resulting from them involved the fundamental 'clash' between the organicist-perennialist and western modernist position. Thankfully, we always managed to keep things respectful, showing (at least in the latter two situations) proper patience and love amidst clear and very serious disagreements. We have definite and deep need of, first, just *understanding* the different paradigms.

Then, and only then, will we be in a position to begin discussing the issues reasonably and effectively with one another. Beyond that, perhaps God will work a miracle in bringing us to some kind of a point of agreement in our respective convictions.

13   The issue of Japan's colonialist takeover of Okinawa and other regions is definitely problematic. Likewise, the problem of the Ainu as an indigenous group in their midst is acknowledged. But these problems should not cloud the fact that the Japanese 'ethnic nation' provides the base for a Japanese 'political nation'. This has been true historically, even before such colonialist expansion and/or displacement of peoples occurred. With respect to the latter issues, our ensuing study would certainly have implications for our view on those matters.

14   Hutchinson and Smith 1996:v; emphasis added. Cf. the remarks of former U.S. President Bill Clinton, who "called ethnic hatred 'the most important issue in the whole world today'" (Burns 1999:1).

Chapter Two

15   Bohannan 1998:3, 18, quoted in Aasland, 2004:1, "Anthropology Addressing Ethnicity," (unpublished paper shared with the author; our gratitude for help in clarifying this important issue; emphasis added).

16   After personal discussions, Aasland (2004:1) verified this view with his own research, noting that: "Anthropologists generally present culture as a tool (Bohannan 1998:7). . . . The metaphors would lead us to believe that culture is something which we can take up and put down like a tool. Geertz confirms this interpretation when he says: 'As an interworked system of construable signs . . . , culture is not a power, something to which social events, behaviors, institutions, or processes can be causally attributed; it is a context, something within which they can be intelligibly—that is thickly, described' (Geertz 1973:14)."

17   Cf. the argument of C.S. Lewis regarding morals in *Mere Christianity*, where he distinguishes between the "is" and the "ought."

18   Cf. Smith 1986:210 on the Parmenidian and Heraclitan paradigms as it relates to the discussion of 'nations'.

19   See quote and surrounding discussion in Ch. 3 of Abdizhapar Abdakimuhli (1997:58), *A History of Kazakhstan*, who notes that the various genealogies of Kazakh tribes demonstrate, amongst other things, that the source-spring of not only the Kazakhs and Turks, but of all humanity is one and the same and that this points back to our human origins in Father Adam and Mother Eve.

20   United Nations High Commissioner for Human Rights, 1995:1, *Fact Sheet No. 9 (Rev. 1), The Rights of Indigenous Peoples*. Cf. again M. K. Simmons, ed., 1995,

Unrepresented Nations and Peoples Organization. (The U.N. *Fact Sheet* was originally referenced by DeLorme 1999:106-7; see discussion in ch 5).

Chapter Three

21 With regard to general Western influence, it is of interest that on the evening of June 26, 2001 NHK ('Nihon Ho-so Kyo-kai') Television network in Japan highlighted the 'global standards' of the economic market for appliances. The Japanese manufacturers *rightfully* complained that, although, the standards and quality of their products are exceptional, even higher than those of Europe and the USA, still the European standards act as 'global standards' and create difficulty and *inequalities* for Japanese exporters.

22 Quoted from an excerpt of Charles Tilley, 1975, *The Formation of National States in Western Europe* (Princeton, NJ: Princeton University Press) in Hutchinson and Smith, eds., 1994:252-3, *Nationalism*; emphasis added. Note that we intend this phrase and the acronym 'LPW' as a replacement for the traditionally used 'Old Testament' (cf. also 'Old Covenant') and its acronym 'OT'. The latter phrase goes back to at least Tertullian in the post-apostolic age, and even Paul himself (2Cor. 3). Nonetheless, in modern-day scholarship the usage of the traditional term 'OT' can create a measure of confusion by its ambiguity and multiple applications as well as potential theological assumptions. One of those possible theological assumptions is that the (old) 'covenant' is directly and fully equated with 'Torah', i.e. 'Law of Moses' (see esp. David Novak, 1995:9-10, 14, 242, 246-8, *The Election of Israel: The Idea of the Chosen People*, Cambridge University Press).

23 James Oliver and Christina Scott, eds (1975:204, 208), *Religion and World History: A Selection from the Works of Christopher Dawson*, Doubleday Image Books.

24 Cp. this with Abernathy's scheme of national-colonial expansion and contraction. He sets forth the overall historical eras as follows: "Phase 1: Expansion, 1415-1773; Phase 2: Contraction, 1775-1824; Phase 3: Expansion, 1824-1912; Phase 4: Unstable Equilibrium, 1914-39; Phase 5: Contraction, 1940-80" (David B. Abernathy, 2000, *The Dynamics of Global Dominance: European Overseas Empires, 1415-1980*, New Haven and London: Yale University Press; taken from Table of Contents; but see "A Classification Scheme: Five Phases" on pp 23-24).

25 Tursin H. Gabitov, Aktolkin T. Kulsarieva, and Zhusipbek Mutalipov (2001), *Madeniettanu*, Almaty: Rarity. (We are currently translating major sections of this book into English; it is scheduled for publication in 2006 under the title *Kazakh Religion, Culture, Society and State in Historical Perspective*. Portions are available online at www.ara-cahcrc.com/CAHCRC. The quote is taken from the English edition from a chapter not included in the original Kazakh edition.)

———

[26] Jadidism was and remains the Turkic Muslim modernist reform movement which arose in the 19th century in the context of other revival and reform movements occurring throughout the Muslim world during that period.

[27] More extensive treatment of this point has been provided in the Kazakh version of this book which also represents 'Part One' of our doctoral dissertation on 'Cultural-Civilizational Foundations of Religious Processes in the Kazakh Nation' (see bibliography).

[28] Vv. 5, 20, and 31; the particular verse used in the text is v. 5.

[29] D.J. Wiseman (1954/79:255-6; cf. also 262), "Genesis 10: Some Archeological Considerations." Interestingly, he suggests that the fluctuation of the order of the three key concepts of "land," "family," and "language" in each summary statement may indicate an intended emphasis on the importance of each concept in relation to the list it concludes. I would not myself put too much weight on this point, but he offers the following helpful comparative table:

Verse 5:	Lands	Language	Families	Nations
Verse 20:	Families	Languages	Lands	Nations
Verse 31:	Families	Languages	Lands	Nations

[30] Akseleu Seidimbek, 1997:64, *Kazakh alemi: etnomadeni paiimdau* [*The Kazakh World: An Ethnocultural Exegesis*], Almaty, Kazakhstan (emphasis added). An English translation of portions of this work are available on the web at www.ara-cahcrc.com/CAHCRC.

[31] Cf. Connor 1994:103, Smith 1999:162-3.

[32] National Geographic, Aug 1999:TOC; de-emphasis on first half mine.

[33] Lucia Mouat. "Indigenous People Press for Rights." In *Christian Science Monitor*. 12 June 1999, pp 9-12; emphasis added.

[34] Tyndale Bulletin 39, 1988:19; emphasis added.

[35] Hans Kohn (1945), *The Idea of Nationalism*, in Hutchinson and Smith, eds., 1994:162, *Nationalism*. Cf. H. Vincent Moses. "Nationalism and the Kingdom of God According to Hans Kohn and Carlton J. H. Hayes." In *Journal of Church and State*, Volume 17(2), 1975, pp 239-258.

[36] Korkut A. Erturk (1999:5), in his otherwise excellent "Introduction" to *Rethinking Central Asia: Non-Eurocentric Studies in History, Social Structure, and Identity*, surprisingly views this through a more modernist paradigm of artificial developmental stages which move strictly from 'the top' academic and political elites 'down' to the social masses. This only goes to show, however, how deeply and widely influential the modernist position is, especially in academic circles. Nonetheless, his categorizing

of ethnonational participants into three distinct groups in relation to their media and means brings helpful clarity to the discussion. He says, "According to Hroch, the first stage of a national movement involves scholarly inquiry into linguistics, folk literature and the culture of the particular ethnic group in question, and leads to a rewriting of history by intellectuals who identify themselves with it, though no political demands are yet advanced. In the second state, political demands are articulated and a programme of action is charted, and leaders tend to be men of action rather than intellectuals. At this stage the movement still lacks a mass following which it acquires only in its third and last stage."

37   K. Karamanuhli, "Tangirge tagzim" ["The Worship of Tengri"], in Akkoshkarov (1997:265), emphasis added.

38   The article is in *Nationalities Papers*, Volume 31, Number 4/December 2003, pp 453-469. The abstract is taken from the journal's website at http://taylorandfrancis. metapress.com/app/home/contribution.asp?wasp=3d325d0qqq2qrv4bhk 91&referrer=parent&backto=issue,4,8;journal,4,22;linkingpublicationresults,1:102227,1. (Emphasis added.)

39   See especially Gerd Baumann, 1999, *The Multicultural Riddle*, who goes to extremes in this direction.

Chapter Four

40   In light of our critique of Olcott below, it is interesting to note that she wrote the 'Foreword' for Poliakov's work, recommending it to the public.

41   In Vitaly V. Naumkin, ed., 1994:21, *Central Asia and Transcaucasia: Ethnicity and Conflict*. (Emphasis added.)

42   Connor 1984:121, emphasis added; cf. Connor 1994:73.

43   Connor 1994:73; cf. N. Baitenova in Gabitov, ed., 2002:256.

44   See Slezkine in Brower and Lazzerini, eds., 1997:28-29.

45   In M.K. Kozibaev, ed., 1998:137, *History of Kazakstan: Essays*, Almaty, KZ: Gilim (The Shokan Ualihanov Institute of History and Ethnology; ed. of Eng. transl. A.K. Akhmetov). We have slightly amended the grammar, etc, of the Eng. transl. while retaining fully the intended meaning of the original. Note that, whatever his particular view, Arne Haugen, 2004, *The Establishment of National Republics in Central Asia* looks like a rather informed read on these issues. The publishers' description notes: "This book . . . argues that the originally nationally minded Soviet communists with their anti-nationalist attitudes came to view nation and national identity as valuable and constructive tools in state constructions." Note the change in attitude which Haugen recognizes and incorporates into his treatment. In one of his sections he asks: "Soviet nationalities policy: tactical concessions or

instrument of modernization?" Until the work can be read, however, his view on the issues is still unclear.

46   Note that the term 'nations' does not explicitly occur in the original (Kazakh form of the) phrase, which is lit. "Avtonomister odagi." 'Avtonomis' ('Autonomous') simply contains the plural ending 'ter' and would more lit. be rendered as 'autonomous ones'. But the term 'avtonomis' itself is understood within the context of the larger Russian empire and even 'decolonializing' world of that day to refer to 'national autonomy', i.e. 'autonomous nations'. 'Nation' is also indicated in the use of '(ethno)national' ('ulttik') as well as 'nation' ('halik', which could also be 'people', but again here is more properly 'nation') within the context of the quote. The use of 'ult' and 'halik' in Kazakh as terms meaning 'ethnic group' and 'people' respectively, *but also 'nation'* in both cases, demonstrates by the way the intimate connection between 'ethnic nations' and 'political nations' in the Kazakh mind and world.

47   The thesis is properly understood as Connor's, though the quotes have been taken from John Noble, John King, Andrew Humphrey, eds., 1996:34, *Lonely Planet travel survival kit: Central Asia* (Australia: Lonely Planet), which also recognizes the essentially rhetorical nature of such "promises".

48   In T. Gabitov, ed., 2002:256, *Filosophia: okulik [A Textbook]*, Almaty, KZ: Karzhi-Karazhat.

49   Barth 1969:15 quoted in A.D. Smith 1999:182.

50   *Bulletin of the Association for Advancement of Central Asian Research* (AACAR), Fall 1995, No. 2, Vol VIII. Available at: http://www.ku.edu/carrie/texts/carrie_books/paksoy-6/

51   Edward Allworth, Gavin R.G. Hambly and Denis Sinor. "Central Asia, history of." In *Encyclopædia Britannica* from Encyclopædia Britannica Premium Service, <http://www.britannica.com/eb/article?tocId=9108340> [Accessed February 3, 2005]. (Emphasis added.)

52   *Bulletin of the Association for Advancement of Central Asian Research* (AACAR), Fall 1995, No. 2, Vol VIII.

53   G. Yesim (1996:59), *Sana bolmisi: sayasat pen madeniet turali oilar [The Essence of Mind: Thoughts Regarding Politics and Culture]*, vol. 2, Almaty: Gilim.

54   In *Turkistan*, No 17-18, 1993, pp 51-56.

55   Gabitov, Kulsarieva and Mutalipov (2001:226-7), *Madeniettanu*. Gabitov is quoting M. Tatimov (1993:82), *Kazakh alemi [The Kazakh World]* (Almaty).

56   Note also here how a network of Islamic militia groups in Uzbekistan have included in their list of demands to the government that Uzbekistan should "stop the policy of drawing close to Turkey" (Abduvakhitov in Malik, ed., 1994:74).

57 In Mircea Eliade, ed., 1987, *The Encyclopedia of Religion*, MacMillan Publishing Co, vol. 7, pp 357-67.

58 Olivier Roy, 2000, *The New Central Asia: The Creation of Nations*, Washington Square, NY: New York University Press. (Quote taken from backcover.)

59 J. Noble, J. King, A. Humphrey, eds., 1996:34, *Lonely Planet: Central Asia*. (Emphasis added.)

60 We realize this language is rather strong and pointed, but we are not alone in 'feeling' this way. The statement stands as a very serious proposal for all of us to carefully and soberly reflect upon.

Chapter Five

61 Sabol's work is a slightly modified version of his 1999 dissertation which originally had the title of M. Dulatuhli's poem *Awake Kazakh!* as part of his own title. He was ultimately unable to treat Dulatuhli within the limit and scope of his work, however, so he removed the title and published, again, with slight modification to the original content. Another article here worth mentioning is Rawi Abdelal, "Memories of Nations and States: Institutional History and National Identity in Post-Soviet Eurasia," (in *Nationalities Papers*, Vol 30, No 3, Sept 2002, pp 459-484). His work only treats Lithuania, Ukraine and Belarus, however, so it does not fall within the scope of our treatment.

62 In *Nationalities Papers*, Vol 32, No 1, March 2004, p 236. (Gratitude is herein expressed to Dr. Sabol for copying and sending this article as well as the articles by Kuzio and Abdelal from *Nationalities Papers*.)

63 See e.g. A.D. Smith, 1986, *The Ethnic Origins of Nations*; Adrian Hastings, *The Construction of Nationhood: Ethnicity, Religion and Nationalism* as well as our forthcoming work, R. Charles Weller, 2006, *A Closer Look at Ethnicity, Nations and Nationalism in the Kingdom of God and World History*.

64 1995:4 and xx. Note that all page number refs. for pages 3- 246 are the same for both the 1987 first edition and 1995 second edition of the work. The differences between the two are that the 1995 edition contains an additional 'Foreword' and 'Preface to the Second Edition' as well as two additional chapters at the end "that cover the history of Kazakhstan since the first edition was published . . ." (1995:xii). Also, the 'Conclusion' to the original 1987 edition has been entirely dropped.

65 Cf. Eremeev and Semashko, "Pastoral and Nomadic Peoples in Ethnic History," who overview "the process of ethnic contact and/or assimilation," mentioning the Kazakhs in the second of the three models they discuss. (In Gary Seaman, ed. 1992:231, *Foundations of Empire: Archeology and Art of the Eurasian Steppes*, Los Angeles: Ethnographics Press).

66   The dates given in this book for the founding of the khanate and the reign of the various khans are based upon M. Koigeldiev and K. Alimgazinov, "Kazakhstan: history," in Burkitbai Ayagan, chief ed., 2003:278-300, *Kazakhstan ulttik [national] encyclopediasi*, vol. 5 (Kokshetau-Kozha), Almaty, KZ: "Kazakh Encyclopediasi."

67   In M.K. Kozibaev, ed., 1998:68, *History of Kazakstan: Essays*.

68   Zh. Kasimbaev, "Kenesari Kasimuhli bastagan kazak xalkining ult-azattik kozgalisi," in Abdimalik Nisanbaev, chief ed., 2002:502, *Kazakhstan ulttik [national] encyclopediasi*, vol. 4 (Zh-K), Almaty, KZ: "Kazakh Encyclopediasi"; Kereihan Amanzholov, 1999:102, *Turki haliktarining tarihi [The History of the Turkic Peoples]*, Vol. 3. Almaty: Bilim; E. Valikhanov, "National Liberation Struggles of the Kazak People Against Russian Colonialism," in Manash K. Kozibaev, ed., 1998:111, *History of Kazakstan: Essays*. Almaty, KZ: Gilim (The Shokan Ualihanov Institute of History and Ethnology; ed. of Eng. transl. A.K. Akhmetov); T. Turligulov, 1998:103, *Kazakh elining kiskasha tarihi [A Brief History of the Kazakh Nation]*, Almaty: Rauan.

69   E. Bekmakhanov, 1947, *Kazakhstan v 20-40 gody XIX veka*, Almaty.

70   From a personal conversation in his office at "Kazakh Encyclopedia," 29 Nov 2005.

71   Cf. e.g. 'Chamber of Commerce'. The combined effort of colonial empire with missions is birthed from the idea of one, glorious 'Holy Russian Empire', which like the other unfortunate cases of colonization undertaken by 'Christian' Europe in roughly the same era (i.e. 1600s - 1800s), envisioned *their* 'nation' (i.e. 'nation-state') as one Christian 'world' which combined socio-politics, economy, education, language, culture and religion.

72   While we would certainly caution against hanging too much on one small point of grammar, grammar remains important as the vehicle through which meaning is communicated. We would at least be justified in asking then why an indefinite article is used here to describe "a Kazakh nation" as opposed to specifying *the* one and only Kazakh nation? Are we dealing with a Western modernist view which sees 'Kazakh nationalism' giving rise to "a" new Kazakh nation?

73   D. Deweese, 1994, *Islamization and native religion in the Golden Horde: Baba Tükles and conversion to Islam in historical and epic tradition*. University Park, Pa.: Pennsylvania State University Press and Bruce G. Privratsky, 2001, *Muslim Turkistan: Kazak Religion and Collective Memory*, Curzon Press.

74   This latter idea is often founded upon the common fallacy of a sharp distinction between the beliefs and values of 'the elite' and the 'common people'. This view is applied to both national political leaders as well as religious 'clergy' and the 'laypeople' of the nation or religious community. On the religious side, scholars

like Peter Brown in his classic treatment of *The Cult of the Saints: Its Rise and Function in Latin Christianity* (Chicago: The University of Chicago Press) have exposed such views as erroneous. See also R. Charles Weller, "An Inquiry into the Socio-Religious and Historical Relation of Ancestor, National Hero and Saint Devotion (with special reference to Israelite-Jewish, Christian and Muslim Traditions)" and "The Christian Cult of the Saints: Its Origins and Development In the Ancient Church and a Comparison with other World Religious Traditions." (Both papers are available at: www.ara-cahcrc.com, "Projects & Publications." They are part of a book being worked on for future publication entitled *Ancestors, Saints, Sacrifice, Communion and Funerary Meals*.)

75 Cf. the perspective on Kazakh nationhood in Steven T. Gilbert, "The Kazaks Under Stalin" (available at: www.ara-cahcrc.com/CAHCRC, "Projects & Publications"). His paper deals with what he considers to be "the most definitive period of the Kazak's history during the modern period—the Stalin era" (p 2). The author himself recognizes, however, that "this paper has predominantly depended on English sources" (p 3), particularly Olcott as well as Akiner (among others).

76 R. Charles Weller (Kzk. Charlz Ueller), "Dini urdisterding ruhani-madeni negizderi zhuninde," in *Adam alemi* [*The World of Man*], a philosophical and social-humanitarian journal, No 2 (24) June 2005, pp 52-60, Almaty, KZ: Institute of Philosophy and Political Science. (We hope to translate this work into English at some point and publish it; check www.ara-cahcrc.com for any updates on progress.)

77 Ibirai Altinsarin, 1988, *Taza Bulak: ulengder, angimeler, hattar* [*Pure Springs: songs, stories and letters*], Almaty: Zhazushi. Altinsarin's personal correspondences with Il'minskii took place between 1860-1899. They are contained on pp 184-314 of his work. They number in the dozens and display a warm, personal friendship with Il'minskii.

78 Among the many editions available, see *Abai: Karasoz*, 1995, Lublyana, Slovenia: Tiskarna Ludska Pravitsa. The English version is *Abai: Book of Words* and the Russian, *Abai: kniga slov*. All three versions were produced in 1995 in honor of Abai's 150th birthday. See esp. "Word 38" regarding Abai's commitment to Islamic faith.

79 Rouland ("A New Kazakstan," p 237) quotes Sabol on this matter as follows: ""Although there was general agreement among the intelligentsia on the causes behind the Kazak's social and economic plight, solutions were disputed, the very language of advocacy was inconsistent, and the lack of consensus was detrimental to unified political action after the 1917 revolution ([2003] pp. 71-72)."" Rouland

then adds: "Whether a unified Kazak intellectual voice could have presented a challenge to the political organization of the Bolsheviks remains a counter-factual question."

80 Available at www.ara-cahcrc.com/CAHCRC under the "Projects & Publications" link.

81 "Tildi bilmegen adam—mentalitetti bilmeidi." In G. Yesim (2002b:63-74), *Sana bolmisi:sayasat pen madeniet turali oilar* [*The Essence of Mind: Thoughts Regarding Politics and Culture*], vol. 7, Almaty: Gilim.

82 In *Nationalities Papers*, Vol 30, No 2, June 2002, p 258. Kuzio references three other scholars apparently taking a similar view, namely P. Kolsto, I. Bremmer and B. Dave (p 264, endnote 97).

83 Cf. DeLorme 1999:89-90; the transl. given is our own based directly on the Kazakh, yet compared with DeLorme's.

84 In *The Journal of Ethnic Studies*, vol 19, No 4, 1992, pp 113-116.

85 R. Stuart DeLorme, 1999, *Mother Tongue, Mother's Touch: Kazakhstan Government and School Construction of Identity and Language Planning Metaphors*, PhD diss., University of Pennsylvania.

86 R. Stuart DeLorme, 04 Dec 2001, personal email correspondence.

87 These chapters are available on the web by DeLorme's permission at: www.ara-cahcrc.com/CAHCRC ("Projects & Publications").

88 DeLorme 1999:83-4; emphasis added. See quote on significance of the Flag for the Kazakhs in ch 8. DeLorme himself quotes from as well as bases his discussion on E. Shajmerdenov (1993), *Kazak elining raemizderi* [*Symbols of the Kazakh Nation*] (Almaty: Balawsa [Fresh Sprig]). See also B.F. Kaiirbekov, Sh.N. Kaiirgali, A.N. Hazarbaeva, 1997, *Kazakhstan Respublikasining memlekettik nishandari* [*State Symbols of the Republic of Kazakhstan*]. (Note that DeLorme translates the booklet title *Kazak elining raemizderi* by Shajmerdenov as "The Kazakh National Symbols". We have corrected it here to read *Symbols of the Kazakh Nation*, with "Kazakh nation" being a common Kazakh phrase used to represent "Kazakhstan" and thus is itself a term which stands at the heart of the critical tensions being discussed.)

89 Personal (email) correspondence, December 01, 2005. Note that our critique in this section was not constructed in consultation with DeLorme, it was written from our own perspective on his work in view of the broader context of the issues being discussed. An advanced copy was, however, sent to him for review and comment before publishing.

90 Uighur and Tatar homelands exist, though they have not yet achieved their desire for independent nationhood. Those who feel the Tatars are entirely content with being an 'autonomous republic' within the 'Russian Federation' need only look at

Chechnaya to understand why the Tatars do express more fully and freely their ethnonational aspirations. Much the same could be said for the Uighurs in China. There are many sympathizers with these ethnonational groups among the native Central Asian population. We likewise express our sympathies and concern for their ethnonational rights and well-being in the modern global age. (See again Mary Kate Simmons, ed., 1995, *Unrepresented Nations and Peoples Organization*).

91   N. Nazarbaev, Nov 1993:8-9, *The Concept of Sociocultural Development in the Republic of Kazakhstan*, as quoted in DeLorme 1999:105-7.

92   The United Nations High Commissioner for Human Rights, 1995, *Fact Sheet No. 9 (Rev. 1), The Rights of Indigenous Peoples* (http://193.194.138.190/html/menu6/2/fs9.htm). This definition is based on the report by the Sub-Commission on Prevention of Discrimination and Protection of Minorities working under the leadership of Mr. José R. Martínez Cobo (Ecuador) as Special Rapporteur, 1971-1984. It conclusions were submitted to the U.N. and published between 1981-84 as "Study of the problem of discrimination against indigenous populations", issued in consolidated form in five volumes as document E/CN.4/Sub.2/1986/7 and Add.1-4.

93   "Kazakhstan Respublikasindagi etnikalik-madeni bilim tuzhirimdamasi" ["A Summary of ethno-cultural education in the Republic of Kazakhstan"], approved by the decision (No. 3058) of the President of the Republic of Kazakhstan on 15 July 1996 and ratified by the National Council on State Policy [serving] beside the President of the Republic of Kazakhstan, *Yegemen Kazakhstan*, 7 August 1996, reprinted in Zh. Naurizbai, 1997:147-159, *Ultting uli bola alsak [If We Can Be Sons of the Nation]*, Almaty: Ana Tili. (Note that we translate 'ult' here as 'nation' according to its contextual meaning; we would normally translate it 'ethnos' or 'ethnonational group', with or without political statehood involved.

94   *Zhalin* journal, No. 7, 2005, front cover (cp. Fierman's perspective on this matter in his quote given earlier in the main text).

95   Gabitov, Kulsarieva and Mutalipov ([2001] 2003:343ff).

96   This is our own translation, done in close comparison w/ DeLorme's (1999:68-69). The "*" marks the refrain. DeLorme's translation better preserves the conciseness and poetic sense. A few minor clarifications are in order in his version and we have provided them here, but the meaning and sense is the same.

97   03 Dec 2005. In that correspondence, DeLorme noted in relation to this issue: "If I were to continue research on 'the question of the indigenous versus the non-indigenous,' I would like to explore drafts, discussions, interviews, etc, with indigenous peoples from around the world who were involved in discussions and drafting resolutions in U.N. sponsored gatherings concerning indigenous or 'first

nations' rights. Perhaps some of those discussions would be framed within a 'Western modernist' paradigm, but I would like to analyze the exact language of various indigenous voices—in translation, of course, but in consultation with them as to the exact meanings of their original languages—to discover some common threads or themes, if any, running through their discourse. (Fishman records from many sources original words concerning the mother tongue, but a similar research method could be used concerning views culled from indigenous peoples around the world concerning their own 'ult' [i.e. 'ethnos'] and the place of other 'ulttar' [i.e. 'ethne'] within a shared politic on their indigenous land)."

[98]   While DeLorme might have done well to clarify this fact when choosing to include it in the final version of his 1999 dissertation, the dating of this observation as part of the field research would have at least been noted within the overall framework of the final version of his work and should have served to warn Olcott (and others) against the dangers of using such outdated, not to mention again merely passing and rather limited, observations as alleged grounds for warning against the dangers of nationalism.

[99]   See *Ana Tili* newspaper, No. 44, 24 kazan (Oct), 2002. The entire edition was dedicated to this problem and entitled: "Tilime til tigizbe, zhetesiz" ["Don't badmouth my tongue, mindless one"]. Not in particular connection with this edition of *Ana Tili* in any way, but regarding the national language issue, it is perhaps worth noting here with respect to the religious dimensions involved, that there are Kazakh Muslims who intentionally and very actively seek to further Arabize the Kazakh language *as an inseparable part* of their 'contribution' to the Kazakh national language cause. This involves terminology as well as at times the Arabic script itself, which was indeed used as the 'official' script for Kazakh (though not its proto-Turkic tongue) from the earliest times all the way down to 1930 when Latin script was introduced for a decade by the Soviets before the imposition of Cyrillic in 1940. Indeed, the Arabic script is still used for Kazakh among China's Kazakh population. Certain Tengrists meanwhile are adamant about the 'restoration' of ancient Turkic script and even terminology, including a 'purification' of 'borrowed' Arabic terms in making their 'contribution' to the Kazakh national language cause. They argue, for instance, that using the Arabic Muslim greeting 'Assalom alaykum' is no better than the Russian 'Zdravstvuitye'. Perhaps it is interesting in this light that, according to Shildebai (2002:78): "The work of Turkic nationalism in Turkey began first and foremost in the field of language. They had to clean up the mixed sour and fresh milk language which until that time consisted of elements from the Turkish, Arabic and Persian (Farsi) languages and turn it into a Turkish language which students and common people

[alike] could equally understand. For since many Arabic and Persian words, phrases and additional [items] were in the Turkish language of that time, only the Ottoman scholars who knew Arabic and Persian understood it, [but] common Turks did not always understand it." I. Altinsarin, in his classic text on Kazakh for the newly developing Kazakh educational system, noted along similar lines that: "Teachers in the places of education, because they have no other option, are using the Tatar language in place of the Kazakh language when instructing the Kazakh children. . . . [But] the literary language of the Tatars, because the educated themselves who came forth from among the Tatars did not pay this language any mind, has become filled with Arab and Persian words; therefore, it is incomprehensible to Kazakhs who have not mastered literature" (*Taza bulak*, [1860-1889] 1988:24). While no should try to set out on a quest to entirely 'purge' or 'purify' Kazakh of any and all Arab, Persian or even Russian loan words, the issue is valid. In the end, whatever exact view or approach one takes, the Kazakh language remains in a deep dilemma and mangled mess in the wake of Russian imperialism.

100 "President Sworn-In to Second Term" http://www.whitehouse.gov/news/releases/2005/01/20050120-1.html.

101 G. Fuller in Malik, ed., 1994:135 (emphasis added).

102 Gabitov et al, [2001] 2006. The quote is taken from the English translation (cf. fn above).

Chapter Six

103 KFWB News Radio, Los Angeles; reported again on Japanese national television, NHK ('Nippon Ho-so Kyo-kai') news broadcast, June 21, 2001.

104 See e.g. Gokhan Cetinsaya. "Rethinking nationalism and Islam: some preliminary notes on the roots of 'Turkish-Islamic synthesis' in modern Turkish political thought." In *Muslim World*, v. 89 no3-4 (July/Oct. 1999) pp 350-76, where he interacts with the whole idea of "Turkish nationalism" exhibiting "schizophrenia" set forth by Hugh Poulton, 1997, *The Top Hat, the Grey Wolf and the Crescent: Turkish Nationalism and the Turkish Republic*, (London).

Chapter Seven

105 Omarov, *Ak Zhol Kazakhstan* (newspaper), No. 30 (152) 02 Sep 2005, p 2.

106 1999:11, *Turki haliktarining tarihi* [*The History of the Turkic Peoples*], vol. 3, Almaty: Bilim.

107 In Robert P. Geraci and Michael Khodarkovsky, eds., 2001:274, *Of Religion and Empire: Missions, Conversion, and Tolerance in Tsarist Russia*, Cornell University Press.

108   "Indian Wars," in Rosenbaum, ed. in chief, [1982] 1993:613-4, *The New American Desk Encyclopedia*, Signet Publishers.

109   See e.g. Malcolm Margolin, ed., [1981] 1993, *The Way We Lived: California Indian Stories, Songs & Reminiscences*, Berkeley, CA: Heyday Books, California Historical Society. See esp. Section X, "The Coming of the Whites." (Special thanks to Dr. Brent Davis for noting this point and bringing this book to our attention.)

110   *http://pqasb.pqarchiver.com/latimes/140522741.html?did=140522741&FMT =ABS&FMTS=FT&date=Jul+22%2C+2002&author=TOM+GORMAN&pub= Los+Angeles+Times&desc=The+Nation%3B+Land+Battle+Splits+Shoshone+ Nation%3B+Compensation%3A+Most+members+want+their+share+of+ %24140+million+the+U.S.+may+pay+the+tribe+for+its+territory.+Others +want+to+keep+fighting* "Land Battle Splits Shoshone Nation" (p A8). The article appears under news for "The Nation." If memory does not fail us here, the *Los Angeles Time Magazine* actually ran a more complete article on the story, using it as a cover article, sometime in August or September that year (2002).

111   Ronald B. Taylor, "Western Shoshones Lay Claim to 24 Million Acres Indian Sisters Spur Land Rights Battle," in *Los Angeles Times*, Mar 24, 1985, p 3.

112   Olcott, 2002, *Kazakhstan: Unfulfilled Promise*. The 11 years are counted from 1991, when Kazakhstan was officially declared an independent (democratic) 'nation', and 2002, when Olcott wrote the book.

113   On the Brooklyn Society for Ethical Culture website (http://www.bsec.org/news/kingpeace.html). Note that we have taken the final sentence from a slightly earlier point in the speech and placed at the end of the quote here.

114   "The Stars and Stripes" on the *Founding Fathers* website (http://www.founding fathers.info/American-flag/stars-and-stripes.html).

115   Cf. "The United States of America" in Rosenbaum, ed. in chief, [1982] 1993:1249-51.

116   A debt of gratitude is herein expressed to Dean Sieberhagen, for taking time out of his busy schedule to sit down for several long hours to talk through these issues. Responsibility for all views expressed of course lies with the author.

117   Paul Stuart, 1989, *Nations Within a Nation*, Greenwood Publishing Group.

118   Martin Hall, Julian R.D. Cobbing, Colin J. Bundy, Leonard Monteath Thompson and Shula E. Marks, "South Africa, history of." In *Encyclopædia Britannica* from Encyclopædia Britannica Premium Service. <http://www.britannica.com/eb/article-9109716> [Accessed 12 Aug 2005]. (Emphasis added)

119   "Homelands," in Robert A. Rosenbaum, ed. in chief, [1982] 1993:580, *The New American Desk Encyclopedia*.

120 Seidimbek, 1997:440-4, *Kazakh alemi: etnomadeni paiimdau* [*The Kazakh World: An Ethnocultural Exegesis*].

121 Note that in using the terms 'dominant' and 'minority' we must be careful how we interpret each one in relation to the other since the primary issue is one of 'power', both political and economic. There are cases where the 'dominant' (i.e. more powerful) group is actually technically the minority in terms of sheer group size. This is certainly often the case in the early stages of colonialism.

Chapter Eight

122 Gabitov, Mutalipov, Kulsarieva ([2001] 2003), *Madeniettanu* (translated into English as *Kazakh Religion, Culture, Society and State in Historical Perspective* for publication in 2006) // D. Kishibekov (1999), *Kazakh mentaliteti: keshe, bugin zhanye erteng*, Almaty: Gilim // Zh. Moldabekov (2003), *Kazaktanu*, Almaty: "Kazakh Universiteti" // K. Zhumadilov (2000), *Kaling elim, kazagim . . .* , "Kazakhstan" Publishers // M. Mamanzhanov (2001), *Engbek ettim elim ushin*, Almaty: "Kazakhstan" Publishers // R. Berdibai (2000), *El bolamiz desek . . .* , Almaty: "Kazakhstan" Publishers // M. Bulutai, 2001, *Musilman Kazakh elimiz* // M. Kozibaev (2001), *Urkeniet zhanye ult*, Almaty: Sozdik-Slovar.

123 The first two publications were edited by A. Kozhamkulov et al and published by "Kazakh Universiteti." The third is due out on the eve of this book's publication. The author has participated in all three conferences, presenting papers (in Kazakh).

124 1998:82-3, *Mother Tongue, Mother's Touch*, quoting E. Shajmerdenov, 1993, *Kazakh elining raemizderi* [The Kazakh national symbols], Balawsa [Fresh Sprig], Almaty.

125 See the classic and only English edition of Robert Dankoff, 1983, *Yusuf Khass Hajib, Wisdom of Royal Glory (Kutadgu Bilig): A Turko-Islamic Mirror for Princes*, Chicago and London: University of Chicago Press. Note that *Kutadgu Bilig* is more literally *Blessed Knowledge*; we have chosen to follow Dankoff's title instead of the more literal rendering because it is already established and made available under that title.

126 "Introduction: the Turko-Persian tradition," in R. Canfield, ed., [1991] 2002:7, *Turko-Persia in Historical Perspective*. See also N.N. Negmatov, "The Samanid State," in M.S. Asimov and C.E. Bosworth, eds. (1998:87, 91-93), *History of the Civlizations of Central Asia: Volume IV: The age of achievement: A.D. 750 to the end of the fifteenth century: Part One: The historical, social and economic setting*, UNESCO Publishing.

127 Soucek is citing Dankoff and Kelly, *Compendium*, vol. I, p. 274; cf. S. Bastug, "Tribe, Confederation and State Among Altaic Nomads of the Asian Steppes," in Korkut A. Erturk, ed., 1999:83-4, *Re-thinking Central Asia*.

[128] Privratsky begins his comments several lines earlier with the statement: "The oppositional context required for the persistence of ethnic identity (Barth 1969; Spicer 1971) has been very strong in the Kazak case." While Privratsky seems to avoid modernist viewpoints in his understanding of ethnonational identity and its historic depth, he *seems* to follow a perennialist view of nationhood, viewing it more as a product of historical circumstances than as something rooted in human society which itself helps produce history.

[129] As noted earlier, the dates given in this book for the founding of the khanate and the reign of the various khans are based upon M. Koigeldiev and K. Alimgazinov, "Kazakhstan: tarihi [Its history]," in Burkitbai Ayagan, chief ed., 2003:278-300, *Kazakhstan ulttik [national] encyclopediasi*, vol. 5.

[130] In M.K. Kozibaev, ed., 1998:62, *History of Kazakstan: Essays*.

[131] In M.K. Kozibaev, ed., 1998:43, *History of Kazakstan: Essays*. Along the lines of the 'single ethnic unity', cf. Sharon Bastug (in Erturk, ed., 1999:92, *Rethinking Central Asia*): "While the scholar must distinguish between kinship, political, economic, and territorial groups, tribally organized peoples are not so constrained. On the contrary, among peoples with segmentary lineage systems, especially those of the Eurasian Steppes, the separate domains of kinship, economic, political, and territorial organization are fused in traditional political economy and culture."

[132] R. Charles Weller, Dina Babasova and Galumzhan Sailauov, 2003:38, *Kazakh halkining ulttik madenieti [National Culture of the Kazakh People]*, Almaty: Central Asian Historical-Cultural Research Center. Note that the actual content of the various sections of this book was left to the decision of Babasova and Sailauov as the two Kazakh authors writing about their own people and nation. Weller's participation was in conceiving, recruiting, outlining the main sections to be covered, guiding and consulting, providing the main resources for the work as well as in selection of particular poems, songs, etc, to be included. The book, therefore, by way of the authors who wrote the actual content and the resources they used, represents a genuine Kazakh viewpoint and not a 'foreign' one—which was precisely the aim of the project.

[133] A.T. Smailova, ed., 2002:4, *Kazakh anderi (zhanye halik kompozitorlarining anderi)*, Almaty, KZ: Kochevniki. See also Weller, Babasova and Sailauov, 2003:115, *Kazakh halkining ulttik madenieti [National Culture of the Kazakh People]*.

[134] While the Kazakh term ('yel') at times might not carry political overtones, of the three Kazakh terms (i.e. 'ult', 'halik' and 'yel') which can all be translated 'people' or 'nation', it is 'yel' which is typically used in a socio-political sense of nationhood. Likewise, while it is used in both a larger national sense as well as a more restricted socio-political sense in relation to one of the three tribes of Kazakh history, the

fact remains that, whatever tribe it may have originated among, the song spread among the entire 'nation' (i.e. all three tribes) and was embraced as pertaining to all of them in relation to the suffering they experienced *as a nation* in the Zhungarian era. That is the understanding which remains in the national collective memory of the present day. There is no thought in the Kazakh mind of the Kazakhs as a strictly non-political 'people' in this era. They view things in combined 'socio-political' terms. Their socio-political nationhood may have been in shambles at this point, but this does not mean for them or for us that it all ideas of political nationhood are lost or abandoned.

[135] Compare the struggles to maintain national unity in ancient Israel in the book of Judges after being established and declared a 'nation' by God (Exod. 19:5-6). Compare also their breakdown of national unity between King Saul and David (2Sam 1-7). The division of the monarchy into two and the much later restoration envisioned in the prophets (Isa. 49:6; Ezek 37ff) can also be considered in ancient Israel's 'long perennial duration' and 'durability' as a nation. The periods of civil war in Spain between 1936-1975 and the United States in the mid-19th century are but a few of the more modern examples which could also be discussed here in the debate over history and nationhood.

[136] In M.K. Kozibaev, ed., 1998:104-13, *History of Kazakstan: Essays*. See also the section on "History: The Struggle of the Kazakh People on the Road to Independence and Political Self-Government," in A. Nisanbaev, chief ed., 2001:81, *Kazakhstan Respublikasi encyclopedialik aniktama* [*The Republic of Kazakhstan: An Encyclopedic Reference Book*], Almaty, KZ: 'Kazakh Encyclopediasi' as well as the chapter on "Kazakhstandagi ult-azattik kozgalistar" ["Ethnonational independence movements in Kazakhstan"] in A. Abdakimuhli (1997:123-134), *Kazakhstan tarihi* [*The History of Kazakhstan*].

[137] Weller, Babasova and Sailauov, 2003:39, *Kazakh halkining ulttik madenieti* [*National Culture of the Kazakh People*]. This view is supported by numerous sources, including Zh. Kasimbaev, "Kenesari Kasimuhli bastagan Kazakh xalkining ult-azattik kozgalisi," in Abdimalik Nisanbaev, chief ed., 2002:502, *Kazakhstan ulttik* [*national*] *encyclopediasi*, vol. 4 (Zh-K), Almaty, KZ: "Kazakh Encyclopediasi"; Kereihan Amanzholov, 1999:102, *Turki haliktarining tarihi* [*The History of the Turkic Peoples*], Vol. 3. Almaty: Bilim; E. Valikhanov, "National Liberation Struggles of the Kazak People Against Russian Colonialism," in Manash K. Kozibaev, ed., 1998:111, *History of Kazakstan: Essays*. Almaty, KZ: Gilim (The Shokan Ualihanov Institute of History and Ethnology; ed. of Eng. transl. A.K. Akhmetov); T. Turligulov, 1998:103, *Kazakh elining kiskasha tarihi* [*A Brief History of the Kazakh Nation*], Almaty: Rauan.

138 Zh. Kasimbaev, "Kenesari Kasimuhli bastagan Kazakh xalkining ult-azattik kozgalisi," in Nisanbaev, chief ed., 2002:502.

139 As noted in the previous chapter, Olcott actually limits Kenesari's aims and efforts, including this demand to the khanate of the Middle Horde, which would follow the old *Kazakh Soviet Encyclopedia* view (see under 'Kenesari').

140 From the section on "History: The Struggle of the Kazakh People on the Road to Independence and Political Self-Government," in A. Nisanbaev, chief ed., 2001:81, *Kazakhstan Respublikasi encyclopedialik aniktama* [*The Republic of Kazakhstan: An Encyclopedic Reference Book*].

141 Sabit Shildebai, 2002, *Turkshildik zhanye Kazakhstandagi ult-azattik kozgalis*, Almaty, KZ: Gilim. See also N. Nurtazina, 2002, *Kazakh madenieti zhanye Islam* (Almaty, KZ: Kazakhstan madeniet zhanye unertanu gilimi-zertteu instituti), section 3.2, "The Spiritual Crisis in the Islamic World and Muslim Reformation (Jadidism)."

142 Cf. Weller, Babasova and Sailauov, 2003:41, *Kazakh halkining ulttik madenieti* [*National Culture of the Kazakh People*].

143 [1903] 1995:134-5, *Abai: Karasoz* (English version, 1995:146-7). The English translation in our main text is a direct translation from the original Kazakh. It differs significantly from David Aitkyn's translation in the 1995 English version because his translation was based on the Russian translation, which itself already has problems. Whether, then, the problem lies in Aitkyn's English or the Russian he based it on is difficult to say, but again, as noted in the first endnote, this whole problem is currently being addressed by N. Rsalieva of Yasawi University (Turkistan, Kazakhstan). She has already written several articles in national newspapers, including her two part piece on "'The Nomads': How is Its English Translation?" ["Kushpendiler: agilshin tilindegi audarmasi kandai?"] (in *Kazakh adebieti*, No. 30 (2930), 29 July—04 Aug, 2005, p 10 and No. 32 (2932) 12-18 Aug, 2005, p 12). *Abai: Book of Words* is one of the translations she is critiquing in her studies as well. Concerning Aitkyn's translation here, it reads: "One should learn to read and write Russian. The Russian language is a key to spiritual riches and knowledge, the arts and many other treasures. If we wish to avoid the vices of the Russians while adopting their achievements, we should learn their language and study their scholarship and science, for it was by learning foreign tongues and assimilating world culture that the Russians have become what they are. Russian opens our eyes to the world. By studying the language and culture of other nations, a person becomes their equal and will not need to make humble requests. Enlightenment is useful for religion as well .... Russian learning and culture are a key to the world heritage. He who owns this key will acquire the rest without too much effort." Aitkyn's latter phrase "acquire the rest without too

much effort" might capture the sense of Abai's "dunie arzanirak tusedi," but it not only somewhat eclipses the direct one-for-one connection intentionally made by Abai of the entire "world" ('dunie') with "the world('s keys)," it also misses the connection with the larger context in which Abai is urging his Kazakh people to "Fear God, be ashamed of [your] sinful human nature [lit. 'pendeden oyal']; if you want your child to be a child, educate him, do not spare your livestock!", i.e. 'do not be selfishly concerned for the expense!' In direct connection with this larger context, we have rendered Aitkyn's "achievements" as more literally "profits" (or perhaps "benefits", Kzk. 'paidasi'; 'achievements' is typically 'zhetistikter' or perhaps 'tabistar'); Abai again seems to be *intentionally* playing off the whole problem of 'expense' in education. Thirdly, a clear difference is seen in Aitkyn's "make humble requests" and our "plead [for help] and be debased [with] exceeding shame." Whether due to Russian and/or Euro-American aversion to it is not clear, but his rendering certainly does not capture the strong sense of 'honor versus shame' which is common in Kazakh society and is surely operating here in Abai's 'Word'. A less important note would be that we have followed Aitkyn in rendering the term "enlightened," which is literally "opened" ('ashilu') on the first occasion, but not the second when it is 'bilgendik' ('Knowledge'). Other variations in Aitkyn which depart just a bit too far from the original at times can also be seen by simple comparison (cp. several notes below re: differences between Aitkyn's and our renderings of Abai's other quote in the main text). Let us note here, by the way, that we are currently translating G. Yesim's commentary on Abai's poems and 'Words' into English to be published sometime in 2006 (see www.ara-cahcrc.com/CAHCRC for updates).

144 *Abai: Karasoz*, [1903] 1995:185-86. (The translation is our own, directly from the original Kazakh, and not based on Aitkyn.)

145 Sorry; we've misplaced the ref.; it seems to have been either Canfield, ed., [1991] 2002 or Khalid in Brower and Lazzerini, eds., 1997.

146 [1903] 1995:90, *Abai: Karasoz*, 'Word Three' (1995:102 in the English version). Our rendering here once again differs significantly from David Aitkyn's translation in the 1995 English version. The phrase, for example, "all the laws passed down from our forefathers," which we have placed before the quote as an introduction to it, occurs in Aitkyn's translation of the passage but is no where to be found in the Kazakh. Of course, the idea is clearly there, which is why we use it as an introduction to the quote, but it is not an idea explicitly expressed in the original. Both the first and last sentences differ significantly as well. His first sentence reads simply "Not everyone is capable of dispensing justice" and his latter sentence is cut down to say "But even these laws have become outdated with the passage of

time and require amendment and infallible interpreters." Again, the sense of this latter sentence is close, but the idea that laws *as a whole* have become completely outdated and require amendment in their entirety does not communicate the actual idea Abai has in mind. Abai rather calls for discerning *which exact portions* of the laws have become outdated and *if* there are any, *then* someone is needed who can discern this and offer "in their place sound judgments put forth [with] full measured authority." Likewise, the idea of their *possibly* not being "in harmony with this new era" is not even hinted at in his translation. Also, in the latter phrase of the middle sentence, the English edition reads: "In order to hold a council 'on top of Mount Kultobe', as we say, . . ." This idea is in the original, but it has become quite twisted and pulled out of its original direct relationship to "Az Tauke khan's 'Seven Decrees'." Finally here, note that we have translated Kasim khan's work as "Straight Path" instead of Aitkyn's rendering of "Radiant Pathway." The original Kazakh 'kaska' can either be taken as 'wise' or 'straight', but 'radiant' does not seem to be an option. Aitkyn, or perhaps the Russian translation, seems to be searching for some meaning which relates to the idea of a 'bald' area around the forehead as 'shiny' or 'radiant' since such a 'bald' area is another usage of the term.

[147] Cf. A. Kasabek (2002:199), *Tarihi-filosofiyalik tanim* [*An Historical-Philosophical Handbook*], Almaty, KZ: KazGZU.

[148] Cf. 1-Chron. 12:32 regarding "the men of Issachar, who understood the times and knew what Israel ought to do."

[149] Zhumagali Ismagulov, ed. in chief, 2002:16, *Mirzhakip Dulatuhli: a 5-volume collection of writings*, Almaty, KZ: Mektep. *Note that our translation "the time" is lit. in Kzk. "zhas," which could be also be 'age' or 'youth'. 'Time' seems the best fit contextually in our opinion. If 'youth' was followed, it would not be intended in Dulatuhli's mind to convey that the Kazakhs were a new, i.e. 'young', nation, but would refer to the 'youth' of the movement, i.e. the movement was still in its 'youth'—fresh, alive and full of vitality—in 1909, invigorated anew with signs of the fall of Tsarist Russia on the horizon, especially following her defeat in the Russian-Japanese war in 1905 (cf. Khalid in Brower and Lazzerini, eds., 1997).

[150] U. Subhanberdina and S. Dauitov, compilers (1995:195), *Aikap*, Almaty, KZ: Kazakh Encyclopediasi. *Note that our rendering of "this hour" is lit. in Kzk. 'zaman', which would normally be 'time', 'period', 'era' or 'age'. 'Hour' fits nicely in the context however, especially for poetic sake in English. Also note that "the exile" is lit. in Kzk. 'alasi'. Some confusion exists over this term, with a few even suggesting that an initial letter may have dropped in transmission somewhere along the line. We would ultimately need to check the original publication if

possible and/or oldest manuscripts to determine that. Until time is found for such, the Kzk term taken as is could grammatically either be from the root 'ala' or 'alas'. We have taken it as 'alas' ('expulsion', 'exile', 'banishment', based on the root of the verb 'alastau', 'to exile, expel, banish').

151 Nurpeisov in Kozibaev, ed. (1998:131-3) and U. Subhanberdina, S. Dauitov and K. Sahov, compilers (1998:405-409), "*Kazak,*" Almaty: Kazakh Encyclopediasi.

152 Indeed, even the Kazakh authors of our own work (Weller, Babasova, Sailauov 2003) took the Soviet view! We will work to change that in the second revised edition, since there is no question in our mind that Babasova and Sailauov both affirm 'Kazakh ethnonationalism', Babasova even participated in the 1986 event! The problem of working through the deep negative impact of both Marxist-Leninist as well as Western modernist views remains a very deep challenge which both we and the Central Asian peoples continue wrestling with.

153 G. Yesim (1997:28-42), *Sana bolmisi:sayasat pen madeniet turali oilar* [*The Essence of Mind: Thoughts Regarding Politics and Culture*], vol. 3, Almaty: Gilim. (We hope to translate this section into English and make it available at www.ara-cahcrc.com/CAHCRC sometime in 2006.)

154 The Kazakh term 'ultshildik' is based in the root term 'ult' or 'ethnos'. They have another term, 'yel', which would more closely correspond to the Western concept of 'political nation'. It is interesting in this light that the Kazakhs choose to translate the Soviet Russian term 'nationalism' with 'ultshildik' and not 'elshildik'. But this is because, again, in their minds the Kazakh 'ult' or 'ethnos' is the proper foundation for both their cultural and political nationhood.

155 Cf. DeLorme 1999:89-90; the transl. given is our own based directly on the Kazakh, yet compared with DeLorme's.

Bibliography

*(An asterik mark * indicates a recommended work)*

Kazakh Sources:

Abai: Karasoz [*Abai: Words*]. 1995. Lublyana, Slovenia: Tiskarna Ludska Pravitsa.

*Abdakimuhli, Abdizhapar. 1997. *Kazakhstan tarihi: erteden buginge deiin* [*The History of Kazakhstan: from early times to the present*], Almaty: Respublikalik baspa kabineti.

Altinsarin, Ibirai. [1860-1889] 1988. *Taza bulak* [*Pure Springs*]. Almaty: Zhazushi. (A small collection of Altinsarin's works, including songs, stories and letters as well as his Kazakh language text.)

*Amanzholov, Kereihan. 1999. *Turki haliktarining tarihi* [*The History of the Turkic Peoples*]. Vol. 3. Almaty: Bilim.

*Berdibai, Rakmankul. 2000. *El bolamiz desek . . .* [*If We Say We Are Going to be a Nation . . .*]. Almaty: "Kazakhstan" Publishers.

Bulutai, Murtaza Zh. 2003. *Burhanizm turali shindik* [*The Truth about Burhanism*]. Almaty: Aris.

———. 2001. *Musilman Kazakh elimiz* [*Our Muslim Kazakh Nation*], Almaty, Kazakhstan: Aris.

Gabitov, T., ed. 2002. *Filosophia: okulik* [*A Textbook*]. Almaty, KZ: Karzhi-Karazhat.

Gabitov, T. H., Aktolkin T. Kulsarieva and Zhusipbek Mutalipov (2001, ch. 12), *Madeniettanu* [*Culturology*], Almaty: Rarity.

Kaiirbekov, B.F., Sh.N. Kaiirgali, A.N. Hazarbaeva. 1997. *Kazakhstan Respublikasining Memlekettik Nishandari* [*State Symbols of the Republic of Kazakhstan*]. Almaty: Aleumettik technologia zhanye okitu ortaligi [Center of Social Instruction and Technology].

Kasimbaev, Zh. "Kenesari Kasimuhli bastagan Kazakh xalkining ult-azattik kozgalisi" ["The National Independence Movement of the Kazakh People Commenced by Kenesari Kasimuhli"]. In Abdimalik Nisanbaev, chief ed. 2002. *Kazakhstan ulttik* [*national*] *encyclopediasi*, vol. 4 (Zh-K). Almaty: "Kazakh Encyclopediasi."

*"Kazakhstan Respublikasindagi etnikalik-madeni bilim tuzhirimdamasi" ["A Summary of ethno-cultural education (policies) in the Republic of Kazakhstan"], approved by the decision (No. 3058) of the President of the Republic of Kazakhstan on 15 July 1996 and ratified by the National Council on State Policy [serving] beside the President of the Republic of Kazakhstan, *Yegemen Kazakhstan*, 7 August 1996 (reprinted in Zh. Naurizbai, 1997:147-159, *Ultting uli bola alsak* [*If We Can Be the Sons of the Nation*], Almaty: Ana Tili).

"Kazakhstan Respublikasindagi aleumettik-madeni damuining tuzhirimdasi / Kontseptsia sotsiokulturnovo razvitija respubliki Kazakhstan [Summary of sociocultural development (policies) of the Republic of Kazakhstan]. "Kazakstan Respublikasining Prezidenti zhanindagi Memlekettik sayasat zhunindegi ulttik kenges" [the National Council on State Policy [serving] beside the President of the Republic of Kazakhstan]. 1993. Almaty: Kazakhstan. (From Delorme 1999.)

*Kishibekov, D. 1999. *Kazakh mentaliteti: keshe, bugin zhanye erteng* [*Kazakh mentality: yesterday, today and tomorrow*]. Almaty: Gilim.

*Koigeldiev, M. and K. Alimgazinov. "Kazakhstan: tarih [history]." In Burkitbai Ayagan, chief ed., 2003:278-300, *Kazakhstan ulttik* [*national*] *encyclopediasi*, vol. 5 (Kokshetau-Kozha), Almaty: "Kazakh Encyclopediasi."

Kozhamkulov, A., ed. 2005. *Kazakhstan Orkenieti: Adamning Auleumettanu men Beiimdelu Maseleleri* [*The Civilization of Kazakhstan: Problems of Socialization and Accommodation of People*]. Conference publication. Almaty: "Kazakh Universiteti."

————. 2004. *Orkeniettik sanani kaliptastiru maselesi* [*The Problem of Forming a Civilizational Mindset*]. Conference publication. Almaty: "Kazakh Universiteti."

————. 2003. *Kazakhstandik Orkeniet zhanye Zhahandanu konteksindegi aikindalu zholdarin izdenis* [*Kazakhstan Civilization in the Context of Globalization and Finding Ways for Cultural Identification*]. Conference publication. Almaty: "Kazakh Universiteti."

*Kozibaev, Manash. 2001. *Orkeniet zhanye ult* [*Civilization and Ethnicity*]. Almaty: Sozdik-Slovar.

Kurmangazi Karamanuhli, "Tangirge tagzim" ["The Worship of Tengri"]. In Yelden Akkoshkarov, compiler, 1997:265, *Kazakh tarihinan* [*From Kazakh History*], Almaty: Zhalin.

*Mamanzhanov, M. 2001. *Engbek ettim elim ushin* [*I Labored for My Nation*]. Almaty: "Kazakhstan" Publishers.

Moldabekov, Zh. 2003. *Kazaktanu* [*Kazakhology*]. Almaty: "Kazakh Universiteti."

Naurizbai, Zh. 1997:147-159, *Ultting uli bola alsak* [*If We Can Be Sons of the Nation*], Almaty: Ana Tili.

Nisanbaev, Abdimalik, chief ed. 2001. *Kazakhstan Respublikasi encyclopedialik aniktama* [*The Republic of Kazakhstan: An Encyclopedic Reference Book*]. Almaty: 'Kazakh Encyclopediasi'.

Omarov, Anuar. "Burin da bolgan, keiin de bola beredi" ["There Before, and Still There Later too"]. In *Ak Zhol Kazakhstan* (newspaper), No. 30 (152) 02 Sep 2005, p 2.

Rsalieva, Nursaule. "Kushpendiler: agilshin tilindegi audarmasi kandai?" ["The Nomads': How is Its English Translation?"]. In *Kazakh adebieti*, No. 30 (2930), 29 July-04 Aug, 2005, p 10 and No. 32 (2932) 12-18 Aug, 2005, p 12.

Satershipov, Bakitzhan. "Kazakh ulti zhanye Kazakhstandik Memleket: Uzindik Yerekshelikteri men kaishiliktari" ["The Kazakh ethnos and the Kazakstan State: Their Own Uniquenesses and Inconsistencies"]. In Aktolkin T. Kulsarieva, ed. 2005. *"Temirkazik" Pikirsaiis klubina—1 zhil* [*The First Year (of) the "Temirkazik" (Scholar's Roundtable) Discussion Club*]. Almaty: Techno Rengau.

*Seidimbek, Akseleu. 1997. *Kazakh alemi: etnomadeni paiimdau* [The Kazakh World: An Ethnocultural Exegesis]. Almaty, Kazakhstan.

Seiitnur, Zharas. "Ulttik 'men'-di kalai saktaimiz nemese kazaktar kimge kedergi bolip otir?" ["How do we preserve our ethnonational selves or (that is) to whom are the Kazakhs being an obstacle?"]. In Aktolkin T. Kulsarieva, ed. 2005. *"Temirkazik" Pikirsaiis klubina—1 zhil* [*The First Year (of) the "Temirkazik" (Scholar's Roundtable) Discussion Club*]. Almaty: Techno Rengau.

*Shildebai, Sabit. 2002. *Turkshildik zhanye Kazakhstandagi ult-azattik kozgalis* [*Turkic Nationalism and the National Independence Movement in Kazakhstan*]. Almaty: Gilim.

Smailova, A.T., ed. 2002. *Kazakh anderi (zhanye halik kompozitorlarining anderi)* [*Kazakh Songs and Song of National Composers*]. Almaty: Kochevniki.

*Subhanberdina, U., S. Dauitov and K. Sahov, compilers. 1998. *Kazak.* Almaty: Kazakh Encyclopediasi.

*Subhanberdina, U. and S. Dauitov, compilers. 1995. *Aikap.* Almaty: Kazakh Encyclopediasi.

"Tilime til tigizbe, zhetesiz" ["Don't badmouth my tongue, mindless one"]. *Ana Tili* newspaper, No. 44, 24 kazan (Oct), 2002.

Turligulov, T. 1998. *Kazakh elining kiskasha tarihi* [*A Brief History of the Kazakh Nation*]. Almaty: Rauan.

Weller, R. Charles (Kzk. Ueller, Charlz). 2006. *Kazak yelindegi dini urdisterding madeni-orkeniettik negizderi* [*Cultural-Civilizational Foundations of Religious Processes in the Kazakh Nation*]. PhD diss. Almaty: Kazakh Ulttik [National] University.

————. 2005. *Kazak pen ortaazialiktarding ulttigi men eldigin korgau* [*Rethinking Kazakh and Central Asian Nationhood*]. Almaty: Central Asian Historical-Cultural Research Center (CAHCRC).

————. "Kazakhstan zhanye demokratianing 'kopulttik' degeni: orindamagan uade me?" ["Kazakhstan and Democracy's (Idea of) 'Multiethnicity': Unfulfilled Promise?"]. In A. Kozhamkulov, ed., 2005, *Kazakhstan Orkenieti: Adamning Auleumettanu men Beiimdelu Maseleleri* [*The Civilization of Kazakhstan: Problems of Socialization and Accommodation of People*]. Conference publication. Almaty: "Kazakh Universiteti".

————. "Dini urdisterding ruhani-madeni negizderi zhuninde" ["Concerning the Spiritual-Cultural (Sources and) Foundations of Religious Processes"]. In *Adam alemi* [*The World of Man*]. No 2 (24) June 2005, pp 52-60. Almaty: Institute of Philosophy and Political Science.

————. "Orkeniettik sanadagi 'halikaralik' degen ogimning shinaii maginasi" ["The True Meaning of 'International' within a Civilizational Mindset"]. In A. Kozhamkulov, ed., 2004, *Orkeniettik sanani kaliptastiru maselesi* [*The Problem of Forming a Civilizational Mindset* [*within Kazakhstan*]"]. Conference Publication. Almaty: "Kazakh Universiteti".

*Weller, R. Charles, Dina Babasova and Galumzhan Sailauov. 2003. *Kazakh halkining ulttik madenieti* [*National Culture of the Kazakh People*]. Almaty: Central Asian Historical-Cultural Research Center (CAHCRC).

Weller, R. Charles and Dina Babasova. 1996. *Kazak tilining grammatikasin mengeru / Using Kazakh Grammar*. Almaty: Orken. (CAHCRC plans to publish a revised edition of this book in 2006.)

Yesim, Garifolla. "Din ideologiyaga ainalsa—kauipti" ["If Religion Turns into Ideology, It's Dangerous"]. In *Turkistan* [newspaper], No. 25 (571) 23 mausim [June], 2005, p. 5.

————. 2002a. *Adam-zat* [*Human-ity*]. Almaty: Gilim.

————. "Tildi bilmegen adam—mentalitetti bilmeidi" ["The Person who does not Know the Language does not Know the Mentality (of the People)"]. In idem. 2002b. *Sana bolmisi:sayasat pen madeniet turali oilar* [*The Essence of Mind: Thoughts Regarding Politics and Culture*], vol. 7, Almaty: Gilim. (Pp 63-74).

*————. "Kazakh ultshil emes, onda kim?" ["(If) Kazakhs are not (ethno)nationalists, then who?"]. In idem. 1997. *Sana bolmisi:sayasat pen madeniet turali oilar* [*The Essence of Mind: Thoughts Regarding Politics and Culture*]. Vol. 3. Almaty: Gilim. (Pp 28-42). (Available at: www.ara-cahcrc.com/CAHCRC, "Projects & Publications.")

————. "Tauelsizdik zhanye Islam." In idem. 1996. *Sana bolmisi:sayasat pen madeniet turali oilar* [*The Essence of Mind: Thoughts Regarding Politics and Culture*]. Vol. 2. Almaty: Gilim.

Zhalin [*Flame*] journal, No. 7, 2005.

Zhumadilov, K. 2000. *Kaling elim, kazagim* . . . Almaty: "Kazakhstan" Publishers.

Zhumagali, Ismagulov, ed. in chief. 2002. *Mirzhakip Dulatuhli: a 5-volume collection of writings*. Almaty, KZ: Mektep.

English Sources:
Aasland, E.A. 2004. "Anthropology Addressing Ethnicity." (www.ara-cahcrc.com, "Projects & Publications").

Abernathy, David B. 2000. *The Dynamics of Global Dominance: European Overseas Empires, 1415-1980*. New Haven and London: Yale University Press.

Abdelal, Rawi. "Memories of Nations and States: Institutional History and National Identity in Post-Soviet Eurasia." In *Nationalities Papers*, Vol 30, No 3, Sept 2002, pp 459-484.

Allworth, Edward, Gavin R.G. Hambly and Denis Sinor. "Central Asia, history of." In *Encyclopædia Britannica* from Encyclopædia Britannica Premium Service, http://www.britannica.com/eb/article?tocId=9108340 [Accessed February 3, 2005].

Anderson, Benedict. 1991. *Imagined Communities: Reflections on the Origin and Spread of Nationalism*. 2nd ed. New York.

Andican, Ahad. "From Central Asian Turkic Republics to the United Turkistan: socio-political analysis of a historical must." In *Turkistan*, No 17-18, 1993, pp 51-56.

*Asimov, M.S. and C.E. Bosworth, eds. 1998. *History of the Civlizations of Central Asia: Volume IV: The age of achievement: A.D. 750 to the end of the fifteenth century: Part One: The historical, social and economic setting.* UNESCO Publishing.

Bastug, Sharon. "Tribe, Confederation and State Among Altaic Nomads of the Asian Steppes." In Korkut A. Erturk, ed., 1999. *Rethinking Central Asia: Non-Eurocentric Studies in History, Social Structure and Identity.* Reading, UK: Ithaca Press. (Pp. 77-109).

Baumann, Gerd. 1999. *The Multicultural Riddle: Rethinking National, Ethnic, and Religious Identities.* New York, NY: Routledge.

Bennigsen, Alexandre and Fanny E. Bryan. "Islam in the Caucasus and the Middle Volga." In Mircea Eliade, ed. 1987. *The Encyclopedia of Religion.* MacMillan Publishing Co. Vol. 7, pp 357-67.

Berger, Peter. "The Four Faces of Global Culture." In Patrick O'Meara, Howard D. Mehlinger, and Matthew Krain, eds. 2000. *Globalization and the Challenges of a New Century, A Reader.* Indiana University Press, p. 419-427.

Block, Daniel I. [1988] 2000. *The Gods of the Nations: Studies in Ancient Near Eastern National Theology,* 2nd ed. Grand Rapids, MI: Baker Academic/Apollos.

Bohannan, Paul and Dirk van der Elst. 1998. *Asking and Listening: Ethnography as Personal Adaptation.* Long Grove, IL: Waveland Press, Inc.

Bowers, Stephen R. "Approaches to the Study of Soviet Ethnic Conflict." In *The Journal of Ethnic Studies*, vol 19, No 4, 1992, pp 113-116.

Brower, Daniel. "Islam and Ethnicity: Russian Colonial Policy in Turkestan." In D. R. Brower and Edward J. Lazzerini, eds., 1997, *Russia's Orient: Imperial Borderlands and Peoples, 1700-1917,* Indiana, USA: Indiana University Press.

Brown, Peter. *The Cult of the Saints: Its Rise and Function in Latin Christianity.* Chicago: The University of Chicago Press.

Buccatteli, Georgio. "Cities and Nations of Ancient Syria: An Essay on Political Institutions with Special Reference to the Israelite Kingdoms." In *Studio Semitici* 26 (Rome: Instituto di Studi del Vicino Oriente, 1967), pp 13-14.

Bush, George W. 2005. "President [Bush] Sworn-In to Second Term" (http://www.whitehouse.gov/news/releases/2005/01/20050120-1.html).

————. 2001. "Statement by the President in His Address to the Nation." (http://www.whitehouse.gov/news/releases/2001/09/20010911-16.html).

*Canfield, Robert L., ed. [1991] 2002. *Turko-Persia in Historical Perspective.* Cambridge University Press.

Cecen, Aydin. "Uzbekistan Between Central Asia and the Middle East: Another Perspective." In Erturk, Korkut A. 1999. *Rethinking Central Asia: Non-Eurocentric Studies in History, Social Structure, and Identity.* New York: Ithaca.

Cetinsaya, Gokhan. "Rethinking Nationalism and Islam: some preliminary notes on the roots of 'Turkish-Islamic synthesis' in modern Turkish political thought." In *Muslim World.* Vol 89, No 3-4 (July/Oct. 1999), pp 350-76.

*Cherry, Conrad, ed. [1971] 1998. *God's New Israel: Religious Interpretations of American Destiny,* 2nd ed. Englewood Cliffs, NJ: Prentice-Hall.

*Connor, Walker. 1994. *Ethnonationalism: the Quest for Understanding.* New Jersey, USA: Princeton University Press.

————. "Nation-Building or Nation-Destroying?" In *World Politics* 24, April 1972:319-55.

*Costello, Paul. 1994. *World Historians and Their Goals: Answers to 20th Century Modernism.* University of Illinois Press.

Dankoff, Robert. 1983. *Yusuf Khass Hajib, Wisdom of Royal Glory (Kutadgu Bilig): A Turko-Islamic Mirror for Princes.* Chicago and London: University of Chicago Press.

Davis, Wade. "Vanishing Cultures." *National Geographic: Global Culture.* 1(196), No. 2, 1999. pp 62-89.

*Dawson, Christopher (ed. by John J. Mulloy). [1958] 2002. *The Dynamics of World History*. Wilmington, Delaware: ISI Books.

DeLorme, R. Stuart. 03 Dec 2005. Personal email correspondence.

————. 01 Dec 2005. Personal email correspondence.

————. 04 Dec 2001. Personal email correspondence.

————. 1999. *Mother Tongue, Mother's Touch: Kazakhstan Government and School Construction of Identity and Language Planning Metaphors*. Ph.D. dissertation, University of Pennsylvania.

Deweese, Devin. 1994. *Islamization and native religion in the Golden Horde: Baba Tükles and conversion to Islam in historical and epic tradition*. University Park, Pa.: Pennsylvania State University Press.

Eremeev, Dmitriy E. and Irina M. Semashko. "Pastoral and Nomadic Peoples in Ethnic History." In Gary Seaman, ed. 1992:223-233. *Foundations of Empire: Archeology and Art of the Eurasian Steppes*. Los Angeles: Ethnographics Press.

*Erturk, Korkut A. 1999. *Rethinking Central Asia: Non-Eurocentric Studies in History, Social Structure, and Identity*. New York: Ithaca.

Fierman, William. (n.d.) "Language and the Defining of Identity in Kazakstan: The Mixed Blessings of Independence." (Unfortunately, no publication information was given in the copy of the paper we received).

*Frye, Richard. 1996. *The Heritage of Central Asia: From Antiquity to the Turkish Expansion*. Princeton, NJ: Markus Wiener Publications.

*Gabitov, Tursin Hafizuhli and Aktolkin T. Kulsarieva, w/ contributions from Nagima Baitenova and Zhusipbek Mutalipov. 2006. *Kazakh Religion, Culture, Society and State in Historical Perspective*. Los Angeles: Asia Research Associates. (Portions available at: www.ara-cahcrc.com/CAHCRC, "Projects & Publications.")

Geary, James. 1997. "Speaking In Tongues." In *Time* (International Ed., "Back to Babel—Special Report: Globalization"). July 7, 1997, pp. 38-44.

———

*Geraci, Robert P. and Michael Khodarkovsky, eds. 2001. *Of Religion and Empire: Missions, Conversion, and Tolerance in Tsarist Russia*. Cornell University Press.

Gilbert, S.T. "The Kazaks Under Stalin." (www.ara-cahcrc.com/CAHCRC, "Projects & Publications").

Gladney, Dru C. 1991. *Muslim Chinese: Ethnic Nationalism in the People's Republic*. London, England and Cambridge, MA: Harvard Council on East Asian Studies.

Gorman, Tom. In *Los Angeles Times*. July 22, 2002, p A8 ("The Nation"). http://pqasb.pqarchiver.com/latimes/results.html?st=basic&QryTxt=The+Danns+and+other+traditional+Shoshone+Indians

Hall, John Whitney. 1970. *Japan: From Prehistory to Modern Times*. Boston, Rutland, Tokyo: Tuttle Publishing.

Hall, Martin, Julian R.D. Cobbing, Colin J. Bundy, Leonard Monteath Thompson and Shula E. Marks. "South Africa, history of." In *Encyclopædia Britannica* from Encyclopædia Britannica Premium Service. <http://www.britannica.com/eb/article-9109716> [Accessed 12 Aug 2005].

*Hastings, Adrian. 1997. *The Construction of Nationhood: Ethnicity, Religion and Nationalism*. Cambridge, UK: Cambridge University Press.

Haugen, Arne. 2004. *The Establishment of National Republics in Central Asia*. Palgrave Macmillan.

*Hutchinson, John and Smith, Anthony D. eds. 1996. *Ethnicity*. Oxford Readers series. Oxford/New York: Oxford University Press.

*————. 1994. *Nationalism*. Oxford Readers series. Oxford/New York: Oxford University Press.

Hutchinson, William R. and Lehmann Hartmut, eds. 1994. *Many Are Chosen: Divine Election and Western Nationalism*. Trinity International Press.

Johnston, Philip and Peter Walker, eds. 2000. *The Land of Promise: Biblical, Theological and Contemporary Perspectives*. Downers Grove, IL: IVP/Apollos.

Kaiser, Walter C., Jr. 1978. *Toward an Old Testament Theology*. Grand Rapids, MI: Zondervan.

Khalid, Adeeb. 1999. *The Politics of Muslim Cultural Reform: Jadidism in Central Asia*. University of California Press.

King, Martin Luther, Jr. 1967. "The Casualties of the War in Vietnam." (Text of speech given in Los Angeles on 25 Feb 1967.) On the Brooklyn Society for Ethical Culture website (http://www.bsec.org/news/kingpeace.html).

*Kozibaev, Manash K., ed. 1998. *History of Kazakhstan: Essays*. Almaty: Gilim (The Shokan Ualihanov Institute of History and Ethnology; ed. of Eng. transl. A.K. Akhmetov).

Kumekov, B. "Problems of Kazak Statehood." In Kozibaev, Manash K., ed. 1998. *History of Kazakstan: Essays*. Almaty: Gilim.

Kuzio, Taras. "History, Memory and Nation Building in the Post-Soviet Colonial Space." In *Nationalities Papers*, Vol 30, No 2, June 2002, pp 241-264.

Liebich, Andre. "Must Nations Become States?" In *Nationalities Papers*, Volume 31, Number 4/December 2003, pp 453-469.

*Malik, Hafeez, ed. 1994. *Central Asia: Its Strategic Importance and Future Prospects*. New York, NY: St. Martin's Press.

Mardin, Serif. "Abdurreshid Ibrahim and Zeki Velidi Togan in the History of the Muslims of Russia." In Korkut A. Erturk, ed., 1999. *Rethinking Central Asia: Non-Eurocentric Studies in History, Social Structure and Identity*. Reading, UK: Ithaca Press.

Margolin, Malcolm, ed. [1981] 1993. *The Way We Lived: California Indian Stories, Songs & Reminiscences*. Berkeley, CA: Heyday Books, California Historical Society.

Mouat, Lucia. "Indigenous People Press for Rights." In *Christian Science Monitor*. 12 June 1999, pp 9-12.

Negmatov, N.N. "The Samanid State." In M.S. Asimov and C.E. Bosworth, eds. 1998. *History of the Civlizations of Central Asia: Volume IV: The age of achievement: A.D. 750 to the end of the fifteenth century: Part One: The historical, social and economic setting.* UNESCO Publishing.

*Nisbet, Robert. "Civil Religion." In *The Encyclopedia of Religion.* In Mircea Eliade, ed. 1987. *The Encyclopedia of Religion.* MacMillan Publishing Co. Vol. 3, pp 524-527.

Noble, John, John King and Andrew Humphrey, eds. 1996. *Lonely Planet travel survival kit: Central Asia.* Australia: Lonely Planet.

Novak, David. 1995. *The Election of Israel: The Idea of the Chosen People.* Cambridge University Press.

Nurpeisov, K. "The Alash Party's Role and Its Place in the Social and Political Life of Kazakstan." In Kozibaev, Manash K., ed. 1998. *History of Kazakstan: Essays.* Almaty: Gilim.

Olcott, Martha Brill. 2002. *Kazakhstan: Unfulfilled Promise.* Washington, D.C.: Carnegie Endowment for International Peace.

————. [1987] 1995. *The Kazakhs.* Stanford, CA: Hoover Institution Press.

*Oliver, James and Christina Scott, eds. 1975. *Religion and World History: A Selection from the Works of Christopher Dawson.* Doubleday Image Books.

Paksoy, H. B. "Nationality or Religion? Views of Central Asian Islam." In *Bulletin of the Association for Advancement of Central Asian Research* (AACAR), Fall 1995, No. 2, Vol VIII. (Available on web at: http://www.ku.edu/carrie/texts/carrie_books/paksoy-6/)

Patai, Raphael. "Folk Islam." In "Folk Religion" in Mircea Eliade, ed. in chief. 1987. *The Encyclopedia of Religion,* MacMillan Publishing Co. Vol 5.

Porkhomovsky, Victor Ya. "Historical Origins of Interethnic Conflicts in Central Asia and Transcaucasia." In Vitaly V. Naumkin, ed., 1994. *Central Asia and Transcaucasia: Ethnicity and Conflict.* Westport, CT/London: Greenwood Press.

Prazauskas, Algis. "Ethnopolitical Issues and the Emergence of Nation-States in Central Asia." In Yongjin Zhang and Rouben Azizian, eds. 1998. *Ethnic Challenges Beyond Borders: Chinese and Russian Perspectives of the Central Asian Conundrum.* Oxford: St. Anthony's College.

*Privratsky, Bruce. 2001. *Muslim Turkistan: Kazak Religion and Collective Memory.* Curzon Press.

Rosenbaum, ed. in chief. [1982] 1993. *The New American Desk Encyclopedia.* Signet Publishers.

Rouland, Michael. "A New Kazakstan: four books reconceptualize the history of the Kazak Steppe." In *Nationalities Papers*, Vol 32, No 1, March 2004, pp 233-243.

*Roux, Jean-Paul. "Tengri" (transl. from French by Sherri L. Granka). In Mircea Eliade, ed. 1987. *The Encyclopedia of Religion.* MacMillan Publishing Co, vol. 14, pp 401-3.

*———. "Turkic Religions." In Mircea Eliade, ed. 1987. *The Encyclopedia of Religion.* MacMillan Publishing Co. Vol 15, pp 87-94.

Roy, Olivier. 2000. *The New Central Asia: The Creation of Nations.* New York University Press.

Sabol, Steven. 2003. *Russian Colonization of Central Asia and the Genesis of Kazak National Conscious.* Palgrave Macmillan.

Shenk, David. 1995. *Global Gods: Exploring the Role of Religion in Modern Societies.* Scottdale, PA: Herald Press.

Sheriffs, Deryck C.T. "'A Tale of Two Cities'—Nationalism in Zion and Babylon." In *Tyndale Bulletin*. Vol 39, 1988.

Shnirelman, Victor A. 1996. *Who Gets the Past? Competition for Ancestors Among Non-Russian Intellectuals in Russia.* Baltimore and London: Johns Hopkins University Press.

*Simmons, Mary Kate, ed. 1995. *Unrepresented Nations and Peoples Organization.* The Hague/London/Boston: Klumer Law International.

Slezkine, Yuri. "Naturalists versus Nations: Eighteenth Century Russian Scholars Confront Ethnic Diversity." In Daniel R. Brower and Edward J. Lazzerini, eds., 1997, *Russia's Orient: Imperial Borderlands and Peoples, 1700-1917*, Indiana, USA: Indiana University Press.

*Smith, Anthony D. 2001. *The Nation in History: Historiographical Debates About Ethnicity and Nationalism.* Hanover: University Press of New England.

*————. 1999. *Nationalism and Modernism: A Critical Survey of Recent Theories of Nations and Nationalism.* London and New York: Routledge.

*————. 1986. *The Ethnic Origins of Nations.* Malden MS: Blackwell.

*Soucek, Svat. 2000. *A History of Inner Asia.* Cambridge: Cambridge University Press.

Soylemez, Orhan. 1995. *Preserving Kazak Cultural Identity After 1980.* PhD diss. NY: Columbia University.

*Stackhouse, Max. "Religion and Politics." In Mircea Eliade, ed. 1987:V11:408-423. The *Encyclopedia of Religion.* MacMillan Publishing Co.

"Stars and Stripes, The." On the *Founding Fathers* website (http://www.founding fathers.info/American-flag/stars-and-stripes.html).

Stuart, Paul. 1989. *Nations Within a Nation.* Greenwood Publishing Group.

Taylor, Ronald B. "Western Shoshones Lay Claim to 24 Million Acres, Indian Sisters Spur Land Rights Battle." In *Los Angeles Times*, Mar 24, 1985, p 3. http://pqasb.pqarchiver.com/latimes/results.html?st=basic&QryTxt=The +Danns+and+other+traditional+Shoshone+Indians

Tilley, Charles. 1975. *The Formation of National States in Western Europe.* Princeton, NJ: Princeton University Press.

United Nations High Commissioner for Human Rights. 1995. *Fact Sheet No. 9 (Rev. 1), The Rights of Indigenous Peoples*. (Programme of Activities for the International Decade of The World's Indigenous People (1995-2004) (para. 4), General Assembly resolution 50/157 of 21 December 1995, annex.) http://193.194.138.190/html/menu6/2/fs9.htm

Valikhanov, E. "National Liberation Struggles of the Kazak People Against Russian Colonialism." In Kozibaev, Manash K., ed. 1998. *History of Kazakstan: Essays*. Almaty: Gilim.

*Weller, R. Charles. 2006. *A Closer Look at Ethnicity, Nations and Nationalism in the Kingdom of God and World History: Rethinking Western Approaches to Nationhood in the Modern Global Age*. Los Angeles: Asia Research Associates. (See www.ara-cahcrc.com).

*———. 2002. "An Inquiry into the Socio-Religious and Historical Relation of Ancestor, National Hero and Saint Devotion (with special reference to Israelite-Jewish, Christian and Muslim Traditions)." (www.ara-cahcrc.com, "Projects & Publications.")

———. 2000. "The Christian Cult of the Saints: Its Origins and Development in the Ancient Church and a Comparison with other World Religious Traditions." (www.ara-cahcrc.com, "Projects & Publications.")

Wiseman, D.J. "Genesis 10: Some Archeological Considerations." In Hess, Richard S. and David Toshio Tsumura, ed. 1994. *I Studied Inscriptions From Before the Flood: Ancient Near Eastern and Literary Approaches to Genesis 1-11*. Eisenbrauns.

*Yesim, Garifolla. 2006. *An Insider's Critique of the Kazakh People and Nation: Abai Kunanbai-uhli and his writings, 1845-1904*. Los Angeles: Asia Research Associates.